90p

(5)

JS

GW00385292

Death of an Idealist

ALSO BY JOHN STONEHOUSE

Prohibited Immigrant

Death of an Idealist

John Stonehouse

W. H. Allen · London
A division of Howard & Wyndham Ltd
1975

*Printed and bound in Great Britain by
Butler & Tanner Ltd, Frome and London
for the publishers W. H. Allen & Co Ltd,
44 Hill Street, London W1X 8LB*

ISBN 0 491 01615 8

Contents

Preface

I FIRST CONCEIVED the idea of this book in the early weeks
of 1975 following my release from the Maribyrnong Detention
Centre. As I was emerging from a deep trauma it was painful
to think about the events I now describe; I broke down many
times. I found it extremely difficult to talk to people, particularly those many insensitives who expected to converse with
a completely rational and coherent person and who could not
accept the fact of my suffering. My recovery was much delayed
by the atmosphere of constant tension created around me. The
British Press were continually harassing me, searching out the
addresses where I was trying to get some peace and pestering,
night and day, anyone who was suspected of being in contact
with me.

I went to Sydney with my wife to stay with friends in
the hope of getting some respite. We tried to travel quietly
but our movements were leaked and the Press surrounded
us at Sydney airport. There were grotesque scenes as the reporters bombarded me with questions which I was in no
condition to answer. For the following four days we experienced a sort of terror as we were pursued through New
South Wales a hundred miles up the coast. Enormous
resources were deployed by certain British newspapers
to find out where we were staying. We avoided them only
by a few hours again and again as we moved from hotel to
hotel. The Australian Police tried to be helpful by escorting
us, but unfortunately their own telephone calls and radio

messages were leaked and they unwittingly led the Press to us.

During the period up to the beginning of February, I stayed at places in and around Melbourne at Yellingbo, Elwood, Tooronga, Brunswick, Mentone, Caulfield (in hospital), Toorak (with the British Consul-General), back to Yellingbo and finally to Hawthorn where I rented a 'unit'. Counting in the hotels and motels, I stayed at fourteen separate addresses over the five weeks. This constant moving to avoid the pressures being put on me did not aid my recovery and certainly did not encourage writing.

One journalist I could talk to was Ian Ward, a correspondent of *The Daily Telegraph*. I wrote an article for that newspaper on the Select Committee then being proposed in the House of Commons to consider my case. As a result of this sympathetic contact I began to think and talk more freely. I made an arrangement to dictate material on to tape with Ian Ward and recorded some 30,000 words. After a period of this collaboration Ward had to return to Singapore and Saigon to report on the Vietnam war.

His withdrawal did me a favour. The material on tape was of indifferent literary quality and work based on it would not have been very good. I have used hardly any of this material in the book you now have before you. I dispensed with tape recorders which I feel tend to create a mechanical barrier to the flow of thought; I wrote this book almost entirely in longhand.

Work could not start on it until the Department of Trade Inspectors had completed interviews with me in connection with the official enquiry into the affairs of my Companies. Although they had indicated they would need only two or three days, I was forced to spend six days under intensive cross-examination. It was a gruelling experience; I again broke down many times.

During that last week of February 1975 I had another shock when the Australian Minister for Immigration, Mr Clyde Cameron, announced that he was refusing my application to be allowed to stay in Australia on the grounds of my mental condition.

The background and the circumstances in which I commenced my writing at the beginning of March were not auspicious. The conditions were also not conducive. At the time I was living with my wife and son Mathew in a very small unit at Number 7, 840 Toorak Road in Melbourne.

I found I could write best in a tiny laundry-room, resting my writing-board on the washing-basket. Sometimes I would sit and write in a small patio to catch the sun before it disappeared behind the roof in the afternoon.

Within two and a half weeks of starting work—and, ominously, four days after the first extract from the book had appeared in the British Press—I was arrested on a warrant from Scotland Yard, who also requested that I should be refused bail. If I had been kept in prison, writing would have been made more difficult, but fortunately, bail was granted by the Australian magistrate. However, the manuscript and all existing material on the book were seized by the police and only returned after a long delay and vigorous protests in public. During the following week Sheila Buckley, my Secretary, was also arrested after she had left New South Wales for Victoria to report to the police and to ensure that her case was defended by my lawyer after hearing charges were being brought against her.

My writing was somewhat dislocated by these events; nevertheless four weeks later the manuscript was completed, on 17 April 1975.

This book has, perforce, many imperfections and I apologise for them. It is written, however, from the depths of my being and with no ulterior motive except to record the events as I experienced them then, and feel them now. Contrary to reports about 'cheque-book' journalism, following the abbreviated extracts which appeared in the *News of the World* by arrangement with my publishers, I have not written this book for money. Some newspapers have made attempts to persuade me to write about matters which are not part of the main story and would only confuse and distort it, but for which vast sums of money would be paid. I rejected these attempts with the contempt they deserve; I have no wish to encourage the British Press in their extravagant and misleading reporting of my case. In due course I hope to be able to describe the extraordinary conduct of the Press in another book to be entitled *Murder by Media*. That book might, with this, chip away at the wall of granite that has been built by the media against me; granite which can only be broken by the laser-beam of truth. As a result of my experiences I have seen truth in greater clarity and in richer colours than I thought possible. Truth is a many-sided diamond and others will, no doubt, look at it through another facet; this book, at any rate, is the truth as I see it. It has been a great release and a therapy to write it. I am well aware, however, that it is too short. There is so much more to say: every chapter could have been a volume. In the interests of space—and time—I have dealt sparingly with some events and in the descriptions of relations with family, friends and business associates. There are also a number of matters that I am unable to discuss at this particular time because of the circumstances in which I find myself. In time I hope to write more, if the fates allow.

I express my grateful thanks to my wife Barbara for her unfailing sympathy and support which helped to make the book possible, and to my solicitor, Jim Patterson, for his generous friendship. I thank Yall and Victa for their promotion of the book, Mr Frank Viner for his introduction to W. H. Allen, the publishers, who have—despite a distance of 12,000 miles—given me a tremendous amount of encouragement, and Mrs Judy Cotton who read my writing skilfully and typed the bulk of the manuscript speedily and efficiently.

John Stonehouse
Melbourne, April 1975

1 *In the beginning*

THE IDEALIST WAS born in the Co-op Halls listening, as a small child, to the Guildswomen discussing good causes and looking at the quaint but telling posters showing the images of Peace or the Tree of Life; the idealist was suckled on the horrors of the Spanish Civil War which he heard from the Basque children brought from Bilbao to Southampton in the old potato boats to escape the horrors of the siege by the Franco Fascists; the idealist sat at the feet of Horace King (later to become an MP and Speaker of the House of Commons, now Lord Maybury-King) when he played his piano and made his appeals for aid to save Freedom in Spain; the idealist went to a hundred primary schools which were all in draughty uncomfortable Labour Meeting-Rooms where the lessons were on the dangers of Nazism or the evils of the ruling class; the idealist went canvassing with his parents at election time and looked into scores of homes of working people and heard them relate their problems, which sometimes they did with strength and courage and which, sometimes, they did with the tears and the anguish brought on by the oppression they suffered. He was impressionable. A kaleidoscopic whirl of events moulded the baby and nurtured the boy. Every day he watched his mother, who was a local Councillor and President of the Southampton Co-operative Society, and his Father— a local Secretary of his Trade Union—painstakingly work to smooth the problems of others. The little front sitting-room of the family home was a local advice centre. Problems, prob-

lems, problems, problems and still more problems, dominated
the family scene. They were everywhere, looming like the long
shadows which hide the warmth of the setting sun, throwing
long bitter fingers of cold. The problems were outside the
family; they affected others. The Spanish democrats, the German Jews, the American negroes, the Indians under the British
Raj, the British unemployed, the Poor and the Blind everywhere and the unenlightened anywhere were the people who
needed sympathy and support, reaching out from that small
Southampton home. And the literature. It was stacked in the
cupboards where the best linen or tea-services should be. Cor-
respondence covered the mantelpieces: the Minutes of Council
meetings, the Agendas and the pathetic letters of appeal from
those who needed support in dealing with the massive, amor-
phous authority with which they could not cope. The idealist
rummaged through the cupboards and read shocking pamph-
lets about the horrors of war; he looked with terror at the
photographs of corpses and mutilated bodies from far-away
places from Spain to Manchuria. Weekly he went with his
mother to the Co-op shops and saw the ritual of the Co-op
divi number recorded on all purchases so the profits of one
shilling in the pound would come back to the member. He marvelled at the oneness, the big familyness of the Co-op, the sense
of belonging not just to a shop, but to a Movement. The Co-
operative Movement. The Trade Union Movement he heard
about from his father who late at night pored over his Trade
Union business. The idealist learnt that the Labour Movement
joined all together in a powerful force which would one day
conquer the world with the power of the working people.

The Movement was a movement towards the better life
where kindness would rule and evil would be banished; the
better life, where men and women would work, not for the
profits of capitalists, but for the goodness of the common
people; the better life where countries would not fight one
another but where all troubles would be solved within the
unity of purpose of the whole human race; the better life where
men would love, not hate, other men. Movement, movement,
movement. Everyday activity hummed around the household,
and every action seemed to have a meaning which, dovetailed
with the thousands of millions of actions of other ordinary folk,
would produce an irresistible force which would change
society. Not by revolution but from within. The Co-op divi

number took on an even greater significance and the idealist learnt it by heart. 9627, 9627, 9627 and 9627 he said to himself as he walked to the shop to buy groceries for his mother, and returning clutching the divi-check and so glad that it was the correct number. He belonged to the great Movement and was proud. He heard that some of the divi money went to education and some to political campaigning and that there were actually ordinary men in Parliament at Westminster sustained by this support who could speak up for the Movement in the highest councils of the land. Trade also had another function: the boycott 'Ban Japanese goods' was the call and 'Help stop the brutal aggression against China.' It seemed there was nothing the common people could not achieve if only their power was organised.

And so, more meetings; every night and every weekend. Whist drives to raise money. The young idealist learnt to play whist to make up the numbers. The fêtes to raise money; the collecting boxes and the side-shows and the speech by the important visitor who intoned like a vicar in a pulpit about the cause and the Movement. Always moving. The Conferences in the seaside towns: Folkestone, Scarborough, Blackpool, Margate, Bridlington and Southsea, where on hot Easter and Whitsuntide holiday weekends, when the thousands of holidaymakers were on the promenades or on the beaches or on the piers, the Movement delegates would sit for hours in the big domed Conference Halls in their thick best Sunday suits or dresses and talk and talk and talk. The idealist could sense that the Conference was the engine room producing the steam power which would drive the wheels of the Movement all over the country for the months ahead. Here was the place where decisions were made but also where faith was renewed. And faith was necessary. Faith to find the strength to fight against the hostile evil world which wanted none of the noble things the Movement worked for. Faith to withstand the propaganda of the ruling class which was fed to the masses by the Press and the radio, although the young idealist never heard the radio as his parents could not afford one. Faith that one day the moral cause would win its true victory and war, hunger, cruelty and squalor would be banished from the face of the earth. The day came when the new recruit would actually join for himself the cause of Idealism.

One evening after school he was taken by his older sisters

to a little wooden hall and was enrolled in the 'Woodcraft Folk'. There were lots of fun things to do like learning to make lino prints and how to put up tents, but also there was the Message. The Folk were part of the Movement which stretched not only through the whole of Britain but across the Channel and through Europe. The young people of other countries were joined to him as brothers and sisters and he must feel for them as for his own family. And their troubles in Europe were terrible.

In Spain the young people had fought with their bare hands on the barricades against Franco; in Germany the young people were being arrested because they believed in the Movement which Adolf Hitler wanted to destroy, and in Italy the youth were being conscripted to fight a dirty war against the gallant Abyssinians. The awful world outside Britain seemed to be dominated by evil. The struggle against it needed all his passionate conviction. The idealist became dedicated. He was given a name. 'Red Falcon' was suggested after the name of the German Social Democratic Youth Movement, but he preferred the more simple 'Falcon', and so 'Falcon' he became even to his brother and his sisters and his Mother and his Father. Everyone had a Folk name and no one was ever called by his real name, and the real names were forgotten, if they were ever known. Falcon called his Mother 'Shamrock', the Folk name she had chosen years before because of her Irish background. Every week the idealist walked to the Woodcraft Folk meetings and passed into another world where there was goodness and generosity, and during the Summer he went to camps in the New Forest where families shared their lives under tents, cooking over fires lit without matches and washing in the cool clear streams that flowed nearby. This was the pure life, away from the noise, the pushing and the antagonisms of the towns. This was the pure life, where people belonged to the community of the human race. One Summer there was great excitement as an International Woodcraft Folk camp was to be held on the Isle of Wight and all could go as it was so near. The site on the cliffs overlooking a perfect bay was magnificent, and there were long walks from it in both directions along the coast. And on the walks the idealist would listen and talk to the youth from other lands. It was wonderful to belong and to feel the bonds growing between peoples. This was the strength which would destroy evil, however strong the jackboots and the poison gas behind it. Around the roaring camp fires the campers sat at night and sang with enjoyment and with passion. They sang the Internationale and the Red Flag and the songs of the working-class movements of Italy and Germany and France and Spain. The initiation was complete and the music of the people was the anointment. It surged through the brain of the new idealist inspiring him as even words could never do. And in the stress and strain of later years it would be this music which would return to the brain to purify the soul and the spirit. The weeks and the months and the years stretched long in the consciousness of the young idealist as they do for the young everywhere, but events were making Time move faster.

Outside his school one day he saw workmen digging long deep trenches. He asked 'Why?' 'War is coming, these are air raid shelters' was the reply. The evil was closing in. But the optimism of the idealists was not to be daunted, and during those years of the late 1930s as the Fascist aggression became even more brutal, there was still hope that the League of Nations would prevent a general holocaust. But the League was a talking shop in Geneva where statesmen in pinstriped trousers and top hats made appropriate noises but did nothing. And the countries went down like ninepins. Spain was followed by the Saar and Albania, attacked by the dictator of Rome on a holy day. Austria was raped and then came the destruction of Czechoslovakia piece by piece. First Sudetenland by Nazi trickery and then the rest of the country, dismembered with the agreement of the English ruling class for the sake of a piece of paper which would give the Establishment in England a few more months respite from the whirlwind of change that would hit it soon. The idealist had parents who wanted for him what they did not have for themselves. The mother had lost her father young and she was left to bring up the family and then find work for herself as a scullery maid in Cowes on the Isle of Wight. The father had been made redundant in the Portsmouth Dockyard in the economy cuts of 1924 and rode on his bicycle thirty miles to Southampton to find work. When the last child and second son was born in the next year, he was in the amazing security of a civil service job as a Post Office engineer. The family lived in a Council house but had ambitions which they eventually reached of buying their own home. The sense of independence can be married to a passion for socialism. And the parents wanted the children to travel, and so at fourteen the youthful idealist set forth to France for an exchange visit to stay with a French family in the Château town of Tours in the delightful centre of the country where the river Indre meets the Loire flowing majestically towards the sea. The visit was a revelation. To see a foreign country from the inside confirmed that basically they are the same with the same hopes, ambitions and even problems. Why could it be that when the peoples are so alike their countries can sometimes be so hostile? As Europe moved towards the Second Great War, which was to start within weeks, German families, Italian families and Polish families would all have the same sorts of emotions. Why then so much antagonism between countries? It could only be the leaders or the systems which were responsible. The ordinary people could never be guilty of such hate. The idealist rode a borrowed bicycle to the great Châteaux, to wander with awe through the great palaces and on to the caves where champagne was made, and to take his first sip with a fit of coughing, and to walk on his own for hours along the banks of the wide Loire, musing on the wonderful beauties of life and feeling at one with the human race. But on the 3rd September war came with a shock. The French family descended nightly to the cellar, where food was stacked as for a siege, and sit around the radio anxiously awaiting news. The trains were requisitioned for troops to go to the front and the young English visitor was caught with the exchange time up. The family decided he must work to pay for the extra time and he was taken to find a job. First it seemed the newspaper shop could provide the best job, that of a newsboy selling 'Paris Soir' on the streets of Tours; then a woman advertised for a strong boy to help in her *charcuterie* cutting up the pork, as her husband had gone to the front, but that had gone to another; and finally a job was found in a photographer's studio, cutting the photos of the wedding groups to size with the serrated edges loved by the French. But this lurch into adulthood was not to last. England was calling. The Vice-Consul insisted the boy should return. With French francs to the equivalent of ten shillings in his trousers he set forth: first to Paris where he stayed the night in a down-and-out hotel for a few francs and to wander the next day all over the city wondering at the sights; and then on to Le Havre by the late train to arrive at one in the morning in time to snatch a few hours sleep on the seats of a pavement cafe.

Returning to Southampton the young idealist found the war was taken so seriously his school was evacuated to Bournemouth, so there he went to watch in helpless horror the Dunkirk disaster and the fall of France. The world of hope was collapsing; the wider ideals had to be shelved until the brutal aggressors were themselves destroyed. At sixteen he was pitchforked into the adult world with his English master—the same Horace King—saying he had limited ability and should be apprenticed to a butcher, little realising how near he had been to that two years earlier. But better fortune prevailed and he joined the Probation Department in the great white stone Civic Centre of Southampton. The Senior Probation Officer needed a clerk and typist at the scale rate of twenty-two shillings and sixpence per week. There were only two other officers, including the Church Army Sister who took care of the delinquent girls, so more responsibility than usual was thrust on the new employee. The idealist loved it for the opportunity to help in the social service was as honey to a bear. Before long he was—in the absence of the officers called to the war—advising married couples on their problems and supervising some of the delinquents who had been put on probation. The kindly Senior Probation Officer gave him much encouragement. In his spare time the idealist helped to form the 'Citizens of Tomorrow', a group of teenagers devoted to talking and thinking about the social problems of the time and the preparations for the years of peace which one day would come. The opportunity for the New World would surely not be for long delayed. It was a joy to meet and work with so many other young idealists, all full of hope for the future. There was Irene Richards who met and married Jack Candy through the COT and went on to become a leading Labour activist in Southampton as Leader of the Council, and Griffin Bartlett who went to Australia to work as an architect and to devote his time to preserving the historic buildings of that young country. And a score of others who carried with them through life the warm experience of that fellowship. It would have been pleasant to carry on that circle.

But the war machine demanded its quota of young men and the idealist went to serve in the blue uniform of the Royal Air Force. This transpired to be a springboard for the future for it took him to the great United States, where he learnt to fly, and through an ex-Serviceman's grant to the London School of Economics and Political Science. He never lived in Southampton permanently again—the wider world was now his stage. And the whole world came to the LSE in the years just after the war. Students from India, America and the unknown colonies in Africa and most students blooded by the experiences of war and anxious to make sure, not only that it did not happen again, but that the roots of society were replanted to avoid the diseases which caused the conflicts leading to war. They sat at the feet of Harold Laski, that great teacher and political philosopher, and they took his lessons to heart. And in every continent his students became the Presidents and Ministers of the newly emergent countries. The hope of idealists was that in such laboratories his noble ideas of democracy could be made to work. The idealist threw himself into political work and became Chairman of the Labour Society, following Sydney Irving (later to become MP for Dartford and Deputy Chairman of Ways and Means) and with Reginald Prentice (later to become MP for East Ham and Minister for Education), Pierre Trudeau (later to become Prime Minister of Canada) and Donald Chesworth (later to be Chairman of the charity War on Want and Trustee of the Bangladesh Fund) as fellow members.

The International Socialist Student Movement opened the doors for the idealist to experience the excitements and inspiration of European socialism. He became active in organising youth and student visits to camps and conferences all over Europe where he found the Movement more passionate and more dedicated than in England. The young in Germany and Austria were recruited to a cause which had lain fallow or suppressed for twenty years and they embraced it with enthusiasm. They wanted to exorcise the evils of Nazism; they were hungry for contacts with the British and the Scandinavians who had so much to teach. There were also the students who had graduated already in the schools of life and death during the war, and now had to graduate in their chosen studies. Men like Helmut Schmidt (later to become Chancellor of Germany): tough and determined to make social democracy work effectively in Germany, so as to hold back the twin evils of Communist or Fascist dictatorship. And the students came from all over the world to the gatherings in the Europe which had been freed.

Vienna, Brussels, Haarlem, Berlin, Hamburg, Oslo, Ebensee, Copenhagen, Amsterdam and Paris were all visited in this pilgrimage in the search for a new spiritual and political relationship between peoples, hopefully putting behind the hatred of war and cruel oppression.

Harold Laski guided his students in politics as well as studies and advised the idealist to stand for selection as the Labour Candidate for the London suburban constituency of Twickenham. With an unrequested letter of recommendation from the Professor he was selected, at the age of twenty-three, as a Parliamentary candidate. The inevitable had happened. He was now firmly launched on a political career. Politics was nothing more, and certainly nothing less, than the expression of idealism in practical deeds. That illusion and that fantasy were to die hard: and a lot was to happen in the meantime.

2 *The challenge of Africa*

MY APPRENTICESHIP FOR the House of Commons was in Africa, in the early nineteen-fifties, in the shanty towns around Nairobi, listening to the earnest pleas for freedom from desperately eager men with determined looks in their eyes; in the wild North of Uganda, snatching a few hours sleep in the simple thatched mud and wattle huts and driving and working by day to create a Co-operative movement which would liberate the peasants from exploitation; at the Jomo Kenyatta trial at Kapenguria giving a character witness for the defence of a friend accused of Mau Mau terrorism.

The apprenticeship had been chosen for me by Fenner Brockway, that grand old man of Labour politics who had himself fought long and hard for Colonial freedom both in India, where he was born, and Africa. I met him at the House of Commons soon after I had been defeated by 700 votes in my second Parliamentary election in October 1951 at Burton. He was forceful yet restrained, thin and wiry yet strong, and, above all, kind. The overriding impression was of a man who felt and cared for others, really cared. He introduced me to the Federation of Uganda African Farmers which had been created to give Africans the economic strength they needed through unity. I became the second white man to be employed directly by Africans in Uganda—the first, George Shepherd, the American and son of a missionary, was already there preparing the ground for our great task.

My wife and two young daughters joined me on the long

voyage to Mombasa—the bustling Kenyan gateway to
Africa—and on the 1,000 mile train journey through to the
interior along the routes where a century before Arab slave
traders had trekked to capture and shackle their human merchandise, and on to Kampala the historic Uganda town built,
like Rome, on seven hills. Historic, because years before the
white men came, the Baganda King, the Kabaka, had his
thatched palace here from which he ruled the vast area around
the north-west of the great lake which became known as Victoria-Nyanza. And our destination was our new home, an African house, standing with dignity, although it was only mud
and wattle and corrugated iron sheets, facing the Kabaka's
compound. We were on a site where history had been made,
but it was a history about which white men knew hardly anything and in which they had played no part. It is a strange and
revealing weakness of white men that they assume, arrogantly,
that all history begins with white men, and that all events must
revolve around white people at the centre as though other
peoples have no function and no purpose unless it serves the
white people.

This attitude of unthinking superiority is so endemic that
graduate teachers today still teach children that Leif Ericcson
or Christopher Columbus discovered America—it doesn't
matter which, for this argument, as neither is true—or that
Captain James Cook discovered Australia, which is equally
false. We lived and worked with Africans long enough to discover how they felt and how they thought and to find a true
identity with them based on that understanding. Above all we
found that the attitude of the liberal do-gooders we had known
in Britain was not only inappropriate but was also, in a way,
insulting. That attitude which subconsciously assumes that all
black people are both more backward and more moral than
white people belies the more simple yet true position that
blacks are, in Uganda and elsewhere, human beings for all that.
With their faults and blemishes as well as their strengths, they
need to be judged. The inverted racial prejudice which gave
blacks a privileged moral position in the eyes of some whites
was as much the result of liberal sentimentalising as the deep
guilt conscience in whites brought on by the years of slavery
and exploitation. Fortunately, I had literally no time for racial
prejudice—simple or inverted—as I was too busy, day in and
day out; travelling, talking, organising and developing the

Movement which would help free the Ugandans from their own ignorance and pathetic inferiority complexes, and give them the tools to build a richer and better life.

My activities came under the scrutiny of the secret police of the Colonial Government who could not understand how any European could work for Africans unless he was a dangerous Communist. Informers fed information on my activities, and, as is usual, such reports were embellished. Inadvertently one day, one of the plain clothes policemen detailed to check on me told my wife about some of the reports. It was clear that these police—like police elsewhere—were getting caught up in a web of their own creation, and the entanglements of intrigue and suspicion which they generated were making it impossible for them to make objective judgements. Before we had left England we were given by friends an introduction to Lady Helen Cohen, the wife of the Governor, Sir Andrew Cohen. That proved to be our saviour from further police harassment. One evening we turned out of our house to drive the twenty miles from Kampala to Entebbe, the administrative capital on the shores of Lake Victoria-Nyanza, to have dinner with the Governor and Lady Helen. The police car, which usually followed us, pulled out behind and kept a discreet distance all the way. But as we went into the spacious driveway leading to Government House and the guards snapped to attention in salute, the other car quietly slipped away, never to be seen again. Someone in authority had decided that, perhaps, after all, we were respectable.

It was these same secret police who reported directly to an Attorney General called Dreschfield and who were mainly responsible for the build-up of intelligence reports that led to the Governor taking the fateful decision to expel the Kabaka Mutesa of Buganda. Relying on informers, who lie freely for money, the police advised that militant public opinion could support the expulsion of the Kabaka as he was an aristocratic playboy without popularity. It was true that 'King Freddie' as he became known in the English Press, was unpopular; I had seen his photographs being burnt on his birthday in the Katwe market place. But when the Colonial power forcibly carried the Buganda King out of his Kingdom almost the whole Baganda nation rallied to his support. Men took to wearing only bark cloth made from the bark of local trees and throwing away their European woollen clothes as a protest.

I remember one magnificent figure wearing a beautifully cut suit made entirely of bark cloth. The protests may have been bizarre but they were genuine for all that.

I was close to Cohen at this time and frequently talked with him about the problems. He welcomed the opportunity to discuss affairs with someone who was not in the administration and who could speak out without being worried about embarrassing promotion prospects within the Colonial service. I told the Governor frankly what I thought about the Attorney General and his advice which I considered to be unfortunate on the expulsion of the Kabaka. Cohen was acutely distressed by the Kabaka affair because he had established such an excellent relationship with the Africans as a progressive Governor. Until the deportation—and even after—they loved him. The isolation of a liberal Governor can be very cruel and Cohen felt it deeply.

The Kabaka deportation split the Labour Party in England. Dick Crossman, then writing for the *New Statesman*, came on a fact finding tour and had lunch with my wife and me. He asked my view. I said firmly 'The deportation was the most foolish act the Government could have done.' Overnight it turned progressive Africans from anti-Royalist to strong Royalist sentiments. They could not stand the affront to Baganda pride to have their King removed by the colonial power, even if before they had themselves wanted to curb the King's power. I told Crossman that the deportation would put back Uganda's development of democracy for years and would lead to disputes for possibly decades. He appeared to understand my points. I was therefore amazed some weeks later to hear from Fenner Brockway about the Labour Parliamentary Party's Colonial group discussion on the issue. The Conservative Government wanted the support of the Labour Party for its action, and the attitude of the Labour Colonial Group of MPs was therefore crucial. Both Fenner Brockway and Jim Griffiths, the humane and sensible ex-miner who had been Secretary of State for the Colonies, opposed the deportation in the group as it was arbitrary, illegal and non-constructive. Others in the group thought otherwise. They considered that an ex-Fabian liberal Governor like Cohen could do no wrong, particularly when dealing with an upstart of a playboy King. The decision could have gone either way when Crossman said, 'I have just come back from Uganda' and looking directly at Brockway 'I was

with your man, John Stonehouse, in Kampala, and he told me
that the deportation was a good policy.' The opposition to the
Tory Government action collapsed at this point and the
Labour Party remained confused about the issue for years
afterwards. I could never discover whether Crossman deliberately misrepresented what I had said, believing that it would
not get back to me, or whether he had genuinely believed I
had said the opposite, wrapped up as he always was with his
own intellectual conceit. Later when I became an MP I tried
to tackle Crossman, but he arrogantly refused to discuss it.

My election in 1957 had come as the result of a by-election
in the Staffordshire constituency of Wednesbury, a grimy industrial place producing car components, nuts and bolts and
locks. The former Member, Stanley Evans, known as 'Feath-
erbed' Evans, because of a famous speech he made attacking
subsidies for farmers when he was a junior Minister, had been
ousted by the Constituency Party as he had supported the
Tory Government on the Suez invasion. My opponents at the
Selection Conference included Ray Gunter, a powerful figure
in the Labour Party as a Member of the National Executive
Committee and Chairman of a Trade Union as well as being
an ex-MP. He had secured nominations from most constituency party organisations and seemed a certain winner. But
Colonel George Wigg, the MP for the nearby seat of Dudley,
was determined to undo him and circulated among delegates
a marked copy of Hansard showing Gunter's Parliamentary
speeches in a very unfavourable light. The support for Gunter
collapsed and he received only four votes. I was selected by
an overwhelming majority and easily defeated Peter Tapsell,
the Tory candidate, at the actual Parliamentary by-election.

Now all the opportunities seemed open. I had arrived at the
Palace of Westminster at my third attempt and, at the age of
thirty-one, had decades of political work in front of me. The
new Member at Westminster can choose between a variety of
courses. The easiest is to tack along doing what the Whips say
and keeping the constituency happy by occasionally asking a
question about local unemployment or the bus service, and
always being available as a glorified welfare officer. In this way
the Member never upsets anyone, is never a threat, is everybody's best friend and ensures his re-selection and re-election
at election after election. Being safe he may be made a junior
or even a senior Minister when his Party wins a majority, but

always ensuring his safety by never putting himself out of line on any major issue and certainly never taking up a cause before it had received the sanctity of official Party endorsement. Such men are the bricks of Parliamentary democracy: solid, heavy and dull. They are essential to any Party as Lobby-fodder. Their most important function is one that is never fully recognised in the unwritten British constitution: that of acting as an electoral college for the election of the Party leader who will, in the event of victory, be Prime Minister. This has become even more evident now that the Tory Party has followed the Labour and Liberal Parties in electing its Leader by secret ballots of the MPs only. This role for MPs ensures that they are courted by prospective Party leaders and made to feel important, as indeed they are.

I felt disinclined to follow the easy course and saw Parliament as a forum in which to further causes and to fight injustice, particularly in Africa, which I loved and which had captured my soul. I became Vice-Chairman of the Movement for Colonial Freedom, of which Fenner Brockway was Chairman. As a result, I was caught in the waves of activity then flowing through British overseas politics as the Great Colonial Power, like a dying dinosaur realising it could no longer exist in a hostile environment, tried desperately to make its death throes more palatable. Most of the African leaders served with us on the MCF Committees: Kenneth Kaunda, who became President of Zambia, Tom Mboya of Kenya who was later to be tragically assassinated, and Hastings Kamuzu Banda the eccentric doctor who became President of Malawi, were among them. Every week a new major issue emerged—a state of emergency in Northern Rhodesia, horrors at the Hola camp for Mau Mau detainees in Kenya or arrests of African leaders in Southern Rhodesia. Day after day a few MPs pursued the issues on the floor of the House, constantly probing and attacking the Government when it failed to guide the situation in a sensible manner.

Looking back just fifteen years or so, it is quite incredible how most Establishment opinion failed to understand the African revolution which is now taken for granted. In the late 1950s nearly all Conservative MPs and most Labour MPs thought that British colonial rule in East and Central Africa could continue for a long period, and at least during their own Parliamentary careers. Some thought that white settler rule was achievable as a lasting solution in Kenya as in the Federation of Rhodesia and Nyasaland, where a rickety constitution gave power to 250,000 whites over eight million Africans. But no one in their right senses should have ignored the sheer arithmetic and the obvious impossibility of a handful of Europeans continuing to dominate millions of Africans, so that they remained, for generations, the servile providers of cheap labour and respectful servants. This fantasy world was bound to collapse just as surely as the slave-owning classes lost their power in the cotton growing Southern United States and Czarist feudalism broke down in Russia. At that time of our campaigning it was surprising how many otherwise sensible politicians assumed otherwise. George Brown, for instance, was convinced that European rule in some form would continue in East and Central Africa. This type of attitude made our job especially difficult within the Labour Party, which in some ways is a curiously conservative and reactionary party resentful and suspicious of change, although many of the active rank and file members were imbued with a moral fervour on the issues and were on our side.

I went to Rhodesia early in 1959 on a tour to see the facts for myself, and naturally spent a lot of time with the African leaders and their followers. After speeches in Bulawayo and Salisbury calling on the Africans to work constructively with their white neighbours to build a non-racial state and saying 'Lift your heads high and behave as though the country belongs to you' I was arrested and deported from the Federation. As the events are fully chronicled in my book *Prohibited Immigrant* I won't deal with them here, except to say that on that occasion I became a catalyst, waking up the Labour Party to take a greater interest in Africa and also helping to galvanise African strength in Rhodesia itself. It was not the only time and certainly not the only issue in which I would be a catalyst.

In the following year I journeyed back to Africa: this time to go further South to stay with my friend Seretse Khama who had been allowed to return to Bechuanaland years after his deportation by a Labour Secretary of State, Patrick Gordon Walker. Firstly, I went to Kenya to meet Tom Mboya. He was one of the brightest of the Africans who emerged in the years following the Mau Mau. He was young enough not to have been tied up with the Mau Mau movement and was incredibly brilliant. He started his working life in Nairobi as a Health

Service officer and graduated from that to organising the municipal employees into Trade Unions. Then he went into politics—a risky exercise because the political parties were then subject to so much control by the Colonial administration. His impact was tremendous despite the fact that he was not from the major Kikuyu tribe.

Kenya then was going through a transition stage. It was clear that the Government had to make some concession to African nationalism, but had not yet decided what it should do. It was prepared to allow men like Tom Mboya, who were considered moderates, to have their small political parties, but they were restricted to small regions rather than being allowed to organise nationwide. So there was a proliferation of parties, and the Government was trying to play one off against the other, so that they could hold the breach. Jomo Kenyatta was still detained and as he was the only man who could unite all these groups, while the Government kept him in prison, they could maintain the balance of power. They were also hankering after allowing the white minority in Kenya to have a substantial say in the future administration of the country.

It was fascinating to see, however, the gradual change in the attitude of the colonial government to African politicians. A few years before, and certainly during the period when I was in Uganda between 1952 and 1954 and when I had attended the Jomo Kenyatta trial in Kenya, the African politicians were subject to rigorous control, and were locked up if they said anything out of line. They were not allowed to visit hotels in Nairobi which were wholly white preserves. The Africans were generally regarded as second-class non-citizens.

The change by 1960 was really quite dramatic. Politicians were allowed to come out with their Party statements, they were allowed to go to Europe, and even to address the Royal Institute of International Affairs. I remember one occasion when Tom Mboya came and spoke there entirely without notes, and had a big audience of industrialists and newspaper men completely captivated, not only by his charm but also by his intellect. His grasp of international politics was quite amazing, when you consider the modest beginnings of this chap. It was a great achievement that he managed to lift himself up to a genuine intellectual appreciation of the relationship between the undeveloped world and their aspirations and the industrial west. I think as a man he could well be compared with Lee Kuan Yew. He had almost congenital intellectual ability.

It was a great tragedy that he was murdered as a result of a tribal as much as a political dispute. He certainly had a lot of enemies, any one of whom could have been responsible for his death. One of his enemies was Oginga Odinga who hated Tom Mboya because he didn't respect the Luo tribal hierarchy. Odinga, being the elder, felt he should have had the respect and submission of Tom Mboya, but Tom forged his own path to success and upset others by being intellectually ahead of Oginga Odinga.

It was suspected that Tom Mboya was being paid by the Americans, and he did certainly receive quite substantial contributions from American institutions. He had, of course, attended an American university and made some close contacts during that period, but whether he was an agent for the CIA or not, I cannot confirm. I doubt it. Through the trade union movement he got money from Walter Reuther, the American trade union leader who ran the powerful Automobile Workers Union. Mboya's trade union activity brought him in quite a good deal of money, and as he lived fairly well, he obviously received money from somewhere.

Odinga resented this and, as a result, he moved towards the Chinese, not because he had any love of Communism, but he had to have a sponsor from somewhere and the Americans were committed to Mboya. On such factors are major decisions of policy and tactics made!

It was fascinating in Nairobi to see these developments, and I spent quite a lot of time with Tom Mboya going round with him to meetings, not only in Nairobi itself, but also up-country. I met a lot of old friends, some of whom had been released from Mau Mau camps. They told me some horrifying stories of the treatment meted out in the camps. I also went to visit some camps myself.

In these Mau Mau camps I saw hundreds of men who had had such traumatic experiences that they could not communicate. They were so resentful of the English Colonial Government which locked them up, misunderstood their motives and forcibly prevented them from realising their aspirations that they became completely mute. Their eyes were glazed when they were cross-examined, they refused to answer questions and gradually became completely disoriented from the society around them.

One camp I visited was just outside Nairobi, and as a Member of Parliament I was given every facility to see the inmates. They were certainly very sullen, but as soon as they realised who I was they began to relax and some even to communicate. On one dramatic occasion when I was walking past a compound there were hundreds of these prisoners about a hundred yards away. When the word went around that I was there, these sullen broken men, who were almost bent over through resentment and the destruction of their spirits, suddenly woke into life. The shout went up 'Stonehouse, Stonehouse', and they ran like one man to that fence to see me. I was able to go over and talk to them. Their sudden change of mood was amazing.

My reputation had obviously preceded me. I had, of course, been campaigning for them to be released, and I had advocated reforms which were nearer their own aspirations than most other things that were being said at that time about them.

The treatment they had had made them more than sullen; they were almost turned into zombies. They had a deep psychological resentment against the colonial régime and did not accept that authority over them in any sense whatsoever. Whereas a prisoner for rape or murder or even political activities of the normal sort, can accept the fact of being a prisoner, the Mau Mau detainee was prepared to accept nothing.

There was a lot of humbug about Mau Mau in Britain. The British take a superior attitude to such movements conveniently forgetting that the idea of a secret society is not confined to Africans by any means. The Freemasons also depend on religious and pagan rites to maintain their hold on their adherents and so do the occult or witchcraft societies. The difference with the African secret society of Mau Mau was that it had a revolutionary purpose. Its object was to get the whites out of the political control of Kenya, to open up the white highlands for occupation by the African farmers, and to give Africans access to all human freedoms which had been denied them by the whites.

The British Press also did its best to misrepresent the true Mau Mau aspirations, preferring to highlight the alleged atrocities against whites, which were actually very few, and almost ignored the massive brutalities against Africans. The

Press taught the public to hate Mau Mau. Rational actions by the local Administration became impossible in these circumstances and the detainees who numbered tens of thousands resorted to a campaign of non-co-operation.

The worst example was at the Hola camp on the site of an irrigation scheme in the hottest part of Kenya. The prisoners were supposed to be working on trenches. When the hard core Mau Mau prisoners refused to pick up their shovels, on the orders of the white prison superintendents they were beaten by the African warders until several of them were left dead in the trenches. It was only one example of the extreme brutality for which the whites in Kenya were responsible, but as it came to the knowledge of Britain it produced an uproar in the House of Commons. A dramatic debate took place and the event was fully ventilated. I remember the debate well. Enoch Powell made a very moving speech condemning the atrocity and demonstrating his independence of mind, not for the first or last time.

3 *Have ideals, will travel*

I WENT FROM KENYA on to Tanganyika where the political development had progressed further. When I arrived in Dares-Salaam, in fact, the first self-government was just about to be installed and Julius Nyerere to become the first Prime Minister. He had been the leader of the Tanganyika African National Union (TANU) and had been able to get a nation-wide political party active, long before this was possible in Kenya where there had been numerous white settlers, and the disadvantage that the Kikuyu and Luo and Khamba tribes were vying with each other for pre-eminence. In Tanganyika there was not this disadvantage of rivalries between major tribes holding back the progress towards a genuine nation-hood.

Tanganyika is a vast country—bigger than France and Germany combined—but it has something like one hundred and twenty-three tribes, and no one tribe is strong enough to dominate the others.

In 1959, on my previous visit, I was received by a colonial civil servant at the airport who gave me a black car and a chauffeur and an apartment to stay in. I had every possible facility in 1959 both before I went to Rhodesia and after I was expelled from the Federation. When I arrived back in Dares-Salaam a year later in 1960, there was nobody to receive me at the airport because the colonial régime was defunct, self-government had emerged and Julius Nyerere had become Prime Minister. When I saw him in his car in the streets he was being driven in the same black car and by the same chauffeur that I had the year before. Circumstances had changed!

I was very pleased to see Africans getting to grips with the problems of running their own country. In Tanganyika the transition from a Colonial Government to self-government was achieved with more peace and more smoothly than practically anywhere else in Africa. It was very successfully done despite the fact that there were very few Africans trained to university standards. The Education Budget was so low that at the time of the final independence there were only three graduates in the whole country. I was told during one of my visits that for many years the Budget for Government House in Dar-es-Salaam, where the Governor lived, was greater than the Education Budget for the whole territory. The Colonial Government relied on the missionaries to provide the education service, but they didn't have the necessary resources for such a vast country.

It was particularly encouraging to me to see the developments in Tanganyika because it typified everything I had worked for. I wanted Africans to come into their own; I felt that unless they had political power they would not be able to improve their economic conditions, and if economic conditions were improved without political power, they would not be able to obtain the fruits of their economic advance. It was, indeed, a question of motivations apart from anything else. If you give Africans the inspiration of running their own country then they work harder to help themselves. They grow better cotton, they market their cotton more successfully, they gin it better, and people are translated from a mere subsistence economy where they are content just to grow their own food to a market economy.

Julius Nyerere is one of the most impressive men I have met in Africa, and he brought together a team of Ministers who were excellent, considering the background of the territory, the limited educational opportunity and the total lack of experience.

Rashidi Kawawa, for instance, was an excellent Minister and is today a competent Vice President. He is a small man standing hardly more than five feet, and always has a puckered expression on his face as though he is thinking deeply about everything said to him. He is indeed a very thoughtful man and much underestimated.

Dar-es-Salaam means the haven of peace and that Arab-derived name is appropriate for a place which has known little violence. There are few countries in the world where the Governor could ride around the town early every morning on his bicycle. Sir Richard Turnbull, who behaved like a kindly headmaster would to a large school, did just that. When I stayed with him at the palatial Government House he insisted that I should accompany him. It was hot and hectic riding through those streets crowded with Africans on their way to work in their tattered clothes. But they liked the Governor's gesture and no one ever harmed him. There might be a lesson in this for rulers elsewhere who cut themselves off from the ordinary people.

Tanganyika is a country of opportunity. It is vast with great agricultural resources. Production of ground nuts, of coffee and cotton could all be increased, and with the improvement of communications a vast interior can be opened up for mineral development as well as farming.

The British had never prepared Tanganyika for independence or development. It was a Trust Territory handed over from the Germans after the end of the first world war, and this gave the British the excuse to neglect it. The Germans had ruled the territory with a rod of iron and there was still ample evidence of their occupation. A German Lutheran Church stands in Dar-es-Salaam near the hotel, 'The New Africa', where I have frequently stayed. The name incidently was rather a misnomer because it was one of the oldest hotels I have ever known. It had mud walls which were two or three feet thick, and the rooms were like cells.

I had planned to fly from Dar-es-Salaam to Blantyre in Nyasaland and then on to Salisbury in Southern Rhodesia, from which I would go by road or train to Bechuanaland. However, the evening before I was due to leave the pilot of the East African Airway's plane came to see me in a state of great agitation. 'Mr Stonehouse,' he said, 'I beg you not to come on my plane tomorrow. I have been warned that if you fly with me into Nyasaland I will be arrested and my plane will be impounded.' I said 'Why is that?' and he said 'It's because the Federal Rhodesian authorities made it clear that you cannot be allowed to come into Nyasaland under any circumstances.'

I was not anxious to give the pilot any problems and so I arranged to go back to Nairobi to try to fly from there. Eventu-

ally I was able to get on a BOAC plane, flying first to Ndola.
The Rhodesian police came on board and I was kept detained
on the plane. Somehow word was passed to the Africans in
Southern Rhodesia that I was arriving in Salisbury, and three
thousand Africans came to the airport to welcome me. They
were packed around the airport terminal. As a result of being
the centre of a tremendous political storm the year before, I
had become a symbol to the Africans and they came to demonstrate their solidarity with me. I was not to see them, except
in the distance. When the plane landed, the other passengers
went to the terminal by airport bus and I was whisked to the
other side of the airport, put on a Royal Rhodesian Air Force
plane and flown, without ceremony, to Bechuanaland. We
arrived at a remote place called Francistown without any sort
of warning; the airport wasn't expecting us and the airport
lights were not on. I was dumped on the airfield by the
Rhodesian pilots who, without more ado, turned the plane
round and took off again. I was left, holding my case, just
standing, with nobody about. It was lonely and desolate to
be left like that in the middle of Africa.

Francistown is a miserable, broken-down, dust-ridden
town, but I found a small hotel and stayed overnight. The next
morning I hitched a lift with a Dutchman who was driving
a truck through Bechuanaland down to Serowe. It was a very
long journey, and very uncomfortable along rough unmade
roads. I arrived in Serowe exhausted after this hot trip and
was very pleased to meet up with Seretse and his English wife
Ruth in their little bungalow. They had been hearing about
my adventure on the radio.

Serowe was a very small sleepy town; just a village really.
There were three or four bungalows with corrugated iron
roofs. Seretse and Ruth had one of these; the rest of the buildings were mud huts. I stayed with Seretse and Ruth for a week
or so, visiting the cattle stations, going to the schools, seeing
the beginnings of the Co-operative Movement and hearing
about the problems of the territory. There was little doubt the
problems were immense.

We ate European foods brought in tins from South Africa
but I also tried my teeth on biltong, a form of dried meat that
is extremely stringy. I did not manage it very well.

Towards the end of my visit there was a phone call to Ruth
from a person who said she had been an old friend of hers.

Ruth, naturally, invited her to visit them. Anyone having driven hundreds of miles could not be sent away without receiving some hospitality. The woman turned up with two men. I should have been suspicious of them, but I took their story at face value. They claimed they were touring the territory with chinchillas in the boot of the car persuading farmers to rear them. It seemed to be a fatuous idea, and if I had known more then about Bechuanaland, which is practically barren without much typical farming, I would have realised that it was quite a ridiculous one.

The visitors were very interested in my future plans and I told them quite willingly what I intended doing. I was going on to South Africa as that was the only way out of the territory for me. I was forbidden to return to Rhodesia unless I flew in to Salisbury Airport and I could not afford to charter an aircraft to do that. My only way out of Bechuanaland was by the train through the long territory into the Republic of South Africa and on to Johannesburg. On the telephone I had booked a place on an aircraft leaving Johannesburg after three days or so of my departure from Serowe.

The visitors, particularly the woman who was a very strong personality, insisted that I visit them in Johannesburg. They would provide every assistance so that I could see something of the country before I left. I agreed to look them up when I got there, but I had doubts whether I would want to spend too much time with them. Later I realised they were the South African secret service.

I was seen off by the Khamas at the station near Serowe. The journey through Bechuanaland is lengthy so I had a sleeper and took myself off to bed. At every stop on the route I was woken up by the District Commissioner banging on the door and saying 'This is the District Commissioner. We have been warned that when you arrive in South Africa you will be arrested. We therefore advise you to leave the train immediately.' I couldn't accept that advice because if I left the train I would be isolated. There was no other way out of Bechuanaland, completely surrounded as it was by South Africa and Rhodesia and Portuguese Angola to the north. I would have to get out somehow. If I was going to be arrested, so be it. It would certainly get me out of the country sooner. I went on with the journey. On the next morning after crossing the frontier into Mafeking I saw two strong Afrikaaner policemen standing and waiting for me on the platform. They looked as though they could be tough rugby players. Without delay they bundled me into a fast American car and drove to Jan Smuts Airport just outside Johannesburg.

At the time I was financing my African journeys by writing articles for *Reynolds News*, the Co-op Sunday newspaper, and as this was Thursday I had a graphic article to write for the following Sunday's edition. As the car sped through the South African veldt, I wrote away sitting on the back seat, with the two Afrikaaners in the front. I produced about fifteen hundred words by the time we arrived at Johannesburg and said to my escort, 'I just want to go into the Post Office for a moment.' They agreed and stood guard at the door. I gave my press card and the manuscript to the counter clerk who was an Afrikaaner and who looked typically thick. He slowly counted the words, obviously without realising their significance, because the first ones were 'I have just been arrested by the South African Police and I am now being taken in a fast car to be expelled from the country.' He did not bat a single eyelid.

I joined up with the policemen and they took me on to the first available plane. I counted my luck that I had, in fact, saved a full day by being escorted in this way. The aircraft was the first Boeing 707 aircraft acquired by South African Airways, and this was the inaugural flight. There was an air of celebration in the cabin. Champagne was served. I sat next to a very distinguished English South African who told me of his brave exploits during the war fighting Rommel, and who also described the great future South Africa had, if only 'We can keep the blacks in their place'. He then started talking about the antics of 'that fellow Stonehouse', and after half an hour of this I amazed him by revealing my true identity. We remained quite friendly and I think that he might have learnt something from the remaining part of our conversation on the way to the first stop of Brazzaville. It is strange that an intelligent man who sacrificed himself to fight a Nazi General does not see the elements of fascism in his own attitude to people he regarded as inferior. After such meetings I can only draw the conclusion that man does not think objectively. Self-interest is so entrenched in the persona that it takes over the thinking apparatus.

I left the aircraft in Brazzaville and spent the night sharing a hotel room with a journalist from a French newspaper. He told me he was intending to slip across the river the next day to Leopoldville. Press passes had been stopped, but as there was no proper supervision because the civil administration was in a state of great disorder, it seemed pretty clear that we would be able to get across to the Congo. The next morning we hired a boat and crossed the river and landed on the Congo side. There were no formalities and no officials at the ferry jetty. We made our way to the main hotel and booked in. It was full of press men from all over the world. The English press were there in great force. It seems that when there is a story which combines all the ingredients of adventure, the collapse of a nation, rapes, brutalities, tribal conflicts, United Nations intervention and the destruction of a leader, the Press could not resist it. All these ingredients were there. But it seemed that the Press treatment was disproportionate to the true importance of the story. *The Times* used acres of space describing the various manoeuvrings within the Congolese Government. Most of the press men did not go for original stories, but rather fed on each other's! There was a great deal of collusion between some of the English reporters in particular. If one man picked up a story he would share it with his friends, so that they could file the same kind of dispatch back to their own newspapers. I soon realised why they did this. They were more anxious to achieve acceptability of their stories in their London office rather than exclusivity. Acceptability was more likely to be granted if the story appeared in other newspapers at the same time, and very often completely inaccurate stories would be reported in several newspapers, based on the activities of just one journalist who had, in fact, got the story wrong and persuaded all the other reporters to file an inaccurate story. So it is that untruth is presented as fact, and because so many newspapers enter into the same chorus, nobody can know what the truth is. They must accept the untruth as truth. Of course, no one will remember the circumstances in which the stories were produced, and the stories go down in history as being the truth.

However, it was still Friday. Only Friday. I had to keep my identity secret. If the newspapers gathered who I was, my story in *Reynolds News* the following Sunday would not be an exclusive. So for three days I lived under a pseudonym, Mr Smith, who was a Pressman. I attended all the press conferences, talked to journalists from England as well as elsewhere, and nobody realised who I was, which was just as well.

There was general chaos. The shops were mostly empty of goods. The troops were obviously in a trigger-happy mood. Every time we passed an army unit it was with great apprehension because the machine guns were always at the ready with the finger on the trigger. There were several people killed in accidental firings. The troops were not being paid so they were in an angry mood.

The maintenance of law and order in the town itself depended on the UN troops who were mostly Ghanaians. I met up with an old friend of mine, Nathaniel Welbeck, who had been appointed as the Ghanaian Ambassador to the Congo. At this time Kwame Nkrumah was extremely friendly to Patrice Lumumba and was trying to afford him some protection, and the UN was the vehicle for this.

I tried to visit Lumumba to have a private interview with him. It proved to be very difficult. I attended a press conference which he addressed, but that did not convey very much. After two days I managed to get into his house. As far as I know, I was the only European allowed to see him on his own for several weeks. He looked extremely sick and his eyes were wild. My French was not good enough for me to talk to him without an interpreter, but, even through the interpreter it was clear the man was beginning to become deranged. He said to me several times very emphatically 'The Congo depends on me. I shall be the saviour of this country.' But the truth of the matter could be seen by looking through the windows. The Ghanaian troops in their blue United Nations helmets were patrolling the gardens. They were the only protection that Lumumba had from his own Congolese troops who no longer accepted his authority, and would have killed him, given half the chance. Later, of course, Lumumba was taken out and murdered. I was one of the last Europeans to see him alive.

On the next day one of the *Daily Express* reporters recognised me. He was amazed that I had been able to stay in Leopoldville with all those press men and to maintain an alias.

I left Leopoldville with a sense of relief. The place was certainly hurtling into even greater catastrophe. What it was like in the up-country areas, of course, I didn't see at first hand, but the reports were quite horrifying. The return to tribalism was a tragedy there. The Belgians passed power over in the

Congo without any preparation. For years they had maintained a strong paternalist domination of this vast country. Until very shortly before Independence, Africans were not allowed to leave the territory or even to go to Belgium to study. There were very few educated Africans in the Congo, and as in Tanganyika, the number of graduates could be counted on the fingers of one hand.

The policy of the Belgians was to keep the Africans in a state of servitude so that Belgian power could be maintained indefinitely. Their policy was in contrast to that of the French territories where Africans were allowed to integrate with Europeans, and encouraged to make visits to France.

In the Congo, however, the resentment against the Belgians was so great, the reaction so strong, that after Independence, within months, complete disorder set in. Colonial rule of this character was a crime against humanity.

I returned to England via Ghana which was ruled then by Nkrumah. It was an interesting visit. I was able to see what happens in a territory after independence has been enjoyed for some years. Nkrumah had been the idol of the Liberals and the Socialists and was a symbol of African freedom. He did not justify in his actions the hope that had been expected of him. Instead of becoming a just democratic leader of Ghana, he increasingly developed megalomaniac tendencies. The economy of the country became warped by his expenditure on prestige projects rather than on essential economic development. There was also a great deal of corruption. He put up a big statue to himself with his fist held high. I had a photograph taken in front of it, but I was not to know that the statue would not last very long. It was pulled down soon after Nkrumah himself had been toppled from power. The military pushed Nkrumah out because they could no longer tolerate corruption in the country.

I had in my visit to Africa covered territories which were going through different stages of development. Some, like Tanganyika, gave me great hope for the future. Others, like the Congo and Ghana, gave me cause for despair. I reflected on my way home what system of Government can best give the ordinary African people the opportunities which they deserve, to help them influence the course of their own lives, to assist them to enjoy the fruits of their own economic activity, and to have the opportunity to develop full personalities and cultural pursuits. The answers to the questions were not simple, because whatever system was used, it could easily be warped by greedy men, not only for economic reward but also for unbridled and corrupting power. The idealist within me was under strain but far from daunted.

4 *The Co-op and the Communists*

When I returned to England from my two years in Uganda working for the African Co-operative Movement, I looked around for a job I could do within the British Co-ops. It was 1954 and I was not yet thirty. The momentum of my idealism was still carrying me over the pitfalls of realism. I believed in human decency and the inevitability of progress if the doors were opened for that decency to express itself. The idea of having a 'career' and working for myself did not appeal to me in the slightest, and I never gave such thoughts any encouragement. My ambition was to serve others and the Co-operative Movement was a natural place to do so. It had no element of exploitation, as the ownership was vested in all the members, and profits were distributed rather than being cornered by clever entrepreneurs as happened in other commercial organisations. I saw an advertisement for an assistant in the London Co-operative Society's Education Department and applied. I could have saved my time. After a week I had a postcard saying the application would be considered by a Committee only after two months.

This was my first personal experience of Co-op Committeeitis in Britain, and certainly not my last. The Committee is, in theory, a wonderful democratic vehicle. Committee Members representing various points of view all have the chance to say their bit and finally a decision emerges which fairly represents a consensus. According to the theory it will be a fair decision, which will be generally acceptable and which will be wise, because so many minds have been applied to the task of reaching it. The theory is fine but the practice is abysmal. It falls down because Committees take time, particularly when composed of voluntary members, and when the cumbersome machine has been applied to calling the Committee, circulating agendas and papers and then actually holding a meeting, the circumstances have changed so much that a decision could be meaningless.

In a fast moving world timing is the all-important factor. In my case, at that time, I could not wait two months before getting work. I looked elsewhere and found two convenient and flexible part-time jobs. They gave me the opportunity of spending most of my time on campaigning within the Co-op for the reforms I thought were vitally necessary, if a great Movement was not to sink without trace into the bogs of committeeitis.

Within a year or so I found myself elected at the age of thirty-one to the Board of Management of the largest Co-op in the world. I was the youngest Director by over twenty years, and the only one who was not an elderly housewife or an employee. The realities and weaknesses of democracy became too painfully obvious. The concept of any member being able to stand for election is wonderful in theory, but the only people who are able to devote the time to the constant electioneering, which goes with an elective position in the Co-op, are housewives, who are active in the Co-op Guild organisations, or employees who are paid and given all the time they need by the Society itself. I was an odd man out and I was made to feel it. How I wished there could be like-minded and younger members on the Board with me. I felt suffocated and frustrated by the attitudes of the diehards of the Committees who had been wrapped up so long in the routine that they could not grasp the fundamental errors which were being made. The sleepy giant of the High Street would not wake up. The chain stores and the dynamic operators like Jack Cohen of Tesco were making big inroads into Co-op trade, and the loyalty of members, which had been the bedrock of Co-op success for a 100 years, was being eroded by the sheer facts of bad service, poor merchandising and sometimes higher prices.

However, I decided not to storm the citadel—which was anyway hardly possible as a lone member—but rather to try to put my reformist philosophy across by stealth. The first essential was to break down the suspicion which most of my new colleagues felt because I was young and, what was even more damning, a graduate. Some of them could not understand how any educated man could have the incentive to serve on a Co-op Committee, where the only material rewards were the perks of the office—an honorarium of twenty pounds per year, plus expenses of fifteen shillings for every meeting attended, plus free food in the Board dining-room, and chauffeur-driven cars. For a housewife committee member a meeting might mean fifteen extra shillings for the housekeeping, a free lunch and a ride in a big car to collect the shopping or the laundry. For the employee member a meeting might mean release from the chores of a job as a bread roundsman or a clerk or a shop assistant. It was no wonder the other Directors looked askance at the thirty-one-year-old economics graduate who could pick up a highly paid job elsewhere. They could not understand my motives. One of my close friends at the London School of Economics, Reg Prentice, came up against a similar misunderstanding of motives when he went for a job at the Co-operative Wholesale Society at their headquarters in Aldgate, London. He was a newly-fledged graduate, but an idealist as well, who wanted to serve the Movement. 'Job?' they said. 'You will not want to work here in the Co-op. You are a graduate.' 'Yes, I do,' he answered. 'I will start at the bottom.' They gave him a job as an invoice clerk, in disbelief, and left him there while others were transferred to gain more experience.

'Why don't you transfer me too?' he asked.

'There is no point in doing that,' they answered. 'You won't be staying, you are a graduate.'

Reg Prentice gave up trying to climb the ladder of the Co-op from the bottom rung, went to the Transport and General Workers Union to work as a clerk in their Legal Department, and eventually became a Trade Union sponsored MP and finally a Cabinet Minister. A Labour Government's gain was the Co-op's loss.

I persevered in my efforts to gain acceptance. For a year I hardly uttered a protest at the stupidities of management, which worried me greatly, or at the inanities of the endless committee system which sapped all initiative. I hoped that my patience would be rewarded, that my colleagues would realise my goodwill and be brought round to accept at least some of my ideas. At the end of the first year as a Committee Member, I was elected as an MP. My Co-op colleagues probably thought 'That will be the end of his Co-op work; he will now take himself off to the higher reaches of Parliament and leave us to our own devices.' No doubt there were hearty sighs of relief at the prospect, because, as an 'odd man' I was an embarrassment to those who could only understand colleagues who fitted into the well-worn pattern of Co-op representation.

But I did not go. I stayed on to press for the changes I felt were essential if the huge London Co-op with its one-and-a-quarter million members was to wake up to the tremendous opportunity of increasing its economic impact. The Society had 1,400 shops, the biggest dairy service in London, and a dozen Departmental stores. It had the sinews of strength if only it would stretch those muscles. On a macabre point, the most successful department was funeral furnishing: burying the co-operators of the older generation who had given the Movement its power in past years. It became evident that reforms would only be possible if the composition of Co-op Committees were changed. The 'old-guard' had to be replaced by younger and more imaginative people who would be less interested in perks and more interested in progress. I knew there were other socialists in the Labour Party who felt as I did that the Co-op could be a practical vehicle for making our ideals of democracy and justice and the avoidance of exploitation actually work in practice. Socialism is not just concerned with legislation and State ownership, it is a way of life. And if the frontiers of the socialist community could be widened by activity on the battlefields of trade, as well as grasping the levers of Power through Parliament, so much the better. It would also be healthier for Co-operative Socialism to succeed in the market place rather than being imposed from the top by decree.

During this time I made visits to both Czechoslovakia and Sweden which were to influence my thinking greatly. In the Communist country the Co-ops were generally dowdy and apathetic as they had a partial monopoly protected by the State, but in Sweden the Co-ops were lively, attractive and enormously successful. The Swedes are vigorous people under that dour exterior, but that could only be part of the explanation for the Co-op emergence as the strongest trading organisation in the country. Structure had a lot to do with its success.

There was professional mangement instead of the amateur committees of the British movement, and the Societies were guided by the Kooperativa Forbundet (KF), the powerful central organisation which was also the wholesale society. I was greatly impressed by the attitude of mind of the Swedish co-operators. They acted as though they had a mission, and that mission was the pursuit of excellence in consumer service. In Britain we had become used to a miserable struggle for mere survival against competition rather than being the pace-maker for new standards which was the Swedish role. I marvelled at the supersmart stores and the automated systems, and thought of some of our own stores where loyalty was sorely strained by poorly designed shops and mediocre standards of merchandise. These were the long years of Labour opposition in Parliament, but I thought that suitably reformed the Co-op Movement could do much to improve Britain itself, without us having to be dependent on political action at the centre. Furthermore, Co-operators elsewhere were waking up to the need for firm action to stop the rot and the fateful decline of Co-op trade.

Hugh Gaitskell was invited to prepare a report on the measures necessary to save the position, and he asked Tony Crosland, who was then not in Parliament, to be the Secretary of the Commission of Inquiry. A valuable report was produced, but instead of embracing it with enthusiasm and getting on with implementing its proposals, the Movement relapsed into the typical Co-op syndrome: it held conferences. There were special Conferences and Congresses to discuss the Gaitskell report, and in the end its wise ideas were buried under a welter of talk and paper. It was left to business pressures— the competition of the market place, which the Co-op theorist is given to abuse—to force the pace of change. The Co-op has suffered from an excess of democracy, helping to prove the old adage, 'You can have too much of a good thing,' and choke on it. I was fed up with the talk, talk and more talk. It reminded me of a meeting I attended in a remote area of Uganda where the tribe was so democratic no decision was possible and no action taken unless every single adult male had said his piece and agreed with the proposal. The meeting went on for three days and still reached no conclusion. The local District Officer, an Englishman, had been tired out by duty and was so exasperated he suddenly jumped into his Landrover and drove at high speed at the crowd, scattering them in all directions.

I felt the great Co-operative Movement, which had grown and prospered for a century since the Rochdale Pioneers, was now drowning in the waters of its own verbosity. Action was the life-jacket as well as the remedy. Action needed decision; decision needed power, and power needed position. It was not sufficient for me to be a lone voice in a Committee of sixteen; I needed allies and I needed to achieve a position which would enable me to influence the Movement's direction. I decided to attempt to win the Presidency of the London Co-operative Society in the coming election. Firstly, I had to be selected by the electoral body known as the London Co-operative Members Organisation (LCMO), because without their endorsement I would stand as much chance of election as a Democratic Party candidate in the New York City of 1940s without Tammany Hall.

For months on end I visited a hundred of the Women's Co-operative Guild branches in the London suburbs stretching from Hounslow to Southend-on-Sea. Thirty years before, as a child, I had achieved my first consciousness of the Co-op at such meetings. Those memories gave me the fortitude to stand the excruciatingly painful boredom, and fortitude was necessary. People who theorise about democracy, and I mean here particularly the intellectuals who live in the ivory towers of the Universities, or the editorialists who preach from the safe and remote pulpits of the Press, never really understand the stresses and strains of democratic activism. They have never had to suffer the weeks and weeks of boring meetings unleavened by the yeast of intelligent controversy. I suffered, willingly—and sacrificed the more interesting time at Parliament—because I had a goal.

I was selected, much to the surprise of the diehards, and then came the election which was more difficult. My opponent was Harry Clayden, a veteran member of the Board, who, as a Grocery Branch Manager had the full endorsement of the Trade Union vote. He was also a long-standing member of the Communist Party and could rely on the Party members coming out to vote for him. They were always instructed to do so. But I worked hard in the campaign visiting over 500 shops and canvassing hundreds of Co-op households. Despite appeals, the local Labour Parties did practically nothing to help, mainly because the Labour Party has never, unlike the social democrats on the continent, understood the Communist Threat. In the Co-ops, as well as the Trade Unions, the Labour Party is soft on Communists. Hugh Gaitskell understood and I had a charming letter of support from him. In the event it was a close run result. I was elected President by a majority of 140 votes in a membership of 1,250,000, all of whom were entitled to vote, but of whom only just over one per cent bothered to do so. I was now, at thirty-seven, the head of the largest retail Co-op in the world, and, in itself, the biggest component of the British Movement. I suffered from one crippling disadvantage. The Communists hated me and were determined to destroy me. And in the Management Committee elections which took place at the same time, all the allies of the Communists were elected. I was the President but a majority of the Board were hostile. It was not a pleasant situation. And the trading position of the Movement was deteriorating. In 1962 even in the food trade, the multiples gained eleven per cent and the Co-ops lost one per cent.

The LCS overall sales had been nearly sixty million pounds in 1957, but by 1962, despite rising prices, sales had fallen back to fifty-six million. I persuaded the Board to adopt more progressive policies, an aggressive sales campaign by cutting prices in the supermarkets, and an advertising campaign to give the Society a new image. The Board appointed an American agency—Batten, Barton, Durstine and Osborn (BBDO)—to handle the campaign. The Communists felt outmanoeuvred as they were not making the running, and feared that a more attractive and lively Society would make it more difficult for their minority to achieve absolute control. Their reaction was vicious, they used some of the same methods as they had adopted in the Electrical Trades Union disputes a few years earlier—vilification of opponents in order to undermine them morally, socially and politically. Les Cannon who had been a Communist but was revolted by their methods resigned to lead the ETU out of the Communist camp. He revealed from his experience just how evil the CP philosophy of 'The end justifies the means' really is. If an opponent has to be destroyed they believe it is acceptable to use everything short of physical assassination to do so—complete character assassination is OK.

Les Cannon sent me several messages of support; he knew what I was up against. He became a most effective Trade Union leader and it was a tragedy that he died comparatively young from an illness that might have been partly caused by the strain of his struggle. I began to suffer the type of attacks he suffered, but like a lapsed monk he probably had more to contend with from his erstwhile Church. I had never been a Communist, despite the attempts to recruit me at University, so they did not hate me quite so much as they hated him and the other former adherents who attacked them. But the attacks were wounding and mostly based on complete fabrication. It was said that I had links with BBDO, the American Company, and that their work was part of a bid to take over the Co-operative Society for capitalism. In fact, I had never even heard of BBDO before they came before the Board for appointment as advertising agents. The later suggestion that the CIA were behind BBDO was equally fanciful. The rumour was spread about that BBDO had bought me a big estate in the country. This was absolute rubbish, they never paid me anything; the truth was that I was forced to sell my home in Canonbury, Islington, to raise the thousands of pounds I spent on Co-op campaigning and forced to buy, on a new mortgage, a cheap tiny place in Potters Bar, twenty miles out of London.

The new home was actually much lower in standards than a typical local authority council home, and there was certainly no 'estate'. They even spread the story that I had a homosexual relationship with one of the American executives of BBDO. The Communists had learnt the Goebbels' trick—the bigger the lie the more likelihood some of it will stick. And they took their campaign to my constituency and tried to persuade the Walsall Co-operative Society, through the local Communists, to drop me as a sponsored candidate for Parliament. No one who has not suffered an orchestrated campaign of vilification can understand how bitter it is. Even some friends began to doubt my intentions: they were falling for the Communists' tactics and did not realise it. In those circumstances it is very difficult, if not impossible, to answer back. The malicious lie has greater currency than the truth, for it is as titillating as the truth is mundane. I was hearing the lies only at fifth or sixth hand after they had gone the rounds, and it was physically impossible to counter them. I went on with the campaign for reform, undeterred, but being a sensitive man I was deeply wounded by the personal attacks made on me.

Fortunately there were one or two members of the Board who could see the situation clearly and were wholly behind me. We arranged a visit to the successful Swedish Co-ops, and particularly to the Stockholm Konsum, to bring back the ideas which could transform the London Society. With less than one fifth of our membership the Stockholm Society's trade was more than London's; their techniques were modern and efficient and, above all, they put emphasis on successful management.

Within the British Movement, management was constantly warped by the intrigue and the infighting which regrettably goes hand in hand with a surfeit of democracy. In Stockholm the elected representatives laid down policy and then allowed the Managers to get on with the job untrammelled by the debilitating farce of amateur elective committees. We brought a 15,000 word report containing detailed proposals before the Board following the Stockholm visit. The Communists and the reactionaries were not prepared to discuss them objectively. It became clear that the struggle for reform could only be won, or lost, in the ballot boxes of the coming elections. No amount of argument or reasoning could change the majority of the Management Committee; they were consumed with prejudice and envy, and much concerned with protecting their own narrow self-interests. Reform, after all, would make it difficult, if not impossible, for people of their calibre to serve on committees with the same self-important role.

Two Board members of the Communist-controlled electoral group, the '1960 Committee', Tom Richardson, a school teacher, and Dorothy Fane, a housewife, resigned to join me in a new Co-operative Reform Group. They announced their disgust with the Communist tactics and their support for Labour Party candidates. They were also disgusted with the Communists for failing to reveal to the members that in the previous six months trading the Society had made a £800,000 loss after making dividend payments. The failure to disclose the truth showed the disdain of the Communists and their allies for the accountability of the Society to its own members. The three of us in the Co-operative Reform Group decided it was our duty to reveal the facts through a minority report. Five minutes before release I was served with an injunction restraining me from publication. The Communists had gone to the capitalist courts—at the Society's expense—to secure their ends. I appealed before the High Court and won the right to publish, and the minority report was released. I was not myself standing for election—my term of office was for three years—but I put all my efforts behind the campaign to defeat the Communists. They were an evil element within any democratic institution. Their candidates included the militant David Ainley, the business manager of the Communist newspaper *The Daily Worker*, and the author of the Party pamphlet 'Class War in the High Street' and Harry Clayden, whom I had defeated the year earlier in the Presidential election and whose photograph was distributed all over the Society in a Communist leaflet. Their motives were clearly outlined by David Ainley who wrote:

> Co-operation alone cannot change society and get rid of capitalism. Only an end of profit making altogether will realise the noble socialist aims for which co-operators have been valiantly striving for over 100 years. This cannot be done just by gradual extension of co-operation, nor yet by nationalisation in the style carried out by the Labour Party in 1945, which left all effective power in the hands of the capitalist class. It can come only by the transfer of political and economic power to the working class, supported by its allies in other sections of the population. Co-operators who want to see their movement launch a stronger fight against the monopolists and take its place in the leadership of the struggle for socialism can do nothing better than join the Communist Party.

Despite this clear statement of faith many social democrats failed to see the dangers of the Communist Party to their own democratic movement. I wrote at the time:

> Those who have studied the development of the international Communist movement tell us that the Communists hate and fear no-one so much as the Social Democrats. In country after country where, after years of co-operating with Socialists, the Communists have succeeded in overthrowing the Government, they have turned like sharks on those Socialists who had been their collaborators. This is because the Communists cannot permit the existence of a reasonable alternative to their method of achieving 'Socialism'.

During the election campaign the reaction of the Communists was vicious in the extreme. In particular, they turned to the staff for support by claiming that a victory for their opponents would spell mass redundancies in the Society. Again the official Labour Party failed to give their own members the support they should have expected. I sent an individual handwritten letter to the Chairmen of forty constituency Labour Parties in the Society's area appealing to their members to vote, and only two bothered to reply. I called on Harold Wilson, now Leader of the Party following Hugh Gaitskell's death, to ask for his support. He was extremely sympathetic but felt unable to intervene in Co-op affairs. It was almost inevitable after the pusillanimity of Labour that the election produced an overwhelming victory for the Communist candidates. I was now even more isolated in the Presidential chair. The trading results continued to show the sad decline of the Society. Opportunities for using the vast resources in terms of underdeveloped land and trading sites were lost. Other traders were booming, we were stagnating. The Communists pushed through the disposal of our one Oxford Street store at a low price for a quiet sale, so as to put the profit proceeds in the current account to distribute as trading dividend to the unsuspecting members. I was powerless against the relentless Communist machine and was eventually forced to resign to allow my Communist opponent, Harry Clayden, to take over the Presidency.

It was 1964 and a Parliamentary General Election was coming after thirteen years of Conservative Government. At least I could now turn to that campaign and to the wider political stage. After the crushing humiliation of defeat, and the destruction of my Co-op idealism, I sorely needed another activity to absorb my energy.

5 *The draughty corridors of power*

AT EVERY GENERAL ELECTION, the civil servants in Whitehall have a respite from Ministers. The Cabinet Committees
no longer meet, except for emergencies, and the cacophony
of Parliament is stilled. For a time the voracious appetite of
legislators for answers to Parliamentary Questions or replies
to debates does not need to be fed with the mountains of words
poured out by the official typewriters. The black ministerial
cars no longer speed their masters from the neat suburban
houses in Surbiton or the flats in Hampstead to the square
mile of Westminster where the wisdom of Oxford, Cambridge—
and sometimes Redbrick—is distilled for the benefit of
Government. The Ministers are on the hustings or, more likely,
preening themselves for the daily appearances before the television cameras which will froth the issues into a soufflé of trivia.

The Mandarins are left on their own, viewing the Election
proceedings with disdain; the country and the commentators
might get excited about elections but the Mandarins and the
lesser-Mandarins are superior to such irrelevancies. They are
self-assured in the knowledge that the real power of Government resides not with the Ministers but with the manipulators;
that behind the colourful scenes of Parliament the decisions
are made by dispassionate men whose loyalty is not to the
ephemeral whims of political parties but to the abiding English
system and to the secure English Establishment. The days are
tranquil and unworried, like a lull before the electrical storm.
Before long the principal actors will return from the provincial

tour to take the stage again in the main theatre, renewed in their confidence, or their arrogance, by the plaudits of the public. The Prime Minister will don the carefully pressed grey-striped trousers and black coat and, shaking off the deadening fatigue of three weeks electioneering, will drive to Buckingham Palace to become, officially, the Queen's first Minister. It will be the well-merited renewal of mandate and return to No. 10 Downing Street or the beginning of an exciting new 100 days. The civil servants will be as civil as ever. 'Yes, Prime Minister.' 'Would you like him called now, Prime Minister?'; the phrases will slip off the tongues without effort, irrespective of the person of the holder of the office.

Such was the arrival of Harold Wilson in the Autumn of 1964. He had thought, mistakenly, that his success, sweeping in like an irresistible tide propelled by his speeches on the white heat of the technological revolution, could create a great impact on the Whitehall machine. But the Mandarins knew otherwise and Harold Wilson as an ex-lesser-Mandarin, with the Order of the British Empire to boot, should have known better. He had fallen into the cardinal error of any politician of believing his own propaganda. His own expectations were therefore too high and this was one of the reasons for his subsequent dismal failure although, consummate conjuror as he was, he continued to juggle the appearance of success as the props and the scenery were crashing all around him.

Sir Alec Douglas-Home had held the election off until the last possible moment, hoping that some issue would avert the erosion of support for the Conservatives. He was much maligned during the election campaign and before partly because, unlike other Party leaders, he was honest. Early in 1964 he said, 'There are two problems in my life. The political ones are insoluble and the economic ones are incomprehensible.' Such frankness is unacceptable to a public fed on the diet of deceit. He had also said something unfortunate about solving economic problems with matchsticks. But his worst crime was not to appear well on television. In these days of electronic electioneering it matters not what qualities a leader possesses if he does not 'perform' in front of the cameras. Obversely, if a mendacious mediocrity appears well on the box he might sweep all before him. In the days of the romantics human society often found itself in a tender trap but today, increasingly, it is caught in a technological trap, doing things which are not necessary and often harmful, simply because the modern invention makes it possible.

Jet travel is another example of opportunity abused. It imposes on leaders the necessity of covering vast distances to hold meetings at inconvenient times when their metabolism has not caught up with the time change and when they are still suffering from the fatigue of the last trip but one. The leaders fool themselves that this frenetic activity is the reality of statesmanship whereas, if truth be known, they have become the sad victims of the public relations syndrome. At every turn, at every airport, the omnipresent cameras will record the journeys of these men not for posterity but simply for a slot in the next news programme. And it is all done not for diplomacy but for the family viewers watching Coronation Street in the terrace houses of Wigan or Warrington who must be impressed that their man is coherent in far-away places from Lancashire.

Harold Wilson was the first fully technological Prime Minister and he used the techniques to the full, arranging his arrivals so they would go out simultaneously by satellite on ITN News or News At Ten or delaying the most telling and polished part of a speech until he had the signal that the TV cameras were on red. Max Frisch once said that technology is the knack of so arranging the world that we don't have to experience it. In Harold's case it has been the treadmill which once trod cannot be left. It is sad because the philosophical man in him has been submerged and warped by the pressures of constant exposure and instant decision-making. Harold would have been a more creative and successful leader if, like Asquith, he had been able to spend four or five months a year away from Westminster. As a general rule the age makes the man. It is an exceptional and rare man who moulds the age. And Harold is, clearly, a product of the technological age— performing to the demands of the media and deluding himself that it is the other way round. In that late Autumn of 1964 the new Prime Minister, the youngest this century, had no appreciation of the problems he was building up for himself. By paying such homage to the mechanisms of the media he enslaved himself to them. But in those heady days few of us realised that the intoxications of communications would be such as to disorient the first Labour Government for thirteen years and would so confuse the century's most intelligent Prime Minister that his capabilities would be warped and wasted. Those were the days of great purpose. The Labour Party and its Parliamentary members were hungry for power but believing genuinely that the formulae they had for the country's ills would work. We were, however, on the horns of a dilemma.

Whilst espousing the noble ideals of equality and fraternity and efficiency we were wedded to a powerful and destructive vested interest in the Trade Union movement which pursued its ends without regard to those ideals: equality was anathema to Trade Unions for each wanted as much for its members as it could get, irrespective of the consequences; fraternity could not mix with the desperate inter-union competition which could stop a whole railway system on a dispute between train drivers and railwaymen, and efficiency could not be achieved with the endless restrictive practices and the blatant over-manning which unions encouraged. The tragedy was that at the grassroots there were many individual union members and even shop stewards who wanted an end to the constant bickering and grabbing. They never had a spokesman because the leaders themselves had a personal interest in the disputes. The disputes gave the Trade Union President or General Secretary a chance to prove to his members his strength in negotiations or his firmness under pressure—all recorded on television, which made compromise more difficult as no leader could afford, with such exposure, to show a hint of weakness. These problems were far from the minds of the Labour Members of Parliament as they streamed back to their homes or to London from the constituency Town Halls where the voting figures had just been announced and they had made the dutiful speeches thanking the Returning Officer and the Police. The country-wide results came over the car radios from the BBC: a cliff hanger and Labour in with a majority of only five seats. The expectant and the hopeful Members stayed at home waiting for the telephone to ring from No. 10 and doing the calculations and making the lists about who would get which job. On the second day of waiting I gave up and took my wife to the local cinema to see Sean Connery as James Bond in 'Goldfinger'—it would be our celebration and compensation for not being offered a post. It was Saturday night and the Government-making would surely be over by now. We returned after 11 pm to hear the surprising news from our fourteen- and thirteen-year-old daughters that the Prime

Minister's office had been on the telephone. The real life had greater tension and excitement than James Bond. The phone soon rang again. 'Harold here, John, will you come and see me tomorrow.'

The door at No. 10 Downing Street was opened to me for my first visit as though I was a well-known regular visitor. At the end of the long ground floor corridor is a round table in an alcove on the left and three or four chairs. This is where the PM's visitors wait, directly outside the Cabinet Room, which has double doors for soundproofing. When I arrived there were two other colleagues waiting and we greeted each other affably, happy in the knowledge that we were all included in the chosen few. Each interviewee spent about five minutes with the Prime Minister who sat at the PM's place in the middle of the long Cabinet table with one telephone, a big ash tray with a pipe, and a copy of the *Life of Lincoln* in front of him. He beckoned me to sit near him and without any preliminaries said, 'I want you to join Roy Jenkins at the Ministry of Aviation; you were a pilot weren't you? You should do well there and I think you can get on with Roy.'

No Member ever gets advance warning of the job to be offered by the new Prime Minister. The discretion lies entirely with him even for the most senior offices and the opportunity for bargaining is limited. For a junior Ministerial job, it is virtually a question of take it or leave it. I was happy to become Parliamentary Secretary to the Ministry of Aviation, which had big responsibilities for the aircraft industry and for civil air transport. It would be a task worth doing, particularly as I would be under a Minister for whom I had a profound respect. On the next day I was picked up by an official car and driven to the vast ugly complex along Whitehall, behind the historic and well-preserved Banqueting Hall, which housed the Ministry of Defence and the Ministry of Aviation. The building had been built post-war to pre-war design and it showed many signs of lack of imagination but my thoughts that day were not on architecture. I remembered coming to the building years before to see Ted Heath when he was President of the Board of Trade and that Ministry was in occupation. And now I was being taken to the same Ministerial offices. My new room was spacious with a large desk in the corner and a highly polished conference table with eight chairs around it. I met my Principal Private Secretary, a career civil servant who is allocated to the

Minister by the Permanent Secretary, the head of the official side of the Ministry. He had been Private Secretary to my Conservative predecessor. It was quite natural for such officers to be translated from one politician to another and to serve them all equally loyally—in their way—whatever the political views of the Minister or Secretary. Such a system keeps the ship of Government on even keel, preventing the violent lurches which could happen if the whole crew were changed at the one time. I was given a heavy red box to carry official papers. I had the suspicion the boxes were heavy and red not so much for security but to ensure that absent-minded Ministers did not forget them in doubtful places.

There was much to read. During the election period the civil servants had been busy filing away in securely locked cabinets all the documents relating to the previous administration just in case they did not come back and preparing new briefs on the Department and its responsibilities for the incoming Ministers in case they were new. The briefs were thick, covering every aspect of the aircraft industry, which had absorbed more public money than any other in Britain, the electronics business—the fastest growing new industry—and the airlines, BOAC and BEA, which also came under our supervision. I went to the Minister's room to talk with Roy Jenkins. He is an urbane, cultured and civilised man and it was a joy to be brought together with him. Roy said, 'I suggest we should divide responsibilities here so you can have some areas which you can run for yourself. I think that is better for you than simply acting as my number two on everything.' I agreed, relieved that I would have some real work to do. 'However,' he added, 'I want you to come in on all the major policy discussions I have and you must say frankly what your view is.' And he was true to his initial word. I participated in all the conferences. The Minister had the capacity for making every one feel his individual contribution was important and valuable. Roy had the rare quality of an intelligence which could be applied to the heart of problems like a rapier thrust—cool, direct and without blood; his intelligence was so acute he could genuinely appreciate and evaluate the thoughts of others. The suggestion often made about him that he is conceited and arrogant is manifestly unfair, coming as it does from jealous rivals who are too unintelligent and insensitive to understand and can only judge by their own inadequate standards. I thought then and consider now that Roy Jenkins could be a brilliant Prime Minister if only the electoral college of Members of Parliament could, for one inspired moment, bury the infighting and elect a leader positively on his individual abilities and qualities rather than as a way of preventing someone else from having the job. It often seemed to me that elections are conducted more on the basis of voting against than for; the secret of success in the democratic process is to choose an opponent who is more disliked than oneself.

When Harold Wilson was selected as Party leader his principal rival was George Brown, the bucolic, eccentric, boisterous yet, in some ways, lovable former fur salesman who became the country's most indiscreet Foreign Secretary. I had backed Harold from the earliest days, believing in his abilities and capacity to lead Britain. When Hugh Gaitskell died unexpectedly of a kidney disease, brought on by the stress of Party squabbles, I telephoned Harold who was then on a lecture tour in the United States and advised his immediate return. I also made a speech supporting Wilson on his own merits. Harold told me later that I was one of the first supporters who had backed him positively rather than merely to stop George Brown. When the election comes for Harold's successor, it is to be hoped that positivism will be evident; then Roy Jenkins would stand a chance and the country would have the prospect of a Prime Minister with a sense of history and one who would not be constantly bogged down in squalid contemporary manoeuvring. He would also be one of the few men, or women, in Parliament with the strength to guide the senior civil service away from its predilection for prissiness and bureaucracy. I saw his capacity as a leader in the Ministry of Aviation and it was impressive.

I concentrated on promoting exports of aircraft, aero-engines and electronics. The first move was to meet the leaders of the British aircraft industry at their headquarters in St James' and to tell them what I had in mind. 'Britain is involved in a struggle for survival,' I said, 'just as surely as during the last war. But the enemy is less obvious than he was then. This time it is an economic and moral war and our enemies, who are legion, want to steal our markets and undermine our economic strength. In these circumstances government and industry must work together to get sales for Britain. The old idea that Ministers and civil servants should keep at arm's length from the squalid commercial world is a nonsense. Selling Britain's products is a noble task and should not be frowned upon. For our part this Government is behind you all the way in promoting British aircraft overseas; you must regard all of us in the Ministry as an extension of your own selling organisation.' Nothing like it had ever been said before by a Minister. It had seemed to me to be self-evident and unexceptional and the fact that my statement was so surprising was a commentary on the way Government, under the guidance of Greek and Latin scholars from Oxford and Cambridge had slipped from providing its obvious function. Two or three generations of senior civil servants, who were slovenly academic about Britain and living in the past dead age of Empire, had created an atmosphere of lackadaisical indifference to the fundamental problem of our country paying its way in a competitive world. Fortunately, for me, there was in the Ministry of Aviation a large number of scientifically trained or influenced civil servants who had not been brought up in what can best be described as the 'Treasury mould'. These men responded well to my new policy directives and some, like John Christie, now Deputy Chairman of the Royal Mint, took to the new ideas with enthusiasm.

I arranged for the Sales Managers of all the aircraft companies to meet monthly under my chairmanship so we could examine world sales prospects, co-ordinate efforts and eliminate the internecine battles which in some markets had let our competitors in. There had been a bad example of this in Brazil a year or so earlier when both Handley Page and Hawker Siddeley were competing for an order and spread damaging propaganda against one another. That nonsense had to stop. At our monthly meetings we would try to decide on a rough justice—giving the most favourably based of the companies all the support of the Government in an attempt to get the order. Within weeks of taking office I heard of a fantastic opportunity for British industry in the sale of an air defence system to the oil rich Saudi Arabia. The information was brought to me by a tall, overweight ex-RAF Group Captain who had been doing a T. E. Lawrence in Arabia, getting close to the Arabs. But his motives were not those of the man who was also 352087 Aircraftsman Ross, because Group Captain Geoffrey Edwards was not a mystic imbued with moral fervour about the Arab cause. He was involved for the money; and the money involved was huge: no less than two and a half per cent to five per cent on orders which could total hundreds of millions of pounds. Most people in Government frowned upon Geoffrey Edwards as an arms salesman grasping after his fat commissions. I did not. In an area such as Arabia much of the commission would any way have to be spent in bribes and, anyhow what was the point of adopting a 'holier-than-thou' attitude when Britain's factories sorely needed that business and our balance of payments needed the foreign currency. Other exporting countries would have no hesitation in providing all possible help to men like Edwards. The United States had a special sales department actually in the Pentagon headed by a Mr Henry Kuss which was fully engaged in promoting arms sales and the French put their full Governmental resources into selling.

I decided the Government should help Edwards and the memoranda whirled around the Whitehall offices like cats among the pigeons. The Foreign Office took strong objection. Firstly they said Britain could never achieve the projected sales of Lightening fighter aircraft and radar equipment because US equipment was better and secondly if we did the resulting political and military commitment to the Kingdom of Saudi Arabia would be too big a price to pay. I answered that it was certainly not our role to bolster foreign goods under any circumstances—the United States was well able to look after itself and, as far as commitments were concerned, none had been suggested and why create problems when possibly they were mere figments of a latter-day nineteenth-century imagination. The Foreign Office objections were somewhat curbed but they were to continue their sniping at the whole project as it progressed. I arranged for John Cronin, the Labour MP for Loughborough, to go to Riyadh to establish our official interest and to prevent the FO from muddying the waters. He did a good job and opened the way for a Ministerial visit. The FO objected again, partly because they did not want to acknowledge defeat and partly because the senior officials had a congenital horror of Government being associated with anything as sordid as trade. Foreign relations to them was simply the graceful gavotte of diplomacy and had as much contact with the real world as the aristocratic dancers in the magnificent ballrooms of the Austro-Hungarian Vienna had with the miserable peasants outside. But I was given permission to go.

I took off for Jeddah, the hot dusty town on the Red Sea which is the point of entry for the annual pilgrimage of millions to nearby Mecca, the secret city of Islam.

I arrived late at night and at the airport to meet me were the British Ambassador, and his Rolls Royce, and an excited Geoffrey Edwards, excited because at last he had secured physical evidence of Government support which was so vital for the conclusion of any deal. We drove off to stay in the Ambassador's Residence, a flat-roofed castle-like place with a camel outside and Ministry of Works interiors.

The next few days were as bizarre as the Thousand and One Arabian Nights of fiction. We flew on to Riyadh, the capital, to see the Ministers and booked into a hotel. Everywhere strict prohibition is imposed. The hotels officially serve only soft drinks. The Ambassador brought whisky with him from the duty free store of the Embassy and in one of our bedrooms we surreptitiously sipped the precious liquid from Scotland. The bottle was smuggled along the corridor in a towel and the glasses were carefully washed by the Ambassador and the military attaché—a distinguished-looking Colonel—as though we were naughty sixth formers having a forbidden midnight feast in the dormitory. Later I was to wonder what all the fuss was about for I went to a Saudi Colonel's home and he had a well equipped bar. I also attended a gruesome sheep-grab where we sat with our Arab hosts on our haunches on the floor drinking contraband whisky run in from Beirut. When the massive sheep was brought in smothered with burnt almonds the Arabs attacked it with their hands, passing to me the delicacies like eyes and items from the nether regions, which I will not describe here.

I spent much of the time in official discussions with the Minister of Defence, Prince Sultan, a well-built man magnificent in his headdress and robes. The Ministry building was situated in an avenue of large Ministerial buildings and all were built according to European designs and were quite unsuitable for the intense dry heat and sun-glare of Arabia. The Prince had his answer to the problem. In his office the heavy curtains were permanently drawn, the artificial lights always on and the air conditioner blaring away as though we were in a factory. It was mightily uncomfortable and somewhat chilly. I longed to get into the warmth of the sun outside. The talks went on for hours and, as usual, were inconclusive.

According to the Arabs, who have infinite patience, it is impolite anyway to reach conclusions at a first meeting. I learnt at least one trick. A small bitter coffee is constantly served to visitors by servants who kneel to pour it from a beautiful silver Arabian pot into tiny cups. I did not find it unpleasant but after several swallows it tended to become boring. Then I realised that a slight shake of the wrist indicates to the servant that enough is enough and he quietly goes away.

It took several visits to make progress and gradually the Saudi requirements emerged. The main threat was not Israel but Egypt and the radar defences were to be aimed at locating enemy aircraft from Cairo, not from Tel Aviv. The Lightnings were to do combat with Russian MIGs in the Egyptian Airforce. Furthermore there was a war by proxy being conducted in the Hashemite Kingdom of the Yemen to the south where the Egyptians had poured in thousands of troops in an attempt to impose the unity of the Yemen within the United Arab Republic. Syria to the north was another arm of the UAR and all was a sinister attempt by Egypt to encircle and dominate the Arab world. The wild broadcasts to the masses in the hovels and coffee shops would also undermine the control by the established Royal Family. Saudi Arabia did not want to lose its special relationship with the United States in concluding any purchase from the United Kingdom. I called on King Faisal and seeing him was rather like an audience with the Pope. He looked so ascetic as to be ill and he seemed to be withdrawn into an unreal spiritual world; as I remember, the conversation itself, which was conducted through an interpreter, was ethereal.

The British Ambassador who, unlike his FO bosses was anxious for our deal to go through, was very pleased with the way things were going. We left Riyadh for Jeddah, but at the airport, after we had booked our baggage on the Saudi Arabian Airways Boeing and had been given our boarding cards, we had the disconcerting vision of a Saudi Prince and ten dark veiled wives going up the steps of the plane with priority and without tickets. When the gates were opened for lesser mortals there was an unholy rush during which the Minister and the Ambassador just made it. I do not know what happened to the eleven unfortunate Saudi passengers who failed to get the seats they had paid for. The philosophy of Government in Saudi Arabia is simple—everything works for the primary benefit of the ruling Royal Family—a blatantly feudal society in a modern world.

After several visits I decided the way to get the order for Britain was to secure the co-operation of the United States, so I went to the Pentagon to see the celebrated salesman Henry Kuss. He was surprisingly affable and agreed to push our case with Robert McNamara, the Defense Secretary. At this time McNamara was trying to soften relations with Britain to get sales for the F111 swing-wing all-purpose aircraft which he was foisting on the American public against some Congressional opposition. McNamara did not say 'no' provided there was an element of US industrial participation. I held a council of war in a Washington hotel bedroom. We were all tense as we knew that hundreds of millions of pounds worth of British exports—the biggest single deal in Britain's exporting history—hung by a thread. If the American companies competing for the sale, and who knew they had it in the bag, thought their own Defense Secretary was making it easy for the Limeys all hell would be let loose and our chances would be lost in a welter of recrimination. The cautious Saudis would also run for cover—buying from us was impossible if it provoked a row in the United States as, at that time, Faisal was in a sense an American protégé. Lord Caldecote attended the bedroom meeting as the representative of the British Aircraft Corporation and he was very sensitive about American industrial espionage. He felt convinced that the bedroom would be bugged—we checked it out, it wasn't. And then someone leapt on a figure behind the curtains; false alarm, it turned out to be one of our own party. We kept tight security, there was no row in the USA—at least not until it was too late—and Britain got the order. It was followed by a similar order by Kuwait, which was made directly on the recommendation of the Saudis, and the total value of the business for Britain amounted to over £300 million. Geoffrey Edwards has gone down in history as the super arms salesman and he made his millions from the commission, but he had to pay out vast sums to all sorts of contact men, including huge amounts for the Royal Family, and to this day he is unable to return to Saudi Arabia because of the endless disputes about money he is expected to pay out. I received a warm congratulatory note from the Prime Minister about all my overseas trips on behalf of exports: for me that was the only reward I wanted.

6 *Government and gorgons*

HAROLD WILSON had one of the most difficult tasks of any Prime Minister in modern times when he took office in 1964. The majority was only five and that was soon reduced to three when Patrick Gordon-Walker, who had been appointed Foreign Secretary without a seat, lost the Leyton by-election on the anti-colour backlash. The pound sterling was under attack. The international money manipulators were selling it short, the multinational corporations were converting to other currencies as quickly as they could, assuming it would soon be devalued, and overseas holders of sterling, even in the Commonwealth, were changing to dollars if they could. The myth of Britain's financial strength was crumbling fast. In the last analysis what matters to a currency's strength is not what the Bankers say but what is happening to the country's economy. And the plain fact was—for all the world to see—that Britain was not paying her way in the world. During 1964 imports exceeded exports by £800 million and that could only be made up by international borrowings, which, in turn, cost money, because of the high interest rates.

Britain was getting more and more in a financial bog. But instead of the British people being told the plain truth that the country was living beyond its means, that the loss of Empire meant British people themselves would have to work harder or more efficiently, and that the delusions of grandeur would have to be discarded, the prevailing mood was one of artificial optimism tinged with only a sprinkling of the phrases about crisis. And the public had heard all those phrases before and they were so inoculated by them that they were immune from shock as the English disease spread further through the country's economic fabric.

The disease took many different forms. Wild cat strikes in the Docks which disrupted the all essential exports, restrictive practices in industry which held back production, speculation in land and property which forced up rents, fiddling by trading companies through undercharging for exports and overcharging for imports, so as to put the proceeds into other currencies, and the opening by directors and professional people of bank accounts in Jersey, the Isle of Man or the Cayman Islands, so as to avoid income tax and to get out of sterling. The common factor in the English disease was the pursuit of narrow self-interest to the detriment of the community and the shirking of responsibility for the country as a whole. The unity of purpose which Churchill had given the British people was gone as the multitude of little vested interests crawled like maggots totally consumed about their own business. It did not matter that the maggots were eating the timbers and that finally the structure must collapse. It was also evident that the Government was, in its way, pursuing its own interest, using the precious months of 1965 not to deal with the fundamental problems but to cover up the wood worm and recharge the myths of Britain's greatness. The Prime Minister even made a fatuous speech about the great British role East of Suez and the need to provide a nuclear umbrella for India. All that was to be scrapped within a year, but at the time it sounded great stuff, and along with other false hopes it served its purpose of deluding the people and disguising the real issues, so as to secure a bigger election victory from the bemused and confused and complacent electorate when the election was sprung early in 1966.

In my job of promoting aircraft exports I came across a lot of noble people who were dedicated to boosting Britain and not deriding her. Men like Sir George Edwards, the designer of the Viscount and the VC10 and head of the British Aircraft Corporation, and Sir Arnold Hall, the brilliant former head of the Royal Aircraft Establishment at Farnborough, who ran the Hawker Siddeley Company. With more men like these, Britain's problems would be less, but there are too few of them, and their efforts are undermined by the others in positions of influence who do not have their vision and patriotism. I was shocked to find that the undertakings under State ownership were often the worst offenders in the insidious game of selling Britain short. It did not tally with my socialist idealism to find that publicly owned undertakings were working against the general public interest.

An example which severely affected our efforts to sell British aircraft was the British Overseas Aircraft Corporation's attitude to the VC10, and it also illustrates the problem of the English disease. Understandably, the Chairman and Directors of BOAC are primarily concerned about their narrow responsibilities to run a major international airline at a profit. In their collective boardroom or in their individual thinking in their own baths, it is this narrow interest which inevitably dominates. They think they will, after all, be judged by the narrow success or failure of BOAC. The word 'narrow' is emphasised because the attitude of mind is narrow like a blinkered donkey which can only move forward in one direction. It is not allowed to see the green grass to the right or the cool water to the left. It must plod the stony path onward and onward and its life is thereby cramped. It is the conventional wisdom that nationalised industries must be operated in this way blinkered and cramped by the rules which regulate everyone to work in their little, or big, watertight compartments, without necessarily being aware of the overriding needs of the nation. And so it was that BOAC with the word British proudly in its name, went about its duty of destroying the credibility of the wonderful British inventions—the VC10 and the Super VC10. It was in its narrow interests to do so. BOAC wanted more Boeing aircraft, subsidised and developed in the wake of a vast United States military programme and said to be marginally more efficient mile for mile than the Super VC10, and they were determined to get them.

The cancellation of BOAC orders for the Super VC10 dealt a body blow just before I took over my job at the Ministry of Aviation. Everywhere I went, in an attempt to press the wonderful virtues of the VC10, I was brought slap up against copies of internal reports by BOAC, slamming the plane. Somehow, Boeing had managed to get hold of these reports and actually circulated them to their own prospective customers. What better recommendation could they possibly have than the fact that British airways preferred Boeings to British planes?

I flew to South America on an inaugural flight of British United Airways flying the VC10 on the route to Rio de Janeiro, Buenos Aires and Santiago de Chile from which BOAC had unilaterally withdrawn. No one in the aviation world could understand why BOAC decided to leave an important flag route for Britain, and it was very good that a private enterprise airline was able to fill the gap, and better still that it was flying a British made aircraft. I travelled with Freddie Laker the flamboyant aviator who had made his first fortune flying supplies into Berlin during the Russian siege and using broken-down second-hand aircraft. Freddie, who was a buccaneer to his fingertips, had a healthy disrespect for civil servants and authority anywhere. He wanted constructive action, not talk, and was exasperated by the type of people who run Government undertakings who are so busy ensuring they never make a wrong move that opportunities flow past them, wasted and lost, and if and when they make a move, it is too late.

BOAC had made it as difficult as possible for BUA to pick up the traffic rights they had renounced in Rio and Buenos Aires, and I had to renegotiate with the Brazilian and Argentine Governments to obtain them. I took the chance in both these countries and in Chile to promote British aviation products. The Brazilian Press got the story slightly wrong. Banner headlines announced 'U.K. Minister arrives to promote V.D.10.'

In Argentina we had a good prospect of selling the VC10 to the national airline Aerolineas Argentinas. The airline had been flying Comets for years and had close relations with Rolls Royce as a result. The country was not so tied to the United States, and the operation of the VC10 on the route to Europe could prove very popular. I decided to ask to see the full board of the airline as it appeared that the case for Britain had not been put. They agreed and I presented the arguments in support of the VC10. Some of the arguments had been suppressed by airline directors but it was clear the board was fairly evenly divided, but what finally killed Britain's chances was the circulation to the directors of the internal BOAC memorandum condemning the VC10's performance. I felt then the truth of that saying 'I can deal with my enemies but heaven save me from my friends.'

I called on the President of Argentina, a frail grey old man who was the most miserable looking head of State I have met apart from King Faisal and, in front of the television cameras, I presented him with a beautiful model of the VC10 for his desk. It was all to no avail because the goose had already been cooked by BOAC and Boeing. After a few days in Buenos Aires I went to catch the plane over the Andes to Chile and, on the roof of an airport building, waited for half an hour for it to arrive. It was twilight on a warm January summer evening, the sky was ablaze with a rosy hue as the sun went down. Then suddenly we saw the plane emerging from the setting sun like a butterfly bursting out of its chrysalis. It was breathtakingly beautiful and, standing there so remote from England, tears came into my eyes at seeing this marvellous British creation coming to South America as an Ambassador for all that was good and positive in my country.

In Chile we had some success in promoting Hawker Siddeley planes, but I was amazed to find how in this, as in other South American countries, the tremendous goodwill for Britain has been neglected by other British companies. I had discussions with Edouard Frei the President—a most impressive man, whom I met again later when he came to London on a State visit. It was a tragedy that he was followed by Salvador Allende, the gentle Communist, who opened the door to workers' control and was incapable of preventing the slide to anarchy and the collapse of the country.

I returned from South America refreshed by my contact with Freddie Laker who was an excellent companion. He introduced me to an exceptional drink he called the Nicolashka. The drinker puts a slice of lemon half covered with coffee grains and half with sugar in his mouth, chews it slightly and then swallows a small glass of neat brandy through the mixture. The result is dramatic, particularly after five or six tries.

I also came back with renewed determination to push the VC10 as much as possible. It was not merely a sentimental exercise. The arithmetic demonstrated that, if the plane had been properly promoted by our predecessors in the Conservative Government, and if BOAC had been instructed to play its part, the aircraft could have been constructed in quantity, which would have reduced costs, rather than being built only to specific orders which was more expensive. And with the Super VC10 available on the shelf, as it were, a lot of sales would have been achieved with airlines which were caught by the boom in passenger transport which came in 1965 and the following years. It is estimated that sales of 200 or more aircraft could have been made over this period and the value, with spares, would have been over £1,000 million.

That sum would have made a sizable difference to British balance of payments over those years and might well have saved the devaluation of the pound.

In the Ministry I gave instructions that we were to look for every possible customer. Most of the airlines were already committed to the giant US companies Boeing or Douglas, but a few smaller companies were not yet equipped with long range modern jets. We turned our attention to two in particular: Middle East Airways, the remarkably successful operator out of Beirut, and CSA, the Czech airline. MEA was run by Sheikh Najib Alamuddin who had created a network out of nothing. I established close relations, meeting with him in both Beirut and London. He told me that he was keen to buy British but needed a token to help him put the case to the Lebanese Government. 'If Britain will agree to allow a small quantity of Lebanese apples to come into the UK market that will swing it in your favour,' he said. The amount involved was indeed small and only a tiny fraction of the cost of the planes. I arranged for a commodity broker who was experienced in barter deals to work with the British Aircraft Corporation who were enthusiastic about the scheme. But again I came up against the problem of petty vested interests. The quotas for apple imports were well organised and the trade did not want the superior Lebanese apple coming on to the British market. Nor did the Press help by printing a story that we were trying to sell planes for apples which was, of course, a distortion. The apples would only be a token in the deal. But I could not get approval for the scheme and the order went to America.

Negotiations with CSA went better and I was able to offer a trade-off of traffic rights for the Czechs to pick up passengers at London for the transatlantic flight if they bought the Super VC10. The airline chiefs were keen to buy but were vetoed by Moscow who did not want that affront to the Soviet aircraft industry which was then developing its copy of the Super VC10—the Iluyshin 62.

During these periods of delicate negotiations I heard that BOAC had circulated papers claiming that the Boeing 707 was more economic on the North Atlantic route than the Super

VC10. This information was very damaging and I tried to check it out, but BOAC refused to give the Ministry the information we needed. I insisted and eventually discovered that an essential fact had been left out of the BOAC calculations. Because the Super VC10 was a more popular aircraft with passengers (and BOAC in its own advertising emphasised this—'Try a little Super VC Tenderness') the load factors were appreciably better than on Boeings. In other words, on scheduled services such as to New York, more seats per aircraft were sold, and so, although the total running costs of the Super VC10 were greater than the 707, BOAC make a higher profit from them. They were also attracting passengers from other airlines which did not fly the Super VC10. I incorporated these facts in a speech I released at the Hanover Air Show—BOAC were not amused.

I moved on from Aviation to a totally different area of responsibility as Under-Secretary of State for the Colonies. I was given an office in Church House in Great Smith Street, just behind Westminster Abbey, but I spent much of my time at Marlborough House or Lancaster House, the stately houses just off St James's Park. There Fred Lee, the Colonial Secretary, and I were engaged in the task of dismantling the residue of the British Empire. They were countries which had been neglected and ignored in the heyday of Empire but which now were almost as difficult to disentangle as the larger states had been. Fiji, for instance: half Fijian and half Indian with the Indians dominating the business life by their superior acumen; Mauritius, a tiny island not much bigger than the Isle of Wight but supporting a population of 750,000 and producing a like amount of tons of sugar; Basutoland, a place of hardy mountain people surrounded by South Africa and the little islands in the Caribbean, each with special characteristics and jealous of their independence. I visited most of these far flung outposts and grappled with the complications of their constitutions. It was not true that smallness means simplicity. Some of the most difficult situations arise in tiny places. Mauritius was a case in point. Britain had taken the island from the French in 1814 after the Napoleonic Wars, but I found the French influence still dominant after a century and a quarter. The local language is a French patois spoken by Indo-Mauritians, Sino-Mauritians and Franco-Mauritians coming from India, China and France respectively. There are Mohammedans from Pakistan, negroes from Africa and Tamils from India and all getting a living from an island strewn with huge volcanic rocks which have been manhandled into piles to enable the precious sugar cane to grow. The cuisine is French, or Chinese, and the well-to-do houses in the high centre of the island at Curepipe look like miniature châteaux. It is an idyllic place with golden beaches and soft warm seas and deer hunting in the forests, which are reminiscent of Scotland. It is a highly polished jewel which, when turned, can show infinite contrasts. But beneath the surface of charm and beauty I found incredible tensions between the races which threatened to explode into violence of the type which afflicted British Guiana some years before. A compromise in the constitution had to be worked out to satisfy the aspirations and fears of each of the communities and preventing any one of them from dominating the others. Without agreement there would have been no progress towards independence and possibly a severe breakdown of law and order. I worked night and day for a week, holding discussions with each leader and each group and gradually edging towards a consensus. It seemed at times the whole effort would founder as passions were so strong.

The Prime Minister was Seewoosagur Ramgoolam, a most resilient Septuagenarian, and a doctor who still liked to practise. His principal opponent was a mercurial mixed blood lawyer called Gaetan Duval who loved the French connection and wanted complete unity with France like nearby Reunion where huge subsidies from Metropolitan France ensured a higher standard of living than that enjoyed in Mauritius. I was greatly helped in my task by friends, such as Harold Walter, the ebullient Minister of Health, with whom I held middle of the night secret discussions. And then at the end of the week the solution emerged. It would provide for compulsory voting across the communities to prevent block domination and ensuring through compensatory seats that every community—including the Chinese with their two per cent of the population—would have fair representation. My scheme would prevent Indians voting only for Indians or creoles only for creoles. The scheme was accepted by all groups and enabled the country to proceed peacefully to Independence.

I returned to England, exhausted, but delighted with my success: I had snatched a complex agreement from the jaws of threatened chaos.. The story did not even rate a paragraph in

The Times and the rest of the Press ignored it completely. If, however, my visit had been accompanied by riots rather than reason, I would have 'enjoyed'·publicity every day of the week and I would have come back a hero to the unsuspecting British public. They do not understand what a fraud the British Press is, concentrating as it does on disorder, scandal, alarm and despondency, and eliminating the positive. The British Ministers who thrive on publicity and whose promotion prospects depend on it learn that there is nothing that succeeds like failure.

One of the most poignant of my journeys was my return to Bechuanaland, which was about to achieve its Independence as Botswana. I had not been there since my visit six years before when the South African Secret Service kept me under surveillance and had me arrested at Mafeking. This time I travelled as a Minister of the United Kingdom Government; it would be difficult for even the South Africans to arrest me this time. Firstly, I went to Swaziland to hold talks on the constitutional developments. Here, as in so many African countries, there was a struggle between the feudal elements around the Royal Family and the pushing nationalists who were influenced by the advances in countries like Kenya and Ghana and who read avidly the papers of the Organisation for African Unity and the Bureaux in Moscow or Peking. The Swazi nationalists wanted all out opposition to South Africa and socialist measures to prevent the exploitation of natural resources. The royalists wanted compromise with South Africa and agreements with the big neighbour on economic development. I met both sides in the dispute. The spokesmen for the Nationalists were smartly dressed in suits and ties and spoke coherently and even intellectually about the country's problems. The Royal opposite could not have been more different. I met King Sobuza in one of his palaces. It was just a medium-sized house but situated in a vast estate. It was a bizarre interview. The King's Ministers sat around the room and all wore suits—one or two with pinstriped trousers and black coats. None of them said a word although there were a few murmurs. The conversation was conducted entirely by the King who was dressed in a piece of multi-coloured cloth slung like a toga over the top of his body and tied with a bow on one shoulder. The chest was half exposed as were the legs and thighs. The King had a magnificent physique although he was well into his fifties, and his skin was velvet like and smooth. In the King's built-up hair were stuck three pieces of wood which could have been small arrows. The room was crowded not only with people but also with about a dozen birds which flew to and from the King's shoulders, on which they perched, in a most disconcerting way. At times I felt the King was willing them to fly straight at my face. The King had flashing eyes and spoke in a most regal way but, unfortunately, in Swazi. The interpretation did not make a great deal of sense to me but that may have been the fault of the interpreter who was crouched in a pathetic way at the feet of the King, and looked extremely frightened. I was glad when that interview was over.

During the few days in Swaziland I went on tour visiting schools where I was welcomed by choirs singing in Swazi, a language which includes an unusual clicking. To hear the clicking in unison from fifty tongues was a sensation never forgotten. I went also to a mountain of iron ore where huge machines were breaking it down as in open-cast mining. The ore was being transported under long term contracts to Japan involving agreements with South African companies. I made calculations on the economics of the operation and discovered that even after allowing for the ploughing back of the reasonably high wages for the Swazi workers, eighty-five per cent of the value of the ore was being taken outside Swaziland. I vowed to myself to try to do something about this neo-colonialist exploitation, but that, regrettably, proved to be impossible, as I did not stay in the same post long enough.

I flew on from Swaziland to Bechuanaland for the Independence Celebrations which were being held at Gaberone, translated overnight from a village to a capital. Princess Marina was the Royal representative and she performed her function with dignity and charm although the conditions were spartan. On the night of the official transfer of power, we went to the hastily constructed stadium just outside the town to watch children performing gymnastics and some tribal dancing. A sand-storm blew up and a biting wind blew across the vast unprotected plateau directly at us. Blankets were obtained and we sat in our morning coats and evening dresses huddled under them. Princess Marina wore her tiara under her blanket and the ceremonies went relentlessly on. It was almost as though we were determined to show the phlegm of the British Empire right to the bitter end.

Botswana emerged as an Independent State and Seretse Khama had moist eyes as I congratulated my old friend on becoming President. Our memories recalled the meeting in Basingstoke, nearly twenty years before, when we were both campaigning for his right to return to his country and everything looked so hopeless. Basingstoke to Botswana was a span, not only of geography and the years, but of anguish and fulfilment.

I left Botswana for Basutoland in the Rolls Royce of the United Kingdom Ambassador to South Africa to drive across the veldt to Johannesburg. This time there were no arrests at the border, and my wife and I were also unmolested at the hotel overnight. We spent the evening at a cinema showing a film in Afrikaans about the South African War. The British were portrayed in the film as boorish and brutal, but the Boers were brave and noble; we reflected on how different history looks from the other side of the fence. The audience hatred against Britain grew more intense as the film went on and we could feel the physical pressure of it enveloping the cinema. We were compelled to leave and there was no doubt the crowd was angry at us as though we were leaving during the middle of a high Church service. To get into the open air was a relief.

Basutoland, or Lesotho as it was soon to emerge, was as different from Botswana as the Welsh mountains from the flat fen country. The people were toughened by the environment of barren hills. Many of them lived on horses wearing colourful blankets as protection against the bitter cold. It seemed to me a deep tragedy that most of the Basuto men had to leave this romantic open country of horses and hills to work in the dark bowels of the earth digging out gold to satisfy the white men's lust and greed. White men, who condemned blacks for their tribal customs, didn't have the sense to realise that the worship of gold is as irrational as the worship of tribal gods, and probably more harmful. What does it benefit the world if thousands of men are cut off for years from families and homes, kept locked in degrading compounds and sent to work for low wages in awful conditions, simply to transfer a useless metal from the tunnels under the Rand to the tunnels under Fort Knox or the Swiss banks. The sum of human happiness is less, not more, as a result of this gold madness which distorts values and warps emotions.

What I had seen in Africa both saddened me and inspired

me. Saddened because there was still so much to be done to improve the lot of Africans, but inspired because political opportunities at last were opening up an escape from the bonds of colonial oppression. But human happiness, like peace, is indivisible and the British Government could not lightly pass over its responsibilities merely by granting titular independence.

7 *The steps to the Privy Council*

IN THE SEYCHELLES, which I was the first Minister ever to visit, I found a rural slum rather than the idyllic paradise I was led to expect. I flew in with an American amphibious aircraft from Mombasa on the coast of Kenya. It was a noisy three-hour flight, and as conversation was impossible, my wife and I played Scrabble. My private secretary at the time was an expert player. He had been Administrator on the remote Tristan Da Cunha, and in the evenings there was nothing to do except play Scrabble. The Seychelles Islands lie in the middle of the Indian Ocean, almost on the Equator, and make a beautiful sight. As the plane banked to find a place to come down on the waters of Mahé harbour, we could see the glorious sandy beaches, the coral reefs, the verdant hills, and all around the huge expanse of deep blue sea stretching without interruption West to Africa, North to Arabia and East to Indonesia and Australia. This was a tiny isolated dot. No wonder that until now it had been lowest on the list for Ministerial visits and never reached. But now my brief was to open it up to encourage travellers from the remote world. The Government had made an agreement with the Americans to develop military establishments on the even tinier coral islands of Diego Garcia. To protect these installations against the eventual protests of nationalists, which had even affected the use of the airport on the Maldive Islands, it was decided to remove the few people on the islands and to create an entirely new constitutional unit to be known as the Indian Ocean Territory.

It could never be independent because it had no citizens and belonged even more securely to Britain than a floating aircraft carrier, which it was devised to replace. The British Empire might be collapsing, but the wisdom was still evident: the ultimate solution to the irritating problems of restless colonies had been found!

Both Seychelles and Mauritius were given large cash sums, provided equally by the US and Britain, to compensate for the loss of territory, and Seychelles was to spend its reward on building an international airport across the coral reefs. This would open the islands to tourism and provide employment for islanders who could no longer make a living picking coconuts. I was shocked to discover that the land speculators had already moved in from Malta and England and were buying up land fronting the beaches for ridiculously low prices. They were splitting it up into villa sites for rich Europeans and Americans who wanted their place on an island in the sun. The fabulous increase in the value of the land which was to come about through the development of the airport was to be creamed off by these foreign entrepreneurs. Here again, as in Swaziland, was another example of neo-colonialism, and the Administration was allowing it to happen. I proposed a stiff capital tax on all land sales, the proceeds of which would be ploughed back into providing decent facilities for the Seychellois. They were terribly neglected. There was no clean water supply, no sanitation or sewage system, and more than half the population suffered from internal parasites which sapped the energy and produced listlessness. The birthrate was too high for local resources to cope with the increase in population, and there was no official birth control policy. I soon found out why. The Governor was the Earl of Oxford and Asquith who was married to an extremely active wife. As devout Roman Catholics they were totally opposed to birth control and would have been unhappy to have seen it introduced. However, the Colonial Office, unbeknown to the Governor, was secretly financing a private family planning clinic being run by a courageous English woman doctor. I proposed to visit her clinic to give her moral support, but when I mentioned her name to the Governor, he would have nothing to do with it, and shut up like a clam. When I walked on my own—for no local Government official would dare come with me— along the little street leading to the clinic, I could feel the eyes peeping from behind the curtains in wonder at the Minister who was daring to defy the Governor, and the Governor's lady.

During the stay we lived in the ramshackle Government House which had the charm and faded glory of an earlier age, but no amenities. One of my suits was left hanging on the verandah at night and was eaten by rats. The water, as everywhere else, was polluted. We heard that Noel Coward who had stayed there before had been violently ill with food poisoning, and we were not surprised.

Over the months we finished our tasks of devising constitutions and arranging independence for the multitude of places which were the left-overs of Empire. Most were successful but one or two were to blow up, unexpectedly, into trouble later. I presided over the conference at Lancaster House which agreed associated status—just short of complete independence—for the group of islands of St Kitts, Nevis and Anguilla. St Kitts and Nevis did all the talking and Anguilla never said a word, and I was therefore amazed years later when Anguilla erupted in delayed protest and declared its own independence.

The Colonial Office, its job completed, was merged with the Commonwealth Relations Office which was finally merged with the Foreign Office, and I was transferred back to an earlier love as Minister of Aviation. The musical chairs of Government provided me with a kaleidoscopic series of contrasting experiences. I now found myself involved in negotiations in Europe on the exciting frontiers of advanced technology. My responsibility was for the British side of the Concorde, the European air-bus, the space programme and the other areas of European technological co-operation. It finally converted me to the belief in the European community which was the only way we could stay in the scientific race increasingly dominated by the giants of the USSR and the USA.

I made frequent visits to Paris to talk to the French on joint military aircraft projects. Sometimes I went in tandem with Denis Healey who was then Minister of Defence. We were both frequently shocked by the blatant duplicity of the French who were secretly developing their own aircraft in competition with joint projects, and then cancelling the Anglo-French project when their own had reached take-off point. Joint schemes were very expensive in terms of time lost and extra research costs trying to fit the product to many different service requirements. Co-operation between the companies was also not easy. I regarded the difficulties as teething problems which would be swept away one day in a united Europe where European institutions would be able to operate continent wide without the complications of national boundaries and sensitivities. Concorde was the biggest and most expensive headache of them all. Cynics might say that supersonic air travel is the most unsocialist policy possible, for it taxes and sonic bangs the many for the privilege of a tiny few. They might also attack the project because it would pollute the environment. However, most technology is polluting. If it were public policy to ban noise-creating transport systems, the internal combustion engine would go, so would the railways and all jet aircraft. And if potentially dangerous emissions were banned we would see the end of aerosols, because the chemicals they release are breaking up the protective layer of the upper atmosphere, not to mention the more obvious alumina plants and power stations. Modern man if he wants the benefits of science must live in a state of compromise with the environment that science creates whilst using, to the utmost, the powers of science to combat the polluting aspects of technology. Every major decision about a new and potentially polluting development should be taken after a total amenity benefit analysis. Government, British or French, never attempted to do that with Concorde. It was another case of 'growing like Topsy': it just grew and grew and grew.

Julian Amery was Conservative Minister of Aviation when the proposal was brought to the Government by a British aircraft industry anxious to be ahead of the Americans in the development of new generation civil aircraft. Britain had been the first to develop the jet engine, but never got the full benefit of this invention as the Comet, the first passenger jet, had disastrous early problems including a crippling crash off Cyprus. The industry leaders argued that breaking the sound barrier for long distance commercial flights would again put Britain in the lead. Amery was in love with technology and agreed; fortunately for him the rest of the Government wanted joint projects with the French, and the concept of an Anglo-French project emerged as a contribution to that *bon-accord*.

It was thought that such co-operation would halve the research and development costs and double the guaranteed market. Both BOAC and Air France would be prevailed upon to buy the aircraft and this, in turn, would put greater pressure on other airlines to match the supersonic service mounted by two countries. The original estimates for the costs of development and production were accepted by the two Governments in faith because they had no means of checking the validity of the industries' figures, unless, of course, they set up parallel undertakings at great expense. The estimators erred on the side of optimism, anxious to get the project approved, but even they did not anticipate the relentless escalation in costs which was to come. In cost benefit analysis it is the marginal, or extra, cost at each stage which has to be weighed in the balance, not the total expense. Money and resources already spent cannot be recovered and is regarded as 'water under the bridge'.

The two Governments decided each time they were presented with a new estimate of increased costs that the benefits of the project in terms of technological progress, prestige and export earnings were greater than the amount of the extra cost. There was never and, given the method of analysis, could never be a justification of the project in terms of total costs except at the beginning when the estimates were guess-work anyway. The weakness in this otherwise fully rational method of decision-making is that the anticipated future escalation of costs is never taken into account. The advocates of a particular programme might argue that no further increases are expected, but with Concorde and similar high technology projects, the likely escalation can be extrapolated from the earlier experience.

In the Labour Governments of 1964 and 1966 there were overwhelming majorities of Ministers opposed to Concorde at every decision point and anxious to secure its instant cancellation. The sponsoring Minister of Aviation or Technology was the only member of the Cabinet to support Concorde for positive reasons; he had support from some other Ministers for peripheral reasons—such as the FO wish to keep good relations with France—and the rest of the Ministers were implacably opposed. They were prejudiced against the aircraft industry and saw the project draining money away from their own pet projects. If it had been a purely British venture, Concorde would certainly have been scrapped. It was saved time and time again by the virtual veto of Elwyn Jones, the Attorney General, who advised the Cabinet that, in the event of unilateral cancellation by Britain, we could be taken to the International Court by the French and made to pay our share of the costs anyway. After the development of the first prototype aircraft, known as 001, which was the limit of the original agreement with the French, the Elwyn Jones advice was no longer valid, as either partner could withdraw without penalty. However, by then, the Labour Government wanted to keep France sweet because of the Common Market application, and, because so much had already been spent, it seemed prudent to delay cancellation until the next crucial stage was reached. Finally, in response to renewed pressure for cancellation, a new formula was devised to enable the programme to continue. It was simple, decisive, and uncontrovertible wisdom. All would depend on airline orders. If they came, the project would continue, if not, it would be cut. The critics were again outmanoeuvred; but soon they had it rubbed in their noses when BOAC were guaranteed subsidies to buy Concorde. It was known that the plane cost more to produce than the buying price, even ignoring the vast research and development expenditure which would never be recovered. In the end Concorde will fly the skies as a tribute to superb British and French technology and also as a living testimony to the breathtaking capacity of Britain to take major decisions entirely based on the wrong reasons. The saying by Lord Leverhulme that half of all advertising was wrong and wasted and the problem was knowing which half could well be applied to Government decisions.

From the start of my Ministerial responsibilities I was sympathetic to Concorde because it was so evidently a brilliant example of technological excellence and Britain sorely needed something to boost its morale. Too many people had been talking Britain down and I was enthused by the contrast I found in the technical branches of the Ministry. The scientists and engineers there were inspired and dedicated. The group, jocularly known as the Welsh Mafia, were particularly impressive, including Morien Morgan, who went on to become head of the Royal Aircraft Establishment and Handel Davies. These were exceptional civil servants believing passionately in the mission to keep Britain in the forefront of technology. It also became clear that although the costs of development would be enormous, the export earnings from Concorde sales could be fabulous. I had the mistakes about the VC10 in my mind. Here might be a chance to redress the balance. Even if the project appeared to 'lose money' in pound sterling terms, the foreign currency earned would be a support to the economy. It could be looked upon as a form of concealed devaluation. This concept I gradually got adopted in Government circles and it became unofficial policy to buy and boost Britain provided the total extra costs did not exceed twenty per cent. The feed back advantages in taxation receipts and employment was certainly worth up to that extra fifth. The formula was later to help me, as Postmaster General, push through the purchase of British ICL computers for the Heathrow airport cargo-handling project LACES, against US competition from Sperry-Univac.

I was glad when I became the Minister responsible for the detailed negotiations on Concorde, with the French; now was my chance to make a worthwhile contribution by assisting its survival. Tony Benn was never involved in the detailed talks but always turned up, as he was entitled to do as Minister of Technology, when there were important public occasions. One of these was the 'roll-out' of the first Concorde at the Sud-Aviation plant at Toulouse. It was a biting cold day on that airfield even in our overcoats in the stands. Two tall flag poles carried the Tricolour and a pathetic Union Jack which looked as if it had been hastily home-made in Toulouse after an eleventh-hour panic order from the French Master of Ceremonies who realised, just in time, that an Anglo-French occasion needed a British as well as a French flag. In his typically able speech Tony announced that the UK, in the interests of amity, would now call Concord, Concorde, conceding the French spelling. It was the touch French pride appreciated.

When the time came for the Ministers to go together to the hangar for the final ceremony I beckoned Julian Amery, who was sitting in the stands as an observer, to join us. He was, I thought, entitled to some recognition for his part in launching Concorde years before. At the ceremony, the French hosts presented Tony with a Concorde model in gold from Cartier in Paris. Later, in a small back room, they presented me with an identical model saying, humorously, that I also deserved it.

Tony flew back to London, the visitors dispersed, the flags and the decorations were removed, and I settled down with the French Minister for the hard bargaining on the future of the project. We met in the Board Room of the French national-ised aircraft company Sud-Aviation. Firstly, French security men checked the room for listening devices possibly left by the company so they could overhear the secret discussions of Ministers. None were found so we felt we could talk freely. It was evident the French Government felt uneasy about the way their own company had spent money with such abandon on the project. We had the same misgivings about BAC and Bristol Siddeley, which produced the engines. The companies operated on a cost-plus basis. They could never lose as there was no penalty if they exceeded their own estimates. For prestige reasons the French Ministers were absolutely committed and the French contractors knew they had them over a barrel. I agreed with the French Minister, Le Chamant, that as our Governments' interests corresponded we should collaborate in detailed checking of the Companies' financial performance. I also agreed with the French that we should have tests on the effects of sonic bangs because the public acceptability of this nuisance was essential if supersonic overland flights were to be allowed. It was a curious physical phenomenon that although an aircraft flying at faster than the speed of sound, was itself not affected, it left behind it a wave which hit the ground thousands of feet below with a bang. It was a noise made, not only as the barrier was broken as some people had assumed, but constantly as the aircraft flew at any speed exceeding Mach One which was the description given to the speed of sound.

I started the process of having tests over British towns so as to assess their effect. The first hurdle was to get the Cabinet's agreement; initially other Ministers were hostile, but I brought them round to my proposal when many of them thought the tests would so inflame public opinion against Concorde as to make it easier to cancel the project. The first tests were over the southern England market town of Dorchester. No advance Press announcement was made; the public did not know the tests were taking place and no complaints about nuisance were received. For the later tests warnings were given to the newspapers. As a result, there were big public protests in Bristol and London, most of them artificially whipped up by sections of the Press and by the anti-Concorde lobby. It has become virtually impossible to discover the true reaction of the general public to new experiences as every issue is clouded and confused by the propaganda and the machinations of anti- or pro-factions, and the inevitable distortion by the media.

One of my disappointments was the cancellation of the official UK share in the European air-bus after I was trans-

ferred from the aviation field to the Post Office. It had seemed
to me that bringing German, French, Dutch and possibly Italian industry together to produce a wide-bodied aircraft would
enable Europe to secure the market for such an aircraft from
the national airlines concerned, so enabling Europe to avoid
complete dependence on US jumbo jets. I secured the initial
agreement in talks held with the German Treasury Minister
Schiller in his Ministry in Bonn and at a beautiful castle just
outside the capital near the Rhine. The French were also there
and guaranteed that French airlines would buy the plane when
it was produced. The Gallic determination to support national
production would not allow Air France or Air Inter any independence. The Germans admitted they would have more difficulties with Lufthansa but thought, in the end, the German
airline would buy. Remembering our own problems with the
VC10 and BOAC, I was also cautious in my assurances about
a guaranteed British market, although, to be fair, BEA was
always better about buying British and had backed Trident
through to its success.

Some of my most interesting negotiations were on behalf
of Rolls Royce, the great aero-engine company which by this
time had absorbed Bristol Siddeley. It was extremely important for the future of the Company that it secured orders for
engines in the new big civil aircraft being developed in the
United States. Apart from some Boeings which had been
refitted with Rolls Royce for BOAC service, no US airframe
company had dared to buy British. It was felt that American
Congressional and public opinion would be angry if the US
companies of Pratt & Whitney and General Electric were
passed over. This was the point that Dan Haughton, the
friendly and drawling President of Lockheed made to me when
I was trying to conclude the deal for the RB211 engine to go
into the new Lockheed TriStar. Somehow we had to devise
an offset arrangement which would get Lockheed off the political hook. Haughton asked for guaranteed orders from British
airlines, but I could not deliver such assurances. Then I hit
on a formula which would satisfy both sides. I persuaded the
British Company, Air Holdings, to agree to take an option on
fifty TriStars on the understanding that any aircraft sold in
co-operation with Lockheed outside the United States—to
Canada for instance—would reduce the commitment. In the
event of the total number not being sold, there would clearly

be a residual financial penalty to be paid by Air Holdings. I made a secret agreement with Rolls Royce that in that unlikely event Rolls Royce would compensate Air Holdings with the full amount. It was a small price for Rolls Royce to pay in securing the biggest ever order for aero-engines.

It was absolutely crazy for the Conservative Government, in later years, to force Rolls Royce into bankruptcy because of the escalation of the costs of developing the RB211 for Lockheed. To besmirch the most renowned firm in British industry, and to destroy a reputation built into a worldwide household name, simply to satisfy the prissy rectitude of Government accountants and Government company lawyers, was the English disease at its worst. Those awful nameless professionals who gave the advice which scared the weak Ministers into their foolish act were burrowing away like maggots doing their own thing with great self-satisfaction, but without any thought or regard for the mighty and valuable tree they would bring crashing down. It would have been possible to renegotiate the contract with Lockheed as they were fully committed to Rolls Royce engines by this time, and Dan Haughton knew the problems of escalating costs only too well from his own experience. The bankruptcy was absolutely unnecessary, as was shown later when a new contract was secured. But the damage to Britain's name was done. One of the extraordinary aspects of this affair was the resultant nationalisation of Rolls Royce by a Conservative Government dedicated to free enterprise, so proving that there is no such thing as principle in modern politics. Pragmatism is the flag which flies at the masthead of all main political parties. The Tory handling of Rolls Royce sent shock waves reverberating through British industry and set in a demoralisation from which the country has not recovered.

During my period as Minister responsible for the aircraft industry, I made many overseas trips, but none were more fascinating than touring Russia as head of a British aircraft industry. mission—seeing, for instance, Concordski (the TU.144) under development in the secret factory just outside Moscow—and following this within a week by a most contrasting tour of American aircraft plants.

In Russia we were all closely watched. This was not surprising as we had with us an undercover agent who was added to our team of industry leaders so he could engage in some industrial espionage. Just before we left Moscow to return home I met some members of the British Press Corps in my hotel suite. They pressed me very strongly to reveal more about Concordski as our party were the first Westerners to see it, but I parried them. There were no Russians present. At a good-bye meeting with the Russian Minister Dementiev on the next day he congratulated me, with a twinkle in his eye, on the way I handled the Press, so confirming that all my conversations were tape-recorded. We all knew that even the cars we used were bugged. So was the British Embassy, and in that building all our exchanges had to be platitudinous. For confidential discussions we had to descend to the lower basement where British workmen had installed a special conversation room. No Russians were ever allowed anywhere near that area. The room was windowless, like a padded cell with its soundproofed walls, and completely suspended within another larger room. When we used it recordings of cocktail party chatter were played in the larger room so as to defeat the most sophisticated listening equipment. It was a most uncomfortable, claustrophobic, place. I felt sorry for the Ambassador who had to dictate all his memoranda cooped up in that tiny room. It is no wonder that the best literary efforts do not emerge from Embassies in Communist countries.

In America, among other companies, I visited General Dynamics in Fort Worth, Texas, and had a nerve-wracking trip in their F111 swing wing aircraft, which Robert McNamara was delighted he had persuaded the British to buy. It was obviously a good public relations exercise to get me, the British Minister, into the co-pilot's seat. I took the controls at supersonic speeds when the wings were effortlessly folded back to reduce drag. It was a deceptively easy plane to fly. Then we came down to a few hundred feet to fly at 500 miles an hour across the mountainous country of Arkansas and Oklahoma without any hands on the controls, using the terrain following radar (TFR) to operate the equipment. Human reactions to the fast looming mountains would have been far too slow at such speeds. But at one point the test pilot suddenly grabbed the controls and took the aircraft up several thousand feet. 'That was a near thing,' he said. 'The plane almost went into a stall.' And at those heights I knew we could not recover from a stall. It is a chastening experience to realise so intensely the fallibility of man-made inventions. In such creations one's life hangs by a single screw or bolt, or the wrongly calculated fatigue life of a small piece of essential metal. In a sense such advanced aircraft are more risky than the Wright Brothers' plane which could fall apart but still be brought down to a safe landing. Coming back to the Fort Worth field I was invited to take the controls for landing. I declined. A few weeks after that trip an F111 crashed doing a similar low flying manoeuvre to ours, and several crashed in Vietnam when the bolts for the swing wings broke.

On the American trip I was accompanied by a Deputy Secretary to the Ministry of Technology who was, not surprisingly for the civil service, a Greek scholar. After I had made several after-dinner speeches including jokes about Guards ties, including one against myself, and adding semi-humorous references to the way a man, or his wife, can be judged by the tie he wears, the Deputy Secretary said, 'Minister, you should call your interest in ties "Desmology" after the Greek word "Desmos" meaning bond.' For the fun of it I agreed. When I returned to the Ministry, word went round about what I had done, and as a result I had several memoranda from other civil servant Greek scholars—including one entirely in Greek—arguing that 'Desmology' was not the correct word and that it should be something else. But I stuck to the original suggestion—mainly because it was the only one I could pronounce—and put it into *Who's Who* as one of my hobbies, much to the confusion of non-Greek readers of that volume.

One day the Prime Minister invited me to join him and Michael Stewart, the Foreign Secretary, for lunch at No. 10. The Guest of Honour was King Hussein, the stocky doughty King of Jordan, who is most English in mannerism and the most pro-British of all the Arab laders. Over lunch the Prime Minister told us that he had decided to recommend my elevation to the Privy Council and added, 'The citation should be "services to export".' I was delighted by this recognition as it was unusual for a Minister to be so elevated without promotion to a Cabinet post. The pomp and circumstance necessary to acquire the honour is shrouded in mystery rather like the rites of secret societies. I suppose in earlier days it made the oaths of loyalty to the monarch more binding. I had to go through two rehearsals with Sir Godfrey Agnew the Secretary to the Privy Council in the Privy Council offices in Whitehall—nothing could be allowed to go wrong in front of

Her Majesty. He said no special clothes were necessary, although striped trousers and black coat were preferable. 'Anyway,' he said, holding his hands up in mock horror, 'Don't worry about that. The Lord President of the Council does not even own such a suit and always seems to wear old clothes when he comes to the Queen!'

On 28 June 1968 I collected with a few Privy Councillors in the ornate halls of Buckingham Palace waiting for the Council to meet at the appointed time of 10.30 am. Half past the hour came and went and still the Lord President had not arrived. Richard Crossman blustered in ten minutes late without any apology for keeping us, or the Queen, waiting. I think he did it on purpose to show off his Republican iconoclasm. As Lord President he went first into the Queen's presence and we followed in order of precedence, dictated not by position but by the length of Privy Council membership. I was last as a new initiate. The ritual, which was the first item on the agenda, involved me kneeling on my right knee towards the Queen, holding up my right hand as the Clerk read the Oath, walking forward and kneeling again to kiss the Royal hand, and then withdrawing backwards. The long, archaic declaration of loyalty was read out with me again holding up my right hand. Then I shook hands with Crossman, Alice Bacon, John Silkin and Bob Mellish, the Privy Councillors in attendance, who had stood in line of precedence during the proceedings. Then the formal business followed; it consisted only of a Rhodesian order in Council, which was somewhat academic as Rhodesia had declared its independence. The Lord President merely read out the title and the Queen said 'Approved'. The formal business over we exchanged pleasant conversation for a few minutes. Sir Godfrey said that at the next Privy Council, 'Your Majesty will be asked to approve the siting of a public lavatory in Guernsey.' Bob Mellish suggested to the Queen that she might consider declining her approval and so make history. The Queen replied with a smile that she would wait for something more important. The rain was pouring down outside, and looking out of the window the Queen said, 'Philip and Charles are in the West country today, but I doubt if they will be able to travel in their helicopter if this continues.' This was our cue to withdraw which we did in reverse order of precedence. The whole event was rather quaint but critics should recognise that such ceremonies are necessary to maintain the mystique of the constitutional Head of State. Queen Elizabeth herself is a warm and human person who does not let the impositions of her rank prevent a closeness to others.

Soon the Prime Minister was to promote me to be the very last of Britain's Postmasters General. Apart from the Privy Council meetings, that position would bring me in a little more contact with the Queen. And I was to have no reason to change my first impressions as her new Privy Councillor. Britain is fortunate in its Royal Family, and the system is infinitely to be preferred to political Presidents, although I wish some of the effete aristocratic hangers-on could be dispensed with. I started my political life as an unmilitant Republican but became converted to pragmatic Monarchism. This could be interpreted either as healthy flexibility or as sinister seduction by the aristocratic system. Naturally, as you would expect, I prefer the former to the latter alternative.

8 *The Czech spy story*

AS POSTMASTER GENERAL my visits to No. 10 Downing
Street were infrequent. I had to attend the occasional Cabinet
Meeting when Post Office business was discussed, but unlike
the days when I deputised for Roy Jenkins or Tony Benn, I
did not have to attend the various Cabinet sub-committees.
The Prime Minister did not make a practice of meeting his
ministers for informal chats and it was possible—I was told
by other ministers—to go for months without ever speaking
to the Prime Minister except at a formal meeting.

Harold Wilson was a particularly tightly controlled head
of Government. He had become intensely suspicious of some
of his colleagues and made a point of never relaxing completely
in their presence. His confidences were reserved for his small
entourage, the most important of whom was Marcia Williams
(now elevated to Lady Falkender) who has been his personal
secretary for many years. She fully justifies her position as a
very close Aide and confidant. But this close relationship put
a great strain on the Prime Minister's civil servants in No. 10.
Michael Halls, in particular, who died in office, found the
strain intolerable, and his widow, Marjory, took the unusual
course of making a claim for compensation.

Harold had a weakness for people who, unlike Marcia, were
unable to give any intellectual stimulus but who were foils to
his private wit and monologues. They were men like Alf Rich-
man, who was seconded from the Mirror Group to advise on
'public presence' and Gerald Kaufman, his public relations

adviser who later became MP for Manchester Ardwick. This 'kitchen cabinet' was a great influence on Harold Wilson, not so much positively as negatively. They mirrored—apart from Marcia—simply what the PM wanted and made no positive contribution themselves. Harold felt he could trust them as they were obviously no threat, whereas men like Callaghan, Jenkins and even Crossman were permanent threats. Of all the senior ministers only Barbara Castle was close to him at that time.

There were certainly very few ministers who were invited in for cosy chats. I remember Dick Marsh, who was Minister of Power and went on to become Chairman of British Railways, scathingly condemning Harold for his isolation. Dick was foolish enough to describe some of his misgivings in witticisms in after-dinner speeches and this did him no good at all with Harold, who bitterly resented this kind of criticism. This was one of the reasons why Dick was fired.

I was therefore not a little surprised when I had a summons to attend at No. 10 one day in 1968. There was no particular crisis in the Post Office and no major Government policy affecting it. It was possible that a Government reshuffle was in the offing. That idea intrigued me, as I hoped I would be translated to a Ministry like the Board of Trade where I would have more constructive work to do. I was driven into a quiet Downing Street at about 11.30 in the morning. The attendant at the door was obviously expecting me and had opened the door almost before I had placed my foot on the first step. I strode into the small entrance hall, which must be one of the most modest of any citadel of power in the world, and walked down the long corridor towards the Cabinet Room, expecting to meet the Prime Minister there. He usually worked at the Cabinet table, but one of the attendants directed me to the sitting room upstairs where the atmosphere was rather typical of a traditional English stately home, with its loose blue and rose chintz covered armchairs. On the mantelpiece there were some rather exquisite antique Chinese vases. Placed strategically around the room there were also framed pictures of world leaders. I remember thinking that the precedences were probably changed frequently, depending on who was visiting at the time. Harold was standing up when I entered and greeted me briskly but affably.

'You know Michael, don't you?' motioning to Michael

Halls, his Principal Private Secretary. 'And this is Elwell of Counter Intelligence,' he said, introducing me to a precisely dressed, clean-cut, sharp-eyed man in his early 40s. He had the manner of an ex-military man and was quietly confident and not at all over-awed by the occasion or the situation.

We spread ourselves around the room on the settee and armchairs and the Prime Minister said, 'There's been a statement made by a Czech intelligence officer who has defected to the West in which you have been named as an informer to the Czech Secret Service.'

I caught my breath. It was unlikely that I was being arrested, otherwise I would not have been sitting there in Downing Street, but my blood ran cold nevertheless. What on earth could this nonsense be?

'As Head of Security I have to take an interest in these matters,' said the Prime Minister. It was obvious he regarded it as serious enough to handle himself rather than leaving it to the Home Secretary who was ostensibly the man in charge of espionage and counter-espionage matters.

Elwell proceeded to read from a report: 'A senior Czech officer has been interviewed and de-briefed by the American authorities, in the course of which he claimed that in addition to Members of Parliament a senior Minister in the Labour Government had provided contact.'

'We must get to the bottom of this,' said the Prime Minister. 'You will appreciate how important it is that you cooperate in investigating these allegations.'

During all these exchanges Michael Halls was busily scribbling everything down in the detailed note he had to keep of every conversation the Prime Minister had. Elwell went on, 'We know that you had lunch with Husak and we have a note of your report on this meeting, but were there other meetings and were there any other meetings with Czech spies?'

My mind flashed back to that and all my other meetings with Czechs over the years, searching for a clue to the present situation. They say a man's life passes through his mind as he is drowning, and that was certainly what happened to me during those few minutes at No. 10. I remembered that my very first meeting with the Czechs was as a member of the Board of the London Co-operative Society when on a delegation with Harry Clayden, one of the Communist Directors of the Board. We spent a week in Vienna and a week in Prague, visiting Co-operative establishments. That was in September, 1957, about six months after I had become a Member of Parliament. The Czechs were extremely friendly to their visitors from the largest retail co-op in the west and gave us the red carpet treatment.

Years before, in 1948, I had felt the tremendous anguish which all democrats felt when the Communists took over the country and put out the flame of democracy of Jan Masaryk. During that coup d'état I was a student under Professor Harold Laski at the London School of Economics, and the Czech experience had the most devastating effect on him. His outlook on life visibly changed. From being a buoyant, optimistic philosopher he became depressed and cynical. Students who went to see him for counsel reported that in fact they found they had to counsel him, such was his heartbreak. Harold Laski never recovered from this experience and died within a few years a deeply disappointed man. Those students who were close to Laski, as I was, could not help but be affected by the reasons for his sadness. Czechoslovakia became the symbol to all of us in the Labour Society at the LSE. It made it all the more important to contest the insidious Communist efforts to take over our own student organisations. Later, indeed, it gave me inspiration to fight the Communists in the Co-operative Movement itself. Czechoslovakia provided an example of what the Communists can do after they have wormed their way into positions of power in coalition with Social Democrats.

During that first visit to Prague I respected our hosts as individuals and I could see that within their limits they were doing their best to help their fellow men. I certainly had more respect for those Communists who were trying to do some positive reconstruction rather than the sinister manoeuvrings of the British Communists.

On the last day of our visit we started, as usual with slivoviça and coffee at the first official appointment. (The drink always flowed very freely.) This being the final day, more toasts than usual were drunk. There was then an official lunch at which our host was Zabotnik, a seventy-year-old Communist pioneer, who had worked his way from the working-class movement from the old days of the Austro-Hungarian empire. The man was stocky and physically extremely tough with that square head typical of the central European peasantry. His handshake was like a vice-grip and his personality was riveting and, although he had no English, he could make his feelings understood to us perfectly. The lunch was lengthy and lavish and we had to drive immediately afterwards to the airport to catch the plane for Brussels and then on to London. But there was a delay. At the airport more drinks were ordered to while away the time, and Zabotnik playfully challenged me to a drinking duel. After several toasts he had to give up and pass the challenge to a colleague.

When the plane was ready to leave and I walked on to the tarmac, I realised just how much I had consumed. The tarmac was very unsteady, but I firmly and deliberately walked over it towards the aircraft steps. I was the last one to reach the aircraft and slowly walked up the steps. At the top I turned round to wave goodbye to our hosts standing by the terminal building. I was very relieved that I had reached the aircraft without any help and so the challenge had been won by the British against the hard-drinking Czechs, but as a mark of respect and friendship to my vanquished hosts I raised my right arm in a clenched fist salute. From 100 yards off a determined Zabotnik, the veteran Communist, raised his arm likewise and for just a moment all barriers between the iron Communist and the Social Democrat were down. We achieved a rare rapport. I never saw Zabotnik again. But could it have been that that one moment had prompted someone in the Czech party to have regarded me as a potential recruit to serve their interests?

It was during this visit that I went on the mandatory tour of Lidice, the village twenty miles out of Prague which had been eliminated by the German SS as a reprisal for the death of Heydrich. Before I left England my people in Wednesbury had suggested that an exchange with a Czech town would be a valuable way of giving ordinary Czechs a view of the outside world and I was asked to look out for a suitable 'twin'. Kladno, the nearest town to Lidice, seemed a very suitable choice. It was an industrial town, dependent on iron and steel, it had a long coal-mining tradition, and there were many other similarities with the Black Country constituency I represented. I spent a day visiting Kladno and was very impressed with what I saw. The standard of housing, at least the flats they showed me, was high and the communal facilities, clubs and sports centres, were excellent. The miners' rest centres had bow-tied waiters serving the miners and everything was spotlessly clean. It struck me that Wednesbury would have a lot to learn from

Kladno rather than the other way round in certain respects. The workers' canteens in Wednesbury were nowhere near the standard of excellence in Kladno.

I went to the Town Hall and established contact with the Mayor. They were delighted with the twinning proposal. Subsequently Wednesbury and Kladno became very close, and frequent visits took place between the two towns. The twinning was a great success until Wednesbury was eventually broken up by the Crossman boundary changes which destroyed the smaller local authorities in the West Midlands. Many individual constituents were still privately keeping up their contacts and making exchanges on their own many years later. One of the keenest on the exchanges was George Thompson, the last Town Clerk of Wednesbury, a Tory by any standards. His life was somewhat transformed by his experiences in visiting Kladno and the realisation that the ordinary people in a Communist country could be just as warm, generous and friendly as any he met back home. One cherished memory of a Czech visit to the Black Country was a traditional charabanc outing to Blackpool to see the lights; cheerfully they followed the example of their British hosts and rolled up their trouser legs, tied their hankies on their heads and played football on the beach. They loved the fish and chips and candy floss but were not too keen on the warm beer.

It is well known that the London diplomatic circle is one of the most strenuous. Every Embassy has its frequent cocktail parties on national days, at the time of special and ministerial visits and for any other convenient excuse they can think of. The diplomats, from the Ambassadors downwards, have to justify their existence, and contacts with representatives of British society are all-important to them. The parties provide an opportunity to make friends. For the Eastern European countries there is a special object in entertaining British politicians in the hope of collecting information. All members of the diplomatic staff work zealously at this cultivation of Western contacts and the most attentive to it are the secret service 'plants' with the diplomatic service. The uninitiated to the circle cannot differentiate between spy and diplomat. Indeed, it is sometimes difficult for the national of the country concerned to do so. It has been rumoured that in some embassies the chauffeur or cypher clerk is more senior in rank than the Ambassador himself. Such stories may be apocryphal but it is certainly true that within the Communist embassies there are agents performing their tasks, sometimes known, other times unbeknown, to their own diplomatic colleagues.

I was not surprised to be approached by Eastern European diplomats with invitations soon after I was elected a Member of Parliament. Other Members had similar invitations. One particularly pushing Czech diplomat I remember was Vlado Koudelka, with whom I had several lunches. He was obviously seeking information on Labour Party activities to bolster up his reports. Whatever I told him was innocent enough and I was pleased to have a contact in the Czech Embassy as it helped the Kladno/Wednesbury relationship and Koudelka was able to give valuable assistance in that respect. As a new Member of Parliament I had invitations not only from Eastern Europeans but also from Russians, Americans, Canadians, French and Germans. The Yugoslavs were especially friendly and, through them, my two daughters arranged to take part in exchange visits with the daughters of the Mayor of Zagreb, Veço Holevac. One year my youngest daughter Julia was exchanged with the daughter of the Yugoslav Minister of Finance, Mincev. When my wife and I went on holiday to Yugoslavia we tried to see her but found she was holidaying on Tito's private island, Brioni. Rather than allow us to visit the island, the authorities laid on a special launch to bring her to see us on the mainland at the Roman port of Pula.

I should not give the impression that my overseas contacts were all with Eastern Europeans as my contacts with Western European countries were much closer. As a Member of the Council of Europe and the European Assembly, meeting frequently at Strasbourg or in Paris, I had almost weekly meetings with Western European Parliamentarians and diplomats. During the two years or so that I served on these bodies I visited every Western European country from Turkey to Norway, and sometimes two or three times in a year. It was, however, the case that the Czechs were particularly persistent in attempting to establish a special relationship with me.

Koudelka, at one time, invited me to a party. I assumed that my wife was also invited and we very nearly attended it but, having gone to see friends at a private party in Twickenham first, we were rather tired and decided to go straight home. Thank goodness we did. Subsequently I learned it had been for male guests only and 'girls had been provided'—I can only imagine what compromising photographs would have been taken if I had gone on my own, whether or not I had participated! As I remember him, Koudelka was a persistent ferret of a man, constantly pushing for the odd scrap of political information, most of which I regarded as totally irrelevant but obviously it must have been important to him because it proved he was justifying his expense account.

In March 1961 I went to the Leipzig Trade Fair in the GDR, flying in with Barbara Castle. On the plane I picked up a tip from her I have found most useful ever since—how to cut out-press cuttings with the aid of a pin—something she spent the entire journey doing, carefully extracting and hoarding a whole stream of useful information for her future political use. There were several other MPs invited from Britain. This was part of the process for the East Germans to make converts to the West and to achieve their eventual acceptance as a sovereign state. The hotel where we stayed was guarded against ordinary East Germans and only VIPs were allowed in. It was hardly a demonstration of Socialist equality. One gets used to such contradictions.

One of the most flamboyant of the British MPs on that occasion was Arthur Lewis, the over-sized MP for West Ham. He had made a speciality of contacts in East Germany and he was like a man transformed in that environment where he was highly regarded by the Government and its different agencies. Another MP who had special treatment given to him was Ian Mikardo, who built up his trading business on contacts in Eastern Europe. But Members of Parliament friendly to the East Germans were not confined to the Labour Party. I well remember Stephen McAdden, the Conservative Member for Southend, greeting Walter Ulbrich at the grand party on the eve of the opening of the Trade Fair, warmly inviting him to visit Britain—a visit he was never to make. Another Member who was very eager in developing contact with the East Germans was Will Owen, who was later to be charged and acquitted of being a spy for the Czechs.

In 1962 I visited the Leipzig Fair again, but this time I had to change planes in Prague, making a one-night stop-over as there were no direct flights to Leipzig at that time. I was very surprised when Koudelka located me at my hotel that night and invited me to have lunch with him the next day before my outward flight. He took me to a restaurant beautifully situated

on the hills overlooking the Vltava. By this time Koudelka
had been appointed to the headquarters of the Foreign Office
staff in Prague and was very anxious to renew his contact with
me, even though it had not been as fruitful to him as he had
obviously wanted in the past. I wondered what would have
happened if I had attended that orgy party without my wife!

During the lunch one of the old waiters, realising I was
English, began to talk to me in extra friendly terms. 'This
Government is terrible!' he said. 'I wish you would tell your
friends in England what a mess they are making of this
country!'

Koudelka smiled, 'You see, the Bourgoisie are still with us!
That old man would have you think he was something important in the old days; he doesn't like his subservient role in this
society, so naturally he resents us.'

'What you must do,' he went on, 'is to come back here on
holiday. We shall be able to give you a really good time! You
can bring your wife and family. We will pay all expenses and
you can stay as long as you like. Then you will see what we
are really doing in this country to make it a very successful
example of Communism at work. Don't listen to these boring
fellows, they are only good enough to be waiters anyway!' I
made a mental note not to take up the invitation on any
account. It would not be much of a holiday to be beholden
to such hosts. I knew, however, that many of my colleagues
had accepted such paid holidays.

Koudelka was very anxious that I should keep in close contact with his successor in London, but apart from one or two
cursory meetings, I did not do so, and I cannot now even remember his name. However, that year at Christmas a black
diplomatic car brought a case of gaily wrapped bottles of drink
from the Czech Embassy. They were sent back unopened.

I had little contact with the Czechs again until I became
Minister in the 1964–70 Labour Government. At a cocktail
party at the old Czech Embassy in Millionaires Row in Kensington, given for some visiting delegation, I was approached
by a tall, handsome and suave Czech who seemed to know
me, although I did not have any recollection of meeting him.
His manner did not attract me to him. In the hubbub of the
cocktail conversation he was trying to push his luck with me.
It turned out that he knew all about Koudelka, Kladno and
my Co-operative background. I did not like being unfriendly

towards anyone, but I did not feel particularly friendly towards him so, when he started trying to make a date for lunch, I allowed myself to be pushed forward in the party mêlée, and so hoped to avoid any commitment. But as I moved forward he pushed an obviously prepared note into my hand with his name on it, 'Husak', and begged me once more to have lunch with him. I did meet him for lunch, but I took the precaution of putting in a full report of our conversation through the Ministry's Intelligence Officer who was then operating under the general supervision of George Wigg, who had been given a watching brief over intelligence matters by Harold Wilson following the Profumo and Vassall security scares of previous Governments.

I saw Husak at several diplomatic functions afterwards and when I was involved in negotiations on the possible sale of VC10s to CSA, the Czech Airline, Husak turned up as an interpreter for the Czech Minister. Subsequently I had to visit Czechoslovakia to sign a Technological Agreement. I stayed with the British Ambassador, Sir Cecil Parrott, in the elegant Ambassador's residence in Prague. The room I was given looked over the beautiful rooftops of old Prague, a truly delightful city. I did not have a chance to visit the architectural sites because of the many official engagements. We went to Government laboratories, the atomic plant at Bratislava which the Russians were building and which turned out to be such a failure and, of course, the inevitable machine tool factories which seemed to me to be remarkably inefficient. Productivity was extremely low and the only explanation for the success of machine tool exports was that they were sold at a subsidised price in order to gain foreign exchange.

I signed the Technological Agreement with my Czech counterpart in a charming ceremony in an old castle just outside Prague. The Czechs set great store by the Agreement as they were anxious not to be totally dependent on Russian technology. This was the beginning of the Dubcek era and already the ice was melting. More freedom of speech was being allowed. Contact with the West was approved. After the signing of the Agreement I gave the first free Press conference for Czech journalists of any Western Ministerial visitor since 1948. The journalists obviously found it an unnerving experience and were not quite sure how they should take advantage of this new found freedom.

I took the opportunity of visiting Kladno again and the Mayor was very pleased, arranging a small function for me at which we exchanged gifts between Wednesbury and its twin town. I had selected as my gift a set of tools made in the constituency by a firm called Elwell's, a family business owned by relatives of my Counter Intelligence friend at 10 Downing Street! The Ambassador came with me and he was deeply moved that we had managed to establish such a relationship. These Communists were so obviously more genuine than those nearer the Diplomatic scene with whom he had to spend so much more time.

As a contrast to the official programme of meetings, the Czechs arranged for our party to visit the Low Tatras to do some skiing. They knew that I was keen to improve my skill at the sport, although judging from the resort they took us to they assumed I was rather better than I was. The hotel was 4,000 feet up on the mountains, isolated by thick snow and absolutely packed with Czechs and East Germans. They seemed different from the Western tourists I had skied with in the Austrian Alps, very much healthier and robust looking. These were the professional classes from the Communist élite, they were as separated from the ordinary working classes as are the professionals in Western Europe. There was a terrific esprit de corps among them and they had a tremendous zest for life, with none of the tensions one would normally have expected in a Communist country. Perhaps the introduction of reforms into Czechoslovakia had helped to induce this relaxed atmosphere—whatever it was they certainly pursued the good life and knew how to enjoy it. Their rude health and high spirits made me feel slightly decadent by comparison and the thought of competing with them on the ski slopes filled me with trepidation.

As I reached the door of my suite in the hotel that night, I turned round and said 'Goodnight' to a member of our party, and went in to the sitting-room. I switched on the light by the door but felt a strange presence in the darkened bedroom beyond. As I went forward I could see two figures sitting in the armchairs. Whoever they were, they were obviously up to no good, I thought, sitting there in the dark waiting for me to return from dinner, and I braced myself for some kind of attack. Instead, one of them turned on the light and, to my amazement, there, sitting comfortably clutching a bottle of wine in one hand and a glass in the other, was Husak! He grinned, no doubt expecting me to be delighted to see him, which I certainly was not. He apologised for his means of entry, explaining that he had come in by using a pass key to the bedroom door.

He had thoughtfully brought a third glass and proceeded to pour me some wine. His friend waved me to a seat and Husak introduced him as a fellow diplomat, about to be sent to London—obviously his successor. We sat and drank the wine through midnight and they both talked enthusiastically about the new Dubček reforms.

'Now we can really do something with this country,' they said.

'With our independence from Russia we will develop a great energy from the Czech people and show the world that Communism can have a sweet and pleasant face.'

'We are so glad you have come to our country at this time and can see for yourself.'

Somehow this conversation did not ring true, and I sat there waiting for the real purpose to reveal itself. These two men were too earnest, too sincere and too obviously saying things they thought I wanted to hear. I astounded them by saying. 'I think Dubček is going too far. You let the lid off a kettle and you can scald yourself! Better the way it is being done in Rumania, rather than rushing things as he is apparently doing.'

My two Czech visitors did not agree with me. 'You'll see. We'll make a great success of it!'

They didn't seem to want to discuss anything more important and finally took their departure about 1 am. I gratefully took to my bed, wondering what it had all been about!

Next morning I went to the ski slopes right at the top of the mountain, reaching it by the ski lift. The sides of the mountain were precipitous but there was a small area where I could do a few practice runs to get my ski legs going. I left my colleagues and gently set off. They were all non-skiers and obviously had no intention of venturing forth too far. They were going back down the mountain by the ski lift that had brought them up, but for me that was the ignominious way down and, even though I didn't like the look of the mountain, I decided that skiing was the only way down for me.

I said goodbye to the others at the ski lift and tentatively set off down the gentle slope. About 200 yards from the ski lift I saw a figure approaching me at speed, obviously a skier of no mean skill. With an expert flourish, he pulled up right beside me and pulled the scarf down from his face. It was my nocturnal visitor, Husak's friend. I could see the pattern developing. An especially close contact was being established between me and this gentleman! He stayed with me for some time but eventually I was able to make my excuses and explain that I could not possibly ski with his skill; he would have to go on without me. He took some persuading, but eventually left me alone. He pulled his scarf up over his face again, made an expert leap to get his skis parallel and was off and out of sight within seconds. That was the last I saw of him in Czechoslovakia.

I slowly plodded back up the mountain to the ski lift where my British colleagues were all stamping about and thrashing their arms around trying to keep warm. Even with my rate of progress it looked as though I might make it to the bottom before the ski lift turned up again. Once again I said goodbye and gingerly set off down the mountain.

The skis the Czechs had lent me turned out to be old fashioned wooden ones and I found them very hard going. A nasty cold mist descended, and as conditions worsened so the mountain seemed to get steeper and progressively more dangerous. I could not ski directly down the mountainside—the drops were eight to two or even nine to one in places. The snow was fresh and in those conditions my control over the skis would have been pathetic. The only way I could get down that mountain was by criss crossing the steep slopes, taking a very gentle pace. I had to hug the side of the mountain, traversing with one ski behind the other and with the mountain on my left practically touching my shoulder. The going was reasonable until I reached the glacier—a sheer stretch of ice which threatened to slip me into the abyss below. This time I could not pick my way gingerly. I had to take courage on both skis and proceed bravely across, praying all the way that I kept my balance. I succeeded in reaching the relative haven of the snow slopes on the other side. The cold isolation of this mountain penetrated to my inner body and soul. It made me realise that whatever the system, capitalist, social democrat or Communist, in the last analysis the individual is on his own. He must find an inner strength to cope with the extreme strains of a hostile environment.

Three hours on the almost bare mountain in conditions of great danger had a salutory effect on me. After this, I felt, one could meet any danger with equanimity. The intensity of the fear I had felt could never quite be the same again. I was grateful to return to the warmth of the hotel.

At the end of the weekend we returned to Prague. I did not see anything more of Husak. It turned out that our Ambassador had his problems. He had just been attacked bitterly by a Left-winger MP. This kindly, hard working Ambassador, who was genuinely trying to achieve better relations with a Communist country, could not understand the vehemence of the attack. I had to explain that politicians often expressed themselves strongly. In fact, it always surprised me that civil servants and diplomats are so worried about congenitally silly outbursts by MPs who are more often than not not really worried about the question which appears to agitate them but are simply using it as a vehicle to gain public exposure or build up support for themselves in some forthcoming election.

I did not see the mysterious man on the mountain again until much later when I attended a dinner party in July 1968 at the Czech Ambassador's home in Hampstead, London. This was an occasion in honour of Dubček's deputy, Dr Ota Sik. Sik was then highly regarded as one of the architects of economic reform in Czechoslovakia and perhaps the man most responsible for the change in political attitudes in the country. He was considered to be an intellectual force behind Dubček. The other guests were Michael Stewart, then Foreign Secretary, Peter Shore who was then in the Department of Economic Affairs, Frank Kearton, the Chairman of Courtaulds, and Fred Catherwood. The Tory MP for the Isle of Wight, Mark Woodnutt, was also there, though I cannot understand why. Sik was very frank about the position in Czechoslovakia. He said that industrial productivity had been dropping under the Novotny regime. 'Czech workers who get across the borders into Vienna had the humiliating experience of finding that the "down trodden" workers in Capitalist countries were enjoying much higher standards than they were,' he added. Sik said that the stagnation was due to the rigid national planning concepts.

'The central direction enshrined in doctrinaire thinking had assumed that human beings were incapable of making sensible decisions, not only in the majority of cases but in all cases.

The structure of a national plan could encourage inefficiency because it provides the ready-made excuses for a slothful bureaucracy.'

Sik went on to describe his own plans for marrying social ownership with market economy and allowing market forces to dictate the production pattern in the country, rather than having it dependent upon central control.

'Each enterprise,' he said, 'will be put on its own merits to succeed or fail.'

Hovering in the background I saw the sinister man on the mountain and he tried to approach me several times during the dinner. Fortunately I was able to appear absorbed by the conversation with the other guests and I did not need to renew our acquaintance. It was not many months after this dinner that the Russians moved into Czechoslovakia, dislodging Dubček and Sik. Sik happened to be in Switzerland where, presumably, he is still in exile. The 'brave new world' of socialist freedom which he had preached that night in July to his audience of industrialists, Ministers and the British Foreign Secretary, was not to be realised.

It was the Russian crack-down which apparently encouraged Major Frolik to defect to the United States and I was to learn later that he was the Czech intelligence officer who had fed information to the CIA about alleged British agents, among them Will Owen, the MP for Morpeth, and myself.

So here I was, sitting comfortably in the Prime Minister's room at No. 10 Downing Street, with all these meetings and experiences going through my mind, wondering what I could possibly have said or done to justify this high level investigation. Everything I had said or done, looking back, seemed innocent enough, if not, in fact, downright cautious and guarded.

Elwell, the Counter Intelligence man, was obviously well informed about all my movements and he was impressed that I had submitted a report on my lunch with Husak. Heaven knows what would have happened or how it would have been interpreted if I had not made that report. Perhaps I would have been charged like poor old Will Owen. Later, Elwell rang me up to warn me that the Ministry of Technology's own Security Officer would be coming to see me to discuss the Husak lunch and my report on it, and on no account was I to tell him of the discussion in No. 10, of which the Security Officer would have no knowledge. There was obviously intrigue within intrigue.

Tony Benn was kept informed of the activities of the Security Officer, as the Minister in Charge of the Department, and when he next saw me complimented me on my attention to the detail of producing reports on meetings with Communist diplomats.

'I'm having lunch with them all the time,' he said, 'and I never make reports about them—do you think I should?'

Over the succeeding weeks Elwell saw me several times, usually meeting me in the deep recesses of the Royal Automobile Club in Pall Mall, of which I was a member. He was checking up on the details of my meetings in Czechoslovakia and obviously working back from the de-briefing which Frolik had given in the United States. He gave me his home number and a secret number in Whitehall for use in emergencies. I never had to use them and never heard of the incident again.

At the end of the meeting at No. 10 the Prime Minister was very concerned about the way I should leave the building, it now being around lunchtime and the press might be interested in my presence there.

'He could go out the back way,' said Michael Halls.

'No, I don't think that's necessary,' said the PM. 'Elwell can go that way and the Minister can go out the front door, the way he came. That would look far less mysterious than if he never came out at all!'

The Prime Minister never discussed the spy issue with me again.

9 *A new nation is born*

EARLY IN 1970 the second Labour Government of Harold Wilson was defeated at a prematurely called General Election. Labour deserved to lose but, unfortunately for Britain, the Conservatives did not deserve to win. The electorate sensed the incapacity of both parties by abstaining in greater numbers than for decades. The public had developed a low opinion of Governments and a disrespect for Parliament because Governments had failed to tell the truth, and Parliament had become an unruly rabble with the Members more interested in scoring party points than in grasping the immense problems afflicting the nation.

The Labour Government had lost its credibility by a series of *volte-face* of policy. Early in its term it pledged to peg the exchange rate of the pound. No devaluation was the call but devaluation came after a series of denials in a way which maximised the losses for Britain. The speculators, who had plenty of advance warning, made a killing. The wages freeze was imposed in an attempt to stem inflation, and the Government followed this by devising a policy which would try to discipline the irresponsible Trade Unions and prevent crippling industrial disputes. The Prime Minister was so determined on this policy that he called some of the leading newspaper proprietors to Chequers, including Max Aitken of the *Express*, to tell them that it was essential to his strategy. Within a few days he was forced by Trade Union opposition to scrap the policy which had been set out in a White Paper called 'In Place of Strife'. But there was to be no end to the strife as the English disease of pursuing narrow vested interests to the exclusion of community, spread still further.

To be fair to Harold Wilson, he did try, on some occasions, to prevent his Ministers from reversing policies on which the Labour Party had made a stand of principle. I remember one such issue vividly. Tony Benn was unable to attend a meeting of the Overseas Policy and Defence Committee of the Cabinet and asked me to attend in his place. The main item on the agenda was a proposal by George Brown and Denis Healey to amend the ban on arms for South Africa, to allow the supply of Nimrod maritime reconnaissance aircraft, some military radars and other sensitive equipment. Both Ministers spoke strongly in support of a change of policy, particularly Denis Healey, who threw all his authority as Minister of Defence into the argument. Neither Minister attempted to justify the proposal in terms of the United Nations resolution which condemned such sales, but pleaded that the supplies could not be used in an anti-insurgent role and, that if Britain did not supply, then someone else would. As South Africa was, at that time, aiding and abetting Rhodesia in her defiance of Britain's legal sovereignty and the blockade of supply ports for Rhodesia was being mounted by the Royal Navy, these seemed to be extraordinary arguments to deploy. However, the proposal was supported by James Callaghan. The Prime Minister was obviously very angry, pointing out that the Labour Party had always opposed arms for South Africa, and the definition always had included defence equipment of the type now being proposed. 'There will be an uproar if we change the policy now,' he said. The other Ministers would not be budged from the proposal saying that the need for exports overrode the Prime Minister's objections. The PM looked to me to contribute and, as Minister responsible for such exports, I could speak authoritatively. I pointed out that most of the equipment on the list—including the complex Nimrod aircraft which would have to be built to order—could not be supplied before five to seven years, and that by then the exports would probably be helping a Conservative Government because the resultant storm from a change in policy would certainly ensure Labour's defeat at the next election. The meeting concluded with agreement that the matter should go to full Cabinet, and it seemed that a Cabinet majority for the proposal would be ensured. The Prime Minister was not to be defeated. He organised for his PPS to get a Commons Motion put down condemning renewed arms sales to South Africa. It received so much support from Labour Members that the proposal had to be abandoned.

I was surprised in the circumstances that after Labour's defeat Denis Healey went to South Africa and took up the progressive cause in order to win popular support within the Party. He was anxious to secure left-wing backing in the National Executive Committee elections, and the anti-apartheid campaign provided a neat and convenient platform. Denis Healey is a perfect example of a career politician.

In a way I was relieved when Labour lost. Opposition would, I thought, help the Party and its Parliamentary members to find the moral basis for their policies and eliminate the humbug and deceit which had characterised major Government actions for the past six years. Opposition also gave me an opportunity to develop other interests. During my whole career in Parliament I had depended on the meagre official pay, plus a few television fees, and a tiny income from books and articles. In earlier years I had spent a lot of my personal resources on campaigning within the Co-ops against the Communists, and I had nothing to fall back on. I noticed how politicians who are discarded are left almost entirely without income. I did not want that and, with frequent boundary changes, one could soon find oneself out of a constituency. I decided to devote some of my time to promoting British exports, a job I had been reasonably good at and which I enjoyed and which was patriotic. I could never understand why the Labour Party was quite happy about its Parliamentarians taking large fees as barristers defending clients they knew to be guilty, or writing memoirs, but became violent about MPs who engaged in trade. The attitude came, I suppose, from the deep-set suspicions about the capitalist system, and any business activity was regarded as a compromise with the enemy.

My company, which was called Export Promotion and Consultancy Services, was very successful from the start and acquired a number of interesting consultancy appointments. As so many actual export sales were being promoted, it was decided to bring in other partners and develop a trading company specialising in exports called Global Imex. This was also successful as I pushed a number of deals into this Company rather than handle them through my wholly owned company. During this period I never lost my interest in politics; indeed it was my intention after a few years to get back into full-time political work supported by financial independence. I never aimed to get a 'fortune', such an idea was against my whole character and upbringing. All I wanted was enough to live reasonably comfortably, to afford to travel and to have the peace of mind to devote myself to political work. My concern for moral issues was in no way dimmed by my commercial activities. An issue was to arise which fired me with emotional concern, with anger at brutal oppression and with passion for justice.

When the Indian subcontinent was granted independence by the Attlee Government of 1945 to 1950, the Moslem religious leader Jinnah secured its fragmentation against the better judgement of most Indian political figures. Pakistan was formed, based on militant Mohammedanism, and its frontiers were decided not on geographical criteria but on the density of the Moslem populations. The rest of the former Indian Empire became the secular state of India where all religions were equal under the law.

As a concept the religious state was irrational, archaic and most likely to fail under the pressure of modern conditions. And as the two halves of Pakistan were separated by a thousand miles of India, it would be a most difficult unit to administer. The situation was further complicated by the fact that the Punjabis, the dominant race in West Pakistan, had as much in common with the Bengalees of East Pakistan as Scandinavians had with Greeks. They were different physically, intellectually, philosophically and culturally. The only common factor was the Moslem religion. Furthermore, although the majority of the population resided in East Pakistan—75 million against 55 million in the West—the political and military control of the entire country was retained, by various tricks, in the hands of the West Pakistanis. The ruling families in the West had wealth, power and prestige and looked down on the Bengalees as peasants and suitable fodder for exploitation. It was colonialism at its worst. Most of the banks, businesses and industries in East Pakistan were owned in the West, and although the East provided a massive share of taxation receipts, most of the budget for education, roads and industrial development was spent in the West despite its smaller population. The Bengalees resented this situation which appeared as if it could never be changed, because most of the senior positions in Government went to West Pakistanis. Even in East Pakistan the power of the Bihari minority, who were pro-West, was enormously greater than their numbers justified. Popular resentment grew after cyclones hit East Pakistan and the coastal region was flooded with the loss of thousands of lives. The world took humanitarian measures to help the victims whilst West Pakistan hardly lifted a finger. Frequent peaceful demonstrations took place in the main towns against the oppression but some turned to violence as Bihari groups retaliated. After a succession of military Governments, free elections were eventually allowed, and these resulted in an overwhelming victory for the Awami League, which represented the Bengali aspirations for home rule. Almost all of the seats in East Pakistan were won by the Awami League under the charismatic leadership of Sheikh Mujibur Rahman. It gave the Awami League a majority of seats in the National Assembly itself.

Rahman should have become Prime Minister of the country but West Pakistanis prevaricated. In particular Mr Bhutto, a Punjabi, who had achieved a certain fame as Foreign Minister, had ambitions for himself and was determined to sabotage any chance of Bengalee ascendancy. Although Bhutto was ostensibly a socialist his socialism did not extend to the lesser breeds outside West Pakistan. Negotiations to reach a settlement were dragged on and the Bengalees were lulled into a sense of security, but meanwhile the West Pakistanis were planning a vicious military crack down on their Moslem partners. That religion preaches goodness and kindness to all humanity and particularly to Moslems, but was not to be applied to Bengalees who stood in the way of Punjabi domination. Yet again religion, however intensely beliefs were held, was shown to be powerless in deflecting power hungry and greedy men from imposing their might on others.

The crack down came one night in March 1971. Talks had just been adjourned in Dacca, the administrative capital of East Pakistan, and most West Pakistani leaders had flown home. Bhutto, however, remained behind in his suite at the Intercontinental Hotel to watch the developments. The Army was moved out of its cantonments in full force to attack the

Bengali police compound, the University and parts of the overcrowded bazaar area of Dacca. No warnings were given. The
police were surprised but attempted to put up some defence,
but they were outnumbered by men and arms; apart from a
few who miraculously escaped, all Bengali policemen in their
barracks were brutally murdered. By the Barracks was a holy
Mosque and a priest was on the steps praying. He, also, was
shot and his body was lying there two days later. At the University the soldiers attacked the student hostel where known
supporters of the Awami League were known to be living—
students were killed indiscriminately. Some students were
made to dig their own graves. One Punjabi soldier told three
students to stand together by a grave so he could shoot them
all dead with one bullet. He shot; they all fell; but the student
in the middle feigned death until he could crawl away to tell
the story.

At the residences of the Professors and lecturers the Punjabi
soldiers went from house to house and flat to flat checking
lists of names of the supporters of the Awami League. When
they found them they smashed the heads of the babies against
the walls and killed the defenceless parents. In the town itself
the horror was intensified. The Army set fire to ramshackle
buildings and then shot down the occupants as they fled.
Dozens of people gathered for safety in an historic Mosque on
the racecourse. The soldiers surrounded it and killed all they
could. Dawn the next morning unfolded on a scene of absolute
horror with corpses strewn around the town and fires blazing
out of control. Some journalists who were staying in the Intercontinental Hotel had seen a lot of the action from their windows; in the morning they were also to see Bhutto coming out
of the hotel to congratulate the soldiers on their exploits. Many
people were fleeing for their lives from the town and thousands
more joined them when the Army lifted the curfew. To escape
from Dacca it is necessary on one route to cross the vast river
of the Buriganga.

Scores of families were waiting by a crossing place when the
Army reimposed the curfew. The men, women and children
in the crowd were surrounded by soldiers armed with machine
guns and grenades and without respite they were all brutally
murdered. Similar atrocities were taking place in other towns
in the main Port of Chittagong, in Khulna and in Jessore—
and as the news spread around the country, panic set in.

Hundreds of thousands of people, simple people who had never been involved in politics as well as intellectuals, doctors and journalists, grabbed what they could and fled towards the arms of Mother India. It became a trek unequalled in human history. And the Indians welcomed the refugees with a generosity which belied the differences of religion.

In London, emergency meetings of the major charities concerned with relief were hastily called as the news of the disaster made its full impact. Two of them, War on Want and OXFAM, asked me to go to the area on a fact finding mission. I quickly got jabs for malaria and smallpox and caught a plane for Calcutta in West Bengal, India. As soon as I arrived I was flung into a catastrophe which had an emotional intensity for me far beyond the realms of my previous experiences. And I had known terrible poverty and disaster in Africa. What I saw and felt in those days was to sear my soul. I was never to be the same man again.

Calcutta is, itself, a monstrous tragedy of a city. It is decaying through the pressures of the twin evils of poverty and the population explosion. The ancient infrastructure left by the colonialists of Victorian England is now trying to cope with a populace many times larger, and the collapse is obvious for all to see. In normal times thousands of poor and debilitated people eke out their lives on the pavements. They are born there, live lives there, scratching for scraps of food; and die there. Such urban poverty is more brutal than the rural squalor of Africa. Nonetheless, Calcutta and overcrowded West Bengal had to accept the refugees streaming across the border. I visited the vast makeshift camps set up on the rice paddies or around the outskirts of the city. Thousands of pathetic families were crowded together and they had the deeply sad look in their eyes of hounded and persecuted people. I remembered the same frightened look in the eyes of the Basque refugee children I had met when I was twelve in the transit camps outside Southampton. This was over three decades on and still man was demonstrating his propensity for brutality. Through interpreters I spoke to many of the refugees. A young woman wearing a soiled sari and clutching a half-dead child described how the Pakistani troops had surrounded her village and ordered the men to sit on the roadway with their hands on their heads. They all obeyed, for they were simple peasant people used to obeying authority. The soldiers then took their pistols and shot the men one by one. The younger women weeping or screaming with anguish were set upon by the soldiers and raped incessantly until all the soldiers had satisfied their lust. A few women, including my informant, slipped through the rice fields to escape. The other women were carried off to the army camps to be kept for regular raping. I talked with old men and young boys who all had similar stories of horror to tell.

I travelled through the countryside towards the border and throughout the journey the narrow roadsides were covered with refugees. They could not easily fan out across the country because the fields were low-lying and waterlogged. In the villages where our car was stopped by the sheer pressure of bodies we were surrounded by hands clutching out for a coin or a piece of paper which would admit them to a camp. And in all the camps the Indian officials were working around the clock to alleviate the suffering.

Before leaving Calcutta I visited the large rambling house where the Pakistani Government had housed its mission. The Pakistani diplomat in charge—being a Bengalee—had defected and declared the mission as the Embassy of the newly independent state of Bangla Desh*. The name was in two words signifying Bengal Land. Indian troops stood on guard outside, and inside the tall garden walls was a hive of activity.

Here was one of the centres of resistance against the Pakistani aggression. Within the borders of East Pakistan such members of the Legislative Assemblies who could be gathered together had made the solemn declaration of Independence, adopted the green and yellow flag, and then dispersed for their lives. Some came to India to join the Government in exile, others joined the guerrilla bands of the Mukti Bahini to carry on the fight against the Pakistani army. Along with Bruce Douglas-Mann the Labour MP for North Kensington, I met two young lawyers from Dacca, Amirul Islam and Moudud Ahmed. They were bearded and intense. 'This is a struggle to

*BANGLADESH: Name of country after independence.
BANGLA DESH: Name of country during independence struggle (East
                      Pakistan).
BANGALEES: Citizens of Bangladesh.
BENGALEES: People from Bengal (East or West) and immigrants in
                      Britain originally from East Pakistan or Bangladesh.
BENGALI: Language spoken by Bengalees.

the death,' they said. 'The Bengali people will never again accept Pakistani rule. We have been oppressed for too long.'

I returned to London determined to do all I could to help these gentle Bengal people who had never deserved the cruelty they were now suffering. Furthermore, I was convinced that a new independent State was the only final answer to the problem. Charity and refugee aid was needed urgently, but that would only be a palliative. Freedom from West Pakistan must also be achieved. My report to War on Want and OXFAM recommended an immediate aid programme of essential supplies of medicines, blankets, milk powder and baby foods, and the despatch of doctors and nurses to assist in the camps. I proposed an approach to the Foreign Secretary to secure an airlift of supplies by the RAF. The report was adopted, and, as proposed, a delegation was seen by Sir Alec Douglas-Home. He was understanding of the problems, sympathetic and warm-hearted. I formed the impression that he did not deserve the image created of him of a bungling and callous reactionary. Within days the RAF had commenced the airlift and Britain became the first Western country to come to the aid of Bangla Desh.

As soon as possible I saw Harold Wilson behind the Speaker's Chair and attempted to raise the problem with him. 'Don't discuss it with me,' he said. 'See Denis Healey, as Shadow Foreign Secretary, he is responsible.' I saw Healey in the corridors and told him I had just returned from seeing a terrible human tragedy. 'What is our concern about that?' he said. 'We have no standing in the matter. Those events are taking place in a sovereign state and we can't do anything about them. Let them sort it out themselves.' I was dismayed, and did not understand how a socialist could behave like that. It seemed to me, rightly or wrongly, that in gaining political power, Healey had lost his soul.

Paradoxically, on the issue of Bangla Desh, the Tory 'man of Munich' had shown genuine human compassion, in contrast to which the Labour man had, in my view, shown indifference. My campaign for Bangla Desh could make no headway, I realised, with the Labour establishment; I would have to make my appeal directly to the bulk of the Labour MPs. Fortunately, most of them were sympathetic, although some from Bradford with Pakistani electors were extremely cautious. Together with Bruce Douglas-Mann I carried the campaign to the floor of the House of Commons. As far as providing aid was concerned we were pushing at an open door: the Conservative Government did practically everything we asked. Political acceptance of a new sovereign state was decidedly more difficult. Some of our Labour colleagues were hostile to independence. Arthur Bottomley, a former Commonwealth Relations Secretary, was much opposed because he thought the breaking up of Pakistan would lead to India following likewise, as the large minorities agitated for sovereign status.

I returned to Bengal many times to keep in touch with the developments, which, from all reports, were getting more horrific. On one trip I went with Ernst Heinsen, a Senator from Hamburg, Germany, who was an old friend from the post-war student days. We were invited to go behind the lines to see a unit of the Mukti Bahini in action. On the journey northeast from Calcutta we passed the long lines of camps and make-shift dwellings where the refugees were hanging on to life by a thread. There were now many more of them. Every week thousands more crossed the border to escape the continuing atrocities being committed by the Pakistani troops in East Bengal. It seemed that the Punjabis had gone collectively mad. What was going on could only be compared to the brutalities of Nazi Germany or Tzarist or Stalin's Russia with a successor to the Marquis De Sade as the organiser of the mass sexual orgies. The stories from survivors made one's blood curdle and one's body became taut with frustrated anger. Eyewitnesses told me that they had been on the banks of the river forming the frontier between West and East Bengal watching the steady stream of refugees crossing by small ferry boats. Suddenly a Pakistan army squad reached the other shore and surrounded a large group of people waiting their turn to get in the boats. They were seen to drag all the girls and young women out of the crowd away from their screaming parents or husbands. Then the troops set up machine guns and shot all the people. A few tried to dash into the water but were also shot like mad dogs. The soldiers then packed up their guns and went off to rape the captured women. They were not at all concerned about the witnesses to their crime who were, of course, powerless to intervene.

We were getting nearer the border and still more refugees were coming. There seemed to be no end to this humanity bleeding out of a country. Close to the border we transferred to a jeep belonging to the Mukti Bahini. The Indian Army escort asked to be excused. 'I cannot come with you across the border,' he said. 'We have strict instructions never to violate the frontier.' The young captain of the Mukti had a Chinese gun, captured from the Pakistani Army, slung over his shoulder. He would now provide our protection. We drove off down a muddy path. 'This is the border,' he said, pointing to a little stick with a handkerchief tied to it sticking up at the end of a paddy field. And we looked into Bangla Desh.

It looked just the same as the Indian side: flat rice fields and a few trees and bamboo plantations. The difference was that this side was empty of people. It was an eerie contrast. The Indian side was so teeming—impossible to see any stretch of country without people. Then we saw a figure stooped under a burden walking towards us along a path. As he approached we saw to our surprise that he was carrying another much older man strung across his shoulder. We stopped him but he did not put down his burden. He looked relieved when told he was so near India. The man was asked the name of the place he had walked from. Then the interpreter turned to us and said, 'It is about 85 miles away.' 'And who is this person you are carrying?' 'He is my aged father,' came the reply. I weep even now as I recall that incident.

We moved into Bangla Desh, occasionally getting out of the jeep to push it through the mud. Finally, about fifteen miles on, we reached a small village with a schoolroom which had been converted into a local command headquarters. The Bangla Desh flag flew from an improvised flag pole. It began to rain and we went into the schoolroom. On the floor were six or seven soldiers dressed in bits of uniforms sleeping soundly, their guns by their sides. 'These are the night patrol. We have to maintain a constant guard against Pak infiltration,' said the Captain. When the rain stopped we inspected the other guerrillas and their captured Chinese-made guns. Some villagers came over to greet us and we shouted 'Joi Bangla' at each other. We returned to the school house to meet the Major in command who showed us maps of the area. The enclave we were in was well protected by the bend of a river, otherwise it would have collapsed long before under the superior armour of the Pakistanis. This enclave was a token, not a serious attempt to invade Pakistan occupied territory. The real battle was far inside the border where guerrillas were sniping at isolated Pak army units, planting bombs and disrupting communications. I asked the Major to endorse our passports which he did. 'Admitted Bangla Desh,' he wrote. Then he marked them with the date stamp '3 July 1971' and the unit stamp for the 'Jessore Sector'. Senator Heinsen and I became the first foreigners to be officially admitted to Bangla Desh.

On the way back to Calcutta we passed again the streaming mass of humanity. It was a strange unreal world after the tranquillity across the border. The car was stopped several times by the congestion on the road. Once I saw a woman carrying her child as though it was sleeping; it had obviously been dead for a long time but nothing could persuade that mother to give up that child freely, and the people around were too apathetic about death to bother.

In Calcutta I met Tajuddin Ahmed, the Prime Minister of the Government in exile, who was leading the Bengalees in place of Sheikh Mujibur Rahman who had been flown to West Pakistan to be kept under guard. Tajuddin was a patient leader and he needed all possible steadfastness. The campaign for independence was not going well. India was getting alarmed at the size of the refugee problem, and no wonder, as upwards of 10 million people were to flee into India. International support was minimal. Only Israel offered support and that would be dangerous to accept as then the whole Arab world would oppose Bangla Desh. Most Arab states were pro-Pakistan, believing that it was the more genuine Moslem country. The United States was behaving in a reprehensible fashion continuing to supply arms to Pakistan.

Later it became clear why the US had adopted this policy. Henry Kissinger was using Pakistan as the stepping-stone to Communist China preparing for President Nixon's visit. Kissinger regarded this ploy as so important he was prepared to sacrifice the Bengalee people in its pursuit. Power politics is so demanding it becomes a grotesque game of its own, ignoring the plight of ordinary people who are caught up in its backlash.

It became clear that the situation would get far worse and the war of liberation could take years to fight. I decided to step up the campaign in Britain and to try to establish such a powerful lobby for Bangla Desh that even Governments would have to listen. I suggested to Tajuddin and Mansoor Ali the Minister of Finance who was also present that Bangla Desh should issue postage stamps which could be used for mail from the liberated areas and which would also be excellent propaganda to establish the fact of the existence of Bangla Desh. They consulted colleagues and told me the next day that the idea had been approved by the Government. They asked me to organise the printing and publishing of the stamps and gave me an official authority stamped by the Government at Mujibnagar, which was the name of the mythical and ever-moving capital of the exile administration.

When I returned to London I contacted Biman Mullick the Indian artist, who is a Bengali from West Bengal, and asked him to design a series of six stamps. Mullick had designed the Gandhi stamp for the GPO when I was Postmaster General and I knew he had the talent. The designs he produced were excellent, depicting aspects of the Bangla Desh struggle, a map of the country and a photo of Mujibur Rahman. I arranged for FORMAT, the Security Printers, to produce a number of sets sufficient for propaganda sales, for distribution to the various missions and to cover the expenses. FORMAT did an efficient job and the stamps were well received when Mr Justice Abu Sayeed Choudhury launched them at a ceremony in the Harcourt Room at the House of Commons. When the stamps went round the world to philatelists, to Governments and to newspapers, they made a tremendous impact. Pakistan complained to the International Postal Union that the stamps were illegal but we were able to demonstrate that envelopes bearing the stamps were posted inside Bangla Desh. Many letters came to me by the International mail, through India, addressed to the House of Commons, and I had the Commons Post Office date-stamp them with the official Seal. There was no disputing that evidence.

I drafted a motion for the Commons Order Paper calling for the end to the genocide in East Pakistan and the recognition of Bangla Desh as an independent state. I discussed it with Peter Shore the MP for Stepney who had become interested in the problems because he had a large Bengalee minority in his constituency. He refused to sign the motion saying that it went too far in calling for independence. 'We must be realistic,' he said. 'I am realistic,' I replied. 'It will be a sovereign state one day and the sooner we achieve it the more bloodshed will be saved.' He never signed the motion, but over a hundred Labour MPs did within days of it being tabled. They included many Privy Councillors and ex-Ministers. We arranged for the

text and the names of all the signatories and their con-
stituencies to go on to a full page of *The Times* as an advertisement. Something had to be done to draw attention to this
dramatic demonstration of support for Bangla Desh; the Press
had ignored it completely in their news columns. *The Times*
page made a big impact and, combined with our continuing
campaign on the floor of the House by questions and debates,
helped to sway more support in our favour. It also had a profound effect on India which had been weighing up whether to
intervene militarily in the situation. Our pressure provided the
turning point; the Indian policy switched to intervention
rather than merely relying on the guerrillas who were assisted
and provisioned from across the Indian border.

Meanwhile, in Britain, I had become a Trustee of the Bangla
Desh Fund of which Mr Justice Abu Sayeed Choudhury, who
later became President of Bangladesh, and Alderman Donald
Chesworth were fellow Trustees. Money was raised from Bengalees all over Britain to pay for arms and supplies for the
Government in Exile. Very little money was spent as arms were
difficult to buy, and India preferred to keep a firm control of
the weapons filtering into the area. They were not a little concerned that some of their own extreme left-wing rebels might
get hold of them.

When the Indian Army moved into East Pakistan it did not
take them long—with the help of the Mukti Bahini—to defeat
the Pak troops who did not have much stomach left for the
fight.

But the atrocities went on to the last day. In Dacca just
before the Pakistan Army surrendered, the fanatical pro-
Pakistan thugs went to the homes of dozens of Bengali intellectuals. They included Professors, editors, poets and doctors
and, not by any means, all mixed up in politics; however they
represented Bengali culture which had to be crushed. The mur-
derers hoped to kill off the flower of the emerging Bengali
nation before it could bloom. The bodies of the men they
slaughtered were taken to the brick-yards at Mohammedpur,
a suburb with a Bihari majority.

The cease fire came unexpectedly on a Thursday late in
December 1971. I was sitting in my office in Dover Street, London, when I heard the news on BBC radio at 1 pm. Immediately I rang the High Commissioner for India, Apa Pant,
my old friend from way back in Kenya in 1952 when he was

Indian Commissioner in Nairobi. 'Can I get out there urgently?' I asked. 'It is difficult,' he replied. 'Most civil aircraft have stopped over-flying Pakistan and India because of the war, but if you can get to Bombay we can get you on from there.' I caught a plane that night for Bombay and was met at the airport by Government officials and taken to stay with the Governor of Maharashtra. He gave me dinner and was most charming. He said he was a Moslem and that now Pakistan was split there were more Moslems in India than in Pakistan. 'Their idea of a religious state is a dangerous fallacy and should never have been permitted by the British Government,' he added.

When I arrived in Calcutta the next day on a crowded Indian Airways internal flight, I was surprised to discover that the Ministers of the Bangla Desh Government were still in Calcutta. It was nearly two days since the cease fire. The Dacca airport was out of action because bombs had made big holes in the runways. However, I decided to get to Dacca somehow, and asked the Indian Government to help. They agreed and asked me to be ready on the next morning at 6 am. It was a Sunday, but even at that time Calcutta was a hive of activity. People were everywhere, constantly milling about the streets. The official Government car drove me through the town to a park which the army had cordoned off. It was a helicopter pad and the helicopter was already waiting, engine running. I climbed in to the one remaining seat. In the other seats were a General, a Brigadier, a Captain and the Pilot. We fastened seat belts and in seconds whirled into the air over Calcutta. We crossed the densely packed houses, the hovels and the temples and soon reached the green country patterned by the lattice work of waterways. I looked at my companions and nodded, it was too noisy for conversation.

The General was the Commander of the Indian Army units which had defeated the Pakistanis, the Brigadier was Chief of the Intelligence, and the Captain, an aide-de-camp. As we travelled they read and checked reports about the disposition of units and the progress of the mopping up operations. Then the Brigadier shouted in my ear 'Look—that is Bangla Desh.' The country below had not changed its appearance but we were across the border and on our way to Dacca. Within a few minutes he shouted again 'Look—there is a village destroyed by the Pakistanis. You will see a lot like that, but many

are already overgrown.' Down below were the shells of buildings, their roofs burnt off. The countryside seemed incredibly
fertile; lush and green all the way. No wonder this land has
been called 'Golden Bengal'.

Soon we crossed a vast sprawling river. Dacca was near and
it came into sight: flat topped buildings clustered closely
together as though they were hugging the slightly higher
ground. We came down on the airport with a thud. There were
some burnt out aircraft on the tarmac; a few Indian Army heli-
copters were parked near the extensively damaged passenger
buildings, but there were no other planes except for a small
ancient DC3 which had managed to avoid the holes in the runway. The General and his party went about their Army business and I was left standing. No one asked for my passport,
indeed there were no obvious officials about. I walked over
to a group of civilians standing by a car. 'Can you give me
a lift to the Government headquarters?' I asked. 'I have just
come in from Calcutta.' They looked amazed. 'You are the first
non-Army man to get in,' they said, 'apart from the advance
party of the Bangla Desh Government which came in yester-
day.' 'Who are you?' they asked. 'John Stonehouse,' I replied.
They all beamed and shook my hands vigorously. 'We are so
glad to see you. Every day we heard your name on the Free
Bangla Desh Radio. Your fighting for us gave all of us hope
and faith when everything was really bad here under the Pakistanis.' They told me they were civil servants and drove me
to the Government offices. On the way we passed crowds of
people cheering and cheering and shouting 'Joi Bangla'. The
least excuse inspired a cheer, but the loudest cheers were for
the trucks carrying Indian soldiers or the Mukti Bahini. The
soldiers held their guns above their heads in cheerful recognition of the crowd's acclaim. My companions said, 'Those chaps
want to be careful, those guns are loaded.' We reached the
offices and I located the small party of officials sent up from
Calcutta. No one had told them I was coming, but they were
delighted to see me. I showed them the piles of stamps I had
brought for them. Some of them I arranged to have over-
printed 'Bangla Desh liberated' in Bengali before my
departure. They were overjoyed. 'You must take them to the
General Post Office. They should replace the Pakistani stamps
immediately.'

We sat and talked about the awful problems the country

faced. Ten million refugees to return to find shattered homes, crops destroyed and cattle lost. Communications to be restored; hundreds of bridges blown up, and in this country of waterways, bridges are essential. And the need for supplies of all descriptions: food, clothing, medicines—the list was endless. 'The Pakistanis have raped our women and raped our country,' they said with feeling. They told me, with tears, about the intellectuals who had been brutally murdered in the last days before the cease fire. 'We will take you to the brick-yards to see for yourself.' We went through the streets of Dacca towards the suburb of Mohammedpur and occasionally I saw a dead body on the pavement. My escort did not seem to notice. I asked him. 'Most of the corpses have been cleared from the streets but there are still some to be removed,' he said. We heard firing in the distance. 'Those are Pakistani soldiers holding out in the Bihari districts. They don't know yet about the cease fire.' As we reached the brick-yards the stench was overpowering. Some bodies had been taken by relatives but many were scattered around in a mutilated state. The heads and faces had been smashed and the stomachs had been eaten by dogs. As I stood by the edge of a pool of stagnant water I noticed a small boy about eight years old coming from the hovels nearby carrying a bucket. He was obviously collecting water for the family. He scrambled down the slope within feet of a grotesque corpse staring with empty eye-pits towards the unseen heavens. He filled his bucket and returned completely unconcerned. 'The children here are oblivious to death,' said my escort. 'They have seen too much.'

I went to the General Post Office to deliver the postage stamps. All top officials had been directed to stay at their posts throughout the weekend after liberation and they welcomed me warmly. One had been seconded to the British Post Office and had been at St Martins Le Grand at the same time as I was there as Postmaster General. 'We must have more of these stamps,' they said, 'they are wonderful.' The Director General of the Post Office gave me a written order for six months supplies of the stamps to be printed in fifteen denominations. I said I would try to get them printed quickly if the Ministers in Calcutta approved. Later Tajuddin endorsed the order and FORMAT printed the supplies in double quick time and I sent some bundles out by air freight. By that time, however, the Director General had been replaced, as he was accused, I think unjustly, of being a collaborator with the Pakistanis. His successor was a man who was imprisoned during the liberation war and he resented his predecessor's actions. He refused to endorse the use of the new series of stamps and went on using hand-overprinted Pakistani stamps from old stocks for over six months. Part of the huge bill for printing was met from the proceeds of the sales of the first series, but I had, somehow, to find the balance of the account. FORMAT, after all, had printed the issue on trust and on my recommendation. I instructed FORMAT to give the rest of the stamps to the High Commission in London and they put them into a garage in Willesden.

A few weeks later I returned to Dacca with my dear friend and fellow Trustee, Donald Chesworth, the Chairman of War on Want. By this time the Government, which had decided to dispense with two words and call the country officially Bangladesh, was well installed and we were able to talk to Ministers about the relief programme then under way to assist the return of refugees as well as other problems. Despite the tremendous tasks in hand, all was hope and confidence; at last the country was free. The Prime Minister invited Donald and me to a dinner party at his house. We were the only guests but all the Ministers were there, and we were made to feel like members of the family. We responded by holding a party at the Intercontinental Hotel to which all the newly arrived diplomatic corps were invited—except the American Ambassador. It was the first diplomatic occasion in Dacca after independence, and so important, the American felt compelled to gatecrash. Tajuddin Ahmed and other Ministers made some very moving speeches.

I was in Dacca when the dramatic news came of Sheikh Mujibur Rahman's release from detention in Pakistan and flight to London. The country was electrified. Although he had been unable to do anything to help the independence struggle, he was still the undisputed leader. Then we heard that the RAF were flying him to Dacca. Hasty arrangements were made for his arrival, but nothing could have been done to prepare for the enormous crowds which came to greet him. At the airport a welcoming line of Ambassadors and Ministers waited to greet the President, but order relapsed into chaos as the crowd surged forward to embrace him. The road to the town was jammed with people and the official convoy made slow progress. I abandoned the car I was in and walked, arriving at the racecourse just before the convoy arrived. The waiting crowd was the largest I had ever seen. Abu Sayeed Choudhury insisted that I should join the Ministers on the platform, which was shaped like a boat—the symbol of the Awami League— and we all sat on our haunches while Mujibur Rahman spoke to his people. It was like a revivalist meeting but with a difference: the prophet was there in person; chiding, guiding and inspiring everyone present. On behalf of the three Trustees, Abu Sayeed presented the President with a cheque for several hundreds of thousands of pounds, collected into the Bangladesh Fund. It was drawn on the National Westminster Bank, Tothill Street, Westminster, and became the first foreign reserve for the new nation. Exhausted by his journey and the speech, Mujibur Rahman went to sleep in the little home from which he had been arrested nine months before. As I was leaving that night for Calcutta on the same RAF Comet that had flown him in, I called to say goodbye. The crowds were still all round the house clamouring to see him. I was shown into a modest bedroom, with the washing hanging all around the room and relatives sitting on the floor, and Mujibur who had been sleeping on the bed in his underwear sat up. 'Thank you,' he said, 'for all you did to help my country and my people. I have heard all about it. You can now regard Bangladesh as your country.'

Within a few days my fellow Trustee, Abu Sayeed Choudhury was installed as the President and Mujibur Rahman became Prime Minister. The invitation to me to become a citizen of Bangladesh was confirmed. 'Not an honorary citizen,' they said. 'We want you to be a full citizen so you stand for Parliament here.' I checked the precedents: it was possible for me to be a citizen of two Commonwealth countries simultaneously, and there were no constitutional objections to being a Member of Parliament in both. I accepted the great honour of citizenship, but declined the prospect of another Parliamentary seat. One was enough.

10 *The painful birth of a bank*

THE CENTRAL LOBBY of the Palace of Westminister is like the nave of a Cathedral, tall and domed, where are held the hushed conversations of the congregation; the mosaic of the four corners of the ceiling pick out the limits of the diocese: St George for England, St Patrick for Ireland, St David for Wales and St Andrew for Scotland; the wide corridors lead to chancels where the clergy and choirs of Parliament perform—east to the low church of the Commons and west to the high church of the Lords. Here is the place where the famous meet the famous, and through which the bishops and priests of politics from one place trundle to the annual ritual of the reading of the Queen's Speech in the 'other place'. Here, almost every weekday, the stern warning rings out to the un-initiated, 'Hats off Strangers' and the Speaker sweeps through, preceded by the mace, on the way to prayers. And here is where the ordinary constituents can come freely from the streets outside, through the St Stephen's Hall, which was once a chapel, and up the steps where the altar once stood into the hall which is the centrepiece of the Mother of Parliaments. At the desk, where stands a friendly policeman, the constituent obtains the instrument which requests his Member of Parliament to appear. It is a simple green card on which is written the name of the Member, the name and address of the visitor and the purpose of the visit. There is a story, which perhaps is not apo-cryphal, that when the playwright, William Douglas-Home, visited his brother, Alec, who was then Prime Minister, he wrote on the green card as his purpose the one word 'assassination'. The card was taken by the attendants—ex-Sergeant Majors quaintly attired in white wing-collared shirts and bow ties, a large medallion of office on their chests and black tailcoats—and solemnly delivered without question.

During my years as a Member I had received hundreds of unexpected visitors in the Central Lobby: schoolteachers, trade union shop stewards, families on holiday trips and people with individual grievances. Some of those seeking help came with unbelievable stories, but everyone must be listened to carefully as it is possible he is right and the powerful but fallible authority about which he complains is wrong. Truth is an elusive quality and can only be distilled by the application of patience. One such visitor was Captain Ernest Law; it was ironic that he complained of unlawful detention. His story was bizarre. After service in the Army, during which he was seconded to Kenya, he became a warehouse supervisor in a prison. This was during the period of the suppression of the Mau Mau uprising by the colonial Government. In the prison, Law saw many atrocities being committed against the African prisoners, including unnecessary beatings and torture. He complained to his superiors but, instead of commendation, he was sacked, and everywhere he went to obtain employment he was blackballed by the white employers who regarded him as a renegade white-man and a troublemaker. After weeks and, when finally completely destitute, he found himself in the White Highlands, a friendly farmer said, 'I couldn't dare to employ you. The best advice for you is to go to Nairobi and ask to be repatriated to the UK as a distressed British subject. Here is the bus fare.' Law went to Nairobi, called at a police station, was put into a barbed-wire compound, and taken before a man in a small room who said, 'Don't worry, we will take care of you.' He was then escorted to a prison and thrown into a cell where he stayed for nine months without trial. During this further period in prison, but from the other side as it were, he saw even worse atrocities than before. All his appeals to the Governor of the prison to be released were ignored. Eventually, with the help of a friendly warder, he smuggled out a letter to Alan Lennox-Boyd, the British Colonial Secretary. Within days he found himself on a plane to London and freedom. Without money, he called at the Discharged Prisoners Aid Society to ask for old clothes, but having heard his story, they refused, saying that as he had never been convicted, he was not eligible.

What Law described to me sounded fantasy. I knew that hundreds of thousands of Africans were kept detained without trial while the British Government preached about the civilising mission of colonialism, but to do it so blatantly to a white man, and a former Captain, was surprising. I checked out the story by asking a series of detailed Parliamentary questions. What Law had told me turned out to be entirely true. He was vindicated and went on to become a messenger for Mr Henry Brooke, Macmillan's Minister of Housing, and I saw him over the months scurrying around the Palace of Westminster, trusted with the red box and the secrets—and sometimes the sandwiches—of the Minister. It says a lot for the Permanent Secretary, Dame Evelyn Sharp, as well as for Henry Brooke, that they backed Law as the grisly details of his experience emerged.

One visitor I received in the Central Lobby was to set in motion a course of events which would entirely change my life, although neither of us had the slightest premonition of it at the time. His card was written simply—K. B. Ahmed, Purpose of Visit—'Bangladesh'. He had with him a tall, lean, bearded Englishman, who had a highly nervous and excitable manner. K. B. Ahmed was neither excited nor nervous. His bearing was cool and collected. He was a youngish man in his thirties, immaculately dressed in the best Bond Street tradition and very good looking with a dark glabrous face. He spoke with quiet confidence and a rationality and absence of excitability which belied his Bengalee background. I was to learn later that port Road in Manchester. As the numbers of migrants in-Pakistan and did not learn Bengali until well into his teens.

I took Ahmed and his solicitor, as the other man turned out to be, to one of the small interview rooms in the bowels of the building, directly under the House of Commons chamber itself. He sat down and quietly outlined his plans.

'You have been one of the leaders of Bangladesh freedom,' he said, 'Now we must establish the institutions which can help make a success of that freedom. We need a bank here in Britain to provide services for the Bengalee migrants who live and work here.'

'Aren't there other banks that can help them?' I said.

'They are simple people. They don't trust other banks as

much as they would their own,' said Ahmed, 'and they certainly don't want to continue to use the Pakistani banks which are associated with the old régime they hate so much.'

'Creating a bank is a most difficult exercise,' I said, 'and I don't really see how I can help.'

'I have sponsors for it,' said Ahmed. 'Leaders of the Bengalee community, including prominent business men. They will back it and make it a success. Because of your name you can help us fight the peace as you did the war.'

When I said goodbye to my visitors I reflected to myself that what they were suggesting was fantasy and it would probably be the last I would see of them. Ever since I had taken up the Bangladesh cause, dozens of Bengalees had come to me with all kinds of proposals, most of them based on fiction rather than fact. But, within a week or so, K. B. Ahmed was back, bringing a deputation of Bengalee businessmen to my office in Dover Street. In the panelled Board Room I listened to their story. Ahmed did most of the talking. He introduced Nazir Uddin, one of the first migrants from East Pakistan and a res-taurateur with a thriving oriental foods business on the Stock-port Road in Manchester. As the numbers of migrants in-creased, so the Nazir Uddin business expanded, and over the years he had become more prosperous.

The delegation proposed that I should become Chairman of the new bank in view of my special standing in Bangladesh. They suggested that the bank would be an important new bridge between the newest independent state and Britain, and would be based on the support of the 83,000 wage-earning Ben-galee migrants in Britain. I replied that I did not wish to take business advantage of my association with Bangladesh and if I accepted any offer of a bank chairmanship, it would be strictly on the understanding that the job would be unpaid. I was conscious that enemies of Bangladesh would certainly want to make capital out of a link which could be represented as based on my own pecuniary interest. I also made clear that the bank could not be launched unless the Bank of England approved of its commencement, and another precondition was that there should be major British institutions involved as shareholders from the very start. I thought the chances of suc-cess on either of these scores was very remote but placated my pressing Bengalee visitors by agreeing to give it a try.

Arranging a meeting with the Governor of the Bank of

England was easier than I had expected. I took with me Nazir Uddin, John McGrath, an old friend who had been the Financial Controller of the British Airports Authority, and K. B. Ahmed. The Bank of England, 'the old lady of Threadneedle Street', is like a fortress. It is an ugly monstrosity of a building with little architectural charm. To penetrate it one has to give some magic names to the splendidly dressed doormen in scarlet waistcoats and bright pink tail-coats. Sir Leslie O'Brien occupied an office, the size of a small house, furnished in a subdued and traditional style as befits the premier bank. He was charm personified, and motioned us to sit on the deep brocade-covered couches. I set out the reason for our visit—a new bank was being proposed which could bring into the banking system migrants who otherwise would not use banks. It would establish a bridge with the new nation of Bangladesh. The Governor was interested. He displayed none of the cool indifference that I had anticipated. After questioning us on different aspects of the proposal, he mentioned that his colleague would be taking care of the arrangements for us and would give us any guidance we felt we needed. The colleague turned out to be Jim Keogh, the Head of the Discount Office and the third most powerful man in the Bank of England. It seemed that our proposals were acceptable; the die was cast—we were set on the road to the creation of a new institution. Jim, as we learnt to call him, could not have been more helpful. He is an engaging bachelor who bravely disguises a false leg and who throughout his years of service was unfailing in his attentions to the banks, both foreign and domestic, which came within his orbit. Unjustly he has been criticised for too lax a supervision of the secondary bank sector. The collapse of this sector would have come anyway following the extraordinary disintegration of the UK financial and property structure. No one man could have stemmed that tide. Jim Keogh mixed genuine friendship and sympathy with the administration of his office and was unlike many others who inhabit the rarefied stratosphere of the financial establishment in the City of London. Jim's advice to us was, 'Get a sponsoring bank to help you through the myriad processes which are necessary.'

I had already been in contact with Jocelyn Hambro, Chairman of Hambros Bank. I had arranged, during the Bangladesh war, for the Hambros Bank in Bishopsgate to have the account of the Bangladesh Fund. It worked very well until hundreds of Bengalees decided to take the trains from Leicester, Bradford and Rochdale, clutching their pound notes and even their unopened pay-packets, to go to the counters of the Bishopsgate headquarters to pay in personally their hard earned contributions to the Bangladesh cause. This went on for days until the cries of protest from other Hambros customers, forced to wait in long queues, led to the account being transferred to the National Westminster Bank. And the Bengalees were then educated in the sophistications of the bank giro paying-in system. They had to be taught that their journeys to Bishopsgate were not really necessary.

Hambro had been keen to take part in the bank exercise and put me in touch with one of his directors, but subsequently this contact cooled off—without explaining why—and we had to look elsewhere. I telephoned Cyril Kleinwort, the head of Kleinwort Benson, another leading city merchant bank. Cyril I had known when I was Postmaster General and he had done excellent work as the Chairman of the Invisible Exports Committee. I had an admiration for his sagacity.

'Now,' he said, 'you cannot really rely on me, I am handing over to Gerald, you know. You speak to him.'

Gerald turned out to be Gerald Thompson, a short, jolly man who gives the impression not so much of a careful city banker as the avuncular public school housemaster. I relish the memory of Gerald carving the beef at the city lunch on the top floors of the magnificent skyscraper Kleinworts share with National and Grindlays Bank. He had invited K. B. Ahmed and me to meet his colleagues, and the lunch, like every other daily lunch in those parts, was a splendid affair. The 'family' and the guests, who have been escorted down the plush carpeted corridors, collect in the beautifully appointed lunch rooms. Cocktails—'anything you want'—'do have another, old chap'—are freely available. There is no haste, no pressure, and everyone seems to have all the time in the world. It is considered bad form to talk real business at this stage. The usual conversation is, 'What are we going to do about the trade unions?' 'They really don't know how to do a fair day's work for a fair day's pay.' 'There is too much malingering nowadays.' 'That fellow Hugh Scanlon needs to be controlled and Jack Jones is a positive menace.' 'You know it's really the Communists who are controlling the trade unions.' 'Joining

Europe will help keep them in order—they're much better organised over there.' And more and more in the same vein.

Our particular meal was arranged buffet style with the hosts serving the guests and with Gerald presiding over it all like the happy housemaster he was. He enjoyed carving the huge side of beef and had a well-practised flourish when sharpening the carving knife. 'Clearly,' I thought, 'there is more to merchant banking than meets the eye.' He introduced K. B. Ahmed and me to the 'family'. Representatives were present from every department of Kleinworts, and Gerald wanted us to be in no doubt that their organisation would be at our disposal.

'And sitting down there at the other end of the table,' he said, 'is Bertie Haynes. Now Bertie is an expert at forming new banks. He has already done it several times for the Americans and I want him to work with you. You could have no better advice. Isn't that right, Bertie?' he called down the long table.

Bertie was in his mid-sixties and could have fooled anyone that he was a merchant banker. He was near retirement and told us that he would regard this operation as his last exercise. He would be taking on a retirement post for the bank in Jersey in the near future.

When Gerald saw us to the lift he again emphasised that he was very keen to help and that Kleinworts would be an excellent body to assist Bangladesh. We went away very encouraged at this declaration of faith, and the advice given by Kleinworts was valuable. However, within a few weeks I had a telephone call from Gerald Thompson which showed that there had been second thoughts in his organisation. He said, 'Well now, we want to help but you cannot quote us as sponsors.' But already we had moved a long way down the road. Prospective shareholders had been approached, the first draft of the prospectus had been prepared and the Bank of England continued daily to be helpful and enthusiastic. So we turned to Barclays Bank to be the receiving bank and in a very practical, matter-of-fact way they took on the job through Barclays London and International.

One of the first prospective shareholders I approached was Ronnie Lyon, the self-made property millionaire. I asked him to join me for dinner at the House of Commons, and I told him all about the proposal. He was quite willing to invest, but said, 'Don't let me be the only one, John. I'll put in £20,000 if you can get other sponsors to participate.' This was very encouraging, coming from such a tough negotiator. My first approach had been successful—if I could obtain a few other sponsors the dream would be off the ground.

My next approach was to Julian Hodge, the 'Welsh Wizard', who had developed his finance business from scratch and was now about to launch a new Bank of Wales. Julian had been proposed to me by Lord Hall as a suitable financial director for the Post Office. I had met him in that connection but did not relish the idea of putting in a part-time director whose main interests would still be in and around Wales.

I travelled to Cardiff to see Hodge with only a limited objective; to persuade one of his organisations to become a founder shareholder in the British Bangladesh Trust. There were large communities of Bengalees in South Wales, particularly in Cardiff and Swansea, and it would make sense for Welsh interests to have a stake in the new body. Hodge received me affably on the top floor of the Julian S. Hodge Building and he introduced one of his colleagues who was responsible for the arrangements in creating the new Commercial Bank of Wales. 'He can be most helpful to you,' he said.

Both of them listened intently whilst I described our plans. I explained that I wanted no more than £20,000 from each founder shareholder as I wanted the interest to be widely spread among various elements in Britain as well as from the Bengalee community itself. Hodge positively sparkled. 'Oh, I think we can do better than that. £20,000 would be too little—count us in for £50,000,' he said.

It is ironic that the first two people I approached and who promised their support enthusiastically were almost the only two from the original list of sponsors who failed in the end to subscribe.

Sir Raymond Brookes, the Chairman of Guest Keen and Nettlefolds, the huge engineering firm, was much more consistent. He was interested from the point of view of strengthening bonds between British industry and the Indian sub-continent. GKN had a big plant in Calcutta and Brookes could see advantages in being associated with a venture that had the object of improving relationships between that area and Britain. His financial director needed a little convincing, so I visited Smethwick, the headquarters of GKN, where during the General Election some years before I had spoken outside the works gates in support of Patrick Gordon Walker in his ill-fated campaign to remain as the Labour Member for that constituency. The GKN board voted to subscribe £30,000.

John Clark, the Chairman of Plessey, invited me to Ilford to lunch with the full Board of his company. Once again I explained the proposal, this time between the soup and the entrée, answered questions over the sweet and during coffee watched as John Clark went around the table collecting the voices. Elworthy, the retired Air Chief Marshal, was in favour. So was Eric Frye, the finance director, who made the point that Bangladesh would be a good country in which to engage in off-shore production of electronics.

'The people are skilled, wages are low and there is no reason why Bangladesh should not provide the same commercial environment for success as Singapore has done,' he said.

Michael Clark was a little less enthusiastic, but John declared the issue as carried. When it came to deciding the figure, the Board were interested only in how much GKN were subscribing, and as they wanted to improve on this, £35,000 was their decision.

I approached the Crown Agents for Oversea Governments and Administrations, not with any expectation of success but merely to go through the form. It might have appeared odd if we had not made the suggestion to them. Claude Hayes, the Chairman, received me in his magnificent office in Millbank. We talked about philately and the Pacific Islands, not to mention Mauritius, Swaziland and other places far afield which Hayes knew well through his frequent visits. The Crown Agents at that time gave the impression of tremendous stability—it had a royal aura about it. No one then realised how shaky the foundations of that immense structure had become and only several years later did it emerge that the Crown Agents had involved itself in disastrous investments in banking and property from which it had to be rescued by the Government with a grant of £85 million. But in July 1972, I had no knowledge of this weakness and I thought I was approaching a mountain of solid financial respectability. I was surprised, a few weeks later, to receive a brief note saying that 4 Millbank Securities Limited, the shareholding arm of Crown Agents, was proposing to invest £50,000 in the bank. We threw our hats in the air—it seemed that now nothing could hold us back from having a success on our hands.

The *Financial Times* carried a paragraph describing the intentions of the new venture and we began to receive inquiries from interested shareholders. It was extremely important to our objectives that the Bengalees in Britain knew just as much about the plans as the readers of the *Financial Times*. Equality of information was essential to the concept of a bridge between Britain and Bangladesh and between Britons and Bengalees. We asked the editor of the Bengali newspaper *Janomot* to prepare a news-sheet in Bengali for distribution to the Bengalees, including in it the facts that had already appeared in the British Press. It was also vital in this handbill to explain to the Bengalees that what was being planned was not a charity or a fund to collect donations like the Bangladesh Fund of which I had been a trustee. They had to understand that it would be a bank and although at the outset the word 'Trust' was in the title, this could be changed to 'Bank' after the various official Bank of England approvals had been obtained. There was no intention to mislead, only a fervent anxiety to inform people as to the facts. No money was invited to be subscribed on the distribution of the news-sheet and none was received, as it was in no sense a prospectus. Bengalee people were simply given the chance of reading what English-speaking people had already read. The Bengali news-sheet was sent, as an example of what we were doing to inform the Bengalees, to the Bank of England, and they did not raise any objection. Indeed, I had the impression, throughout, that they were pleased with our efforts to involve the ordinary migrants.

About this time I was approached by a highly articulate Bengalee called Suhail Aziz, who was an economics graduate, an ex-RAF officer and an official with the Commission on Industrial Relations. He was enthusiastic about our plans and volunteered to do all he could to help by putting his organisation, a section of the Awami League in Britain, at our disposal. 'We all admire what you have done for Bangladesh, we must support you in making a success of the new bank,' he said.

He brought groups of Bengalees to my office so they would hear more about it and organised a meeting at Aldgate in East London where I spoke. The chairman of the meeting, who was also the Chairman of the Aziz section of the Awami League, advised all present to support the proposed bank. Other meetings were organised to take place all over the country where Bengalees live: in Bradford, Sheffield, Birmingham, Manchester, Rochdale, Portsmouth, Newcastle-on-Tyne, Swansea, Cardiff, Bristol, and other places. Meanwhile Suhail Aziz applied for a job with the new British Bangladesh Trust. He seemed to be an ideal person to appoint: enthusiastic, energetic, enterprising and qualified, but unfortunately we could not meet his terms.

I attended all the meetings up and down the British Isles, explaining to the Bengalee migrants how the plans for BBT would provide an opportunity for better links between their mother country and their host country, but certain opponents of our plans had travelled the country before me, spreading rumours, and the meetings were mostly poorly attended. In one town, Rochdale, nobody—except a couple of reporters— turned up at all. Something, clearly, was going wrong but I was powerless to do anything about it. The promises of massive support from tens of thousands of Bengalees, which their leaders had given me a few months before, were not materialising. We were already committed to establishing the Bank; the prospectus was printed and on the advice of solicitors a minimum shareholding of £500,000 was fixed; the building for the Bank had been acquired and refurbished in a very attractive semi-eastern style with the two flags of Britain and Bangladesh furled on a pole above the crest of the Bengal tiger outside; and senior staff recruited. I had needed to make myself, or my companies, responsible for all this expenditure in the event that the launching was not successful and all the subscriptions returned.

However, the interest of the financial community was very favourable and a number of British institutions approached us to acquire options on large blocks of shares. One merchant bank wanted 10 per cent of the issued capital. We turned down these proposals as they were not consistent with our plans for a wider based British shareholding. But it was cruelly disappointing that the Bengalee community were being turned against us. I had never wanted to be the promoter of just another Bank. As the one Englishman who was a citizen of both Britain and Bangladesh my concern was to secure a genuine commercial partnership between the two peoples.

At one of the meetings—I think it was in Bradford—a reporter from the *Sunday Times* turned up. He was Anthony Mascherenas, a Goan who had been with the Pakistan Army, and who had written a splash story for the *Sunday Times* on

'Genocide in East Pakistan'. Some weeks before 'Mac' Choudhury, the information officer at the Bangladesh High Commission, had told me that Mascherenas had made enquiries from him about my business activities. 'Mac' Choudhury, who had known Mascherenas years before in Karachi as a fellow journalist, asked him why he wanted such information. Mascherenas replied that it had been decided at the *Sunday Times* to investigate the affairs of Labour MPs in business as had been done, for example, in the case of Reginald Maudling, a leading Conservative, whose name had been associated with Poulson, the architect who was convicted of corruption. 'We have to keep the political balance,' said Mascherenas. My wife told Beryl Maudling about this conversation. She was not surprised and said, 'Look what they've done to Reggie.'

Despite my misgivings, I gave Mascherenas as much information as possible, and, in particular, supplied him with a list of the British institutions who were proposing to be shareholders. During the next week I was shaken to hear that these companies were being telephoned by another *Sunday Times* reporter, Richard Milner, to confirm whether they really intended to subscribe to the new bank.

It became clear that Milner and Mascherenas were preparing an article critical of our enterprise and this was confirmed when they came to our offices. They were not well disposed towards us, and many of their questions seemed to me to be of the trick 'when did you last beat your wife?' variety. We were coming near to the end of November 1972 and to the time for the public subscription for shares. A hostile article at this stage in an influential paper like the *Sunday Times* would do incredible harm.

I decided I should see Harold Evans, the Editor of the *Sunday Times*, to tell him what was going on. Harold welcomed me to his office—we were old friends and used to play squash together at the Royal Automobile Club in Pall Mall.

'We are doing well on the thalidomide case,' he said. 'They are trying to stop publication but we will win in the end.'

We then turned to the reason for my visit. I told him that an article was being produced within his organisation which I had reason to suspect would be so damaging that it would, through its effects, destroy all our efforts to create an institution which would link Britain and Bangladesh and that it would, furthermore, destroy me publicly, financially and politically. I would be completely ruined if it appeared.

'Nonsense,' he said. 'You are well respected and well known as an outstanding politician and a good Minister. One article would not ruin you.'

I could not agree. Harold Evans did not want to admit the power of the press. A hundred favourable articles may not make a career, but one devastating article can ruin one just as surely as a damning from a mediaeval pulpit could condemn a witch or sorcerer, however unjustly.

Evans checked up and discovered that the article was planned to go into the Business News section of the *Sunday Times* on the Sunday a week before the subscriptions opened. The unfortunate timing would do the maximum damage. It would appear too late for any effective reply to be circulated.

He said chirpily, 'Ring me up on the Saturday and I will read the article over to you before it goes to print.'

I left the offices of the *Sunday Times* in Gray's Inn Road a dazed man; I felt a foreboding of impending disaster.

We were given no advance information on what would appear in the article and I had to wait until the appointed Saturday. I was returning from my constituency, driving down the M1, and at every service area I stopped to telephone Harold Evans. Each time he told me the article had not yet 'come down'. At this rate, there would be no possibility of major amendment or legal injunction until it was too late.

At the last service area I got through, and this time Evans had the article in front of him, as promised. 'Here it is,' he said, and read it to me. I was flabbergasted. It was far worse than anything I had expected. There was not a single good word to say for all our work, and our motivations were completely misunderstood. Harold Evans said it was impossible to replace the article; it was going in. At least, I asked, remove the false statement about Rowe Rudd the stockbrokers withdrawing as shareholders. He agreed to do that.

Late that Saturday night I went to Ludgate Circus to buy the first edition of the *Sunday Times*. It was as if a condemned man were collecting his death warrant. In print the article looked even more unjust to me, and I had reason to believe that one at least of the informants was no friend of mine, and had a vested interest in my failure. The *Sunday Times* had not presented us with a list of their charges, or given us an opportunity to refute them. Such a technique would of course have meant a more balanced article, but would, I suppose, have hurt the image of crusading journalism.

During the night I prepared a reply so that on the Sunday it could be distributed to all the daily newspapers. Apart from *The Guardian*, which had a far less damaging piece, none of the Monday papers reported anything adverse about us. *The Daily Telegraph*, whose city editor Kenneth Fleet had taken the trouble to find out all the facts about our venture, made some very favourable references to it. It was pleasing that not everybody followed the *Sunday Times* lead, but the pall of gloom settled on Dover Street. My hard work, without pay or reward over nine months, was now crushed like a cruel schoolboy tears apart in seconds the nest a bird has taken ages to build.

As a result of the *Sunday Times* campaign many of the expected applications for shares did not materialise—we shall never know how many. The article was severely damaging because it went beyond journalistic criticism of a suspected bad business venture. It specified alleged malpractices in recruiting support for the project. Most seriously the article accused us of company fraud in circulating a Bengali prospectus containing false statements. Here again the *Sunday Times* was in gross error. There was never a prospectus in Bengali; there was merely a news-sheet in Bengali distributed many weeks before the official prospectus. The news-sheet contained information which had appeared in the English Press and included the essential point for the Bengalees to understand that the Trust was to operate as a bank and could be renamed as 'Bank' if the Bank of England approved. As the Bank went on to gain all the official recognitions possible during its first two years of operation, and in his letters at the time Keogh of the Bank of England wished the 'bank' success, this was certainly no extravagant or misleading claim. For the *Sunday Times* to brand us openly as guilty of fraud was to strike at the roots of our integrity and credibility. And they failed to notice the key point in our position, which would confirm absolutely our innocence of fraud: no money at any time had been subscribed on the Bengali news-sheet; all subscriptions were still to be made and would be made on the basis of the official prospectus.

When the subscriptions for shares was opened shortly afterwards we waited in great apprehension. Everything now depended on the public subscription. We had laboured long and hard to create a structure from a noble idea and now we wanted to put life and meaning into the symphysis between peoples that we called, meaningfully, the British Bangladesh Trust. Would our efforts have been in vain?

When the first subscriptions were opened by Barclays Bank it was clear the issue was not the success we had expected. Many of the companies we had managed to contact with our reply to the *Sunday Times* article were standing firm. Plessey, GKN, De La Rue, Trust Houses Forte and the Crown Agents were all subscribing. So were many individuals who knew and respected us: Sir Lew Grade, the entertainment king; Sir Charles Forte, the great hotelier; Sir John Clark, the head of Plessey; Sir Herbert Ashworth, the President of the country's third largest Building Society; Tony Rampton, the chairman of the biggest mail-order company, and many others. When all these people had such confidence and faith, how could we let the ideal fail? As there were two days in hand before subscriptions closed I decided to throw all my personal and companies' resources into the subscription, and by borrowing from other banks to maximise my applications for shares. I asked personal friends and family to do likewise, believing that as the Bank was proved successful within a few months there would be a healthy demand for the shares.

When we analysed the Bengalees' applications they amounted—apart from K. B. Ahmed's—to a mere £15,000, which was a far cry from the £500,000 the original documents had led me to expect. Only the last-minute subscription I had organised saved BBT from being aborted.

I had saved the day but in the process I had shackled myself to the wheel of a chariot; and as the wheels turned the spikes dug into me, slowly draining me of blood, and preparing me for a final sacrifice at a Roman circus.

11 *Enter Scotland Yard*

DECEMBER 1972, was a month of deceptive calm. The Bank had been launched; its doors were open, and business, although slow, had started. Some inter-bank relations, which enable one bank to lend or borrow from another at will up to specified limits, had been established. A few deposits came in from customers, and the Bank did some lending. My exporting companies continued to operate very successfully and they were encouraged to open accounts with the Bank and to use its facilities to help the new institution to get into orbit. Above the ground surface of manufacturing or commercial enterprises, which mainly operate on the earthy basis of making a profit on invested capital, there are hovering in the financial air a large number of banks, merchant banks, secondary banks, fringe banks, bucket shops and money-lenders who do not base their activities on such solid soil at all. They depend, not so much on invested capital, but on taking in the money flow like blood to a heart and pumping it out again, re-oxygenated, at a higher rate of interest, towards the arteries of business who are the customers. The speed with which that pumping takes place propels the financial rocket—or racket—away from the earth-bound orthodoxy towards the heavens where only the incorporeal condition of the money market exists. Once off the surface of the earth, the new addition to the money solar system hopes to join others in a perpetual and comfortable suspension well away from the harsh environment of the brutish world below. The successful banks are those which have become permanent satellites glowing in the skies like planets reflecting the glory of the sun.

The early nineteen-seventies followed a period of excess currency supply and a high velocity of money, as Chancellors released the blood flow in an attempt to keep businesses fully active and employment booming. The banks, of all shapes and sizes, prospered in these conditions as the pumping of their busy organs circulated the money and took from each flow the relevant tithe of interest.

Property lending had also become a source of wealth for the money operators. Property was a tangible security, constantly increasing in value like the inevitability of inflation, and usually providing the lending bank with a big slice of the capital profits.

It was not our wish in the BBT to join the less reputable banks in a purely satellite role, but if we could get into the acceptability of orbit it would be much easier for us to perform our task of assisting the Bengalee migrants as customers and encouraging trade between Britain and Bangladesh. That was why we made every effort to get the Bank off the ground. In those first weeks we, at least, established a launching pad.

At the modest Christmas Party we held for the staff and families in the basement of our offices, with hot, hearty food delivered in buckets by the outside caterer, we celebrated our initial success. We looked to 1973 as the year for steady progress towards a status which would enable us to perform our chosen role. But 1973 became the year when our early progress was shattered and our hopes dismayed. The seeds of distrust, which had been planted by the *Sunday Times*, began to sprout at the beginning of January. At Dover Street one day we had a visit from a tall, bulky man of about fifty-five with a friendly manner and big feet. He introduced himself as Mr Newman, ex-policeman and now an investigating officer for the Department of Trade and Industry. 'What can we do for you?' I asked, thinking that he had enquiries to make about one of our customers. 'I have been asked,' he said, 'to look into this serious allegation which appeared in the *Sunday Times*.' He brought out a clipping of the article, marked in places with black ink. 'They say here that your Company issued a prospectus in Bengali and that it contained false statements and that you committed a fraud under the Companies Act. These are most serious charges coming from a responsible paper like the *Sunday Times*, so we are bound to investigate them.'

I was amazed. 'Do you mean to say that you spend your valuable time following up such slanted stories?' I asked.

'We have to be careful,' he answered. 'Someone, some day, might ask why we hadn't made our own investigation. The *Sunday Times*, itself, might attack us.'

'Why did you leave it so long? The article appeared six weeks ago.'

'We thought we would let you settle in first,' he beamed, wanting to be chummy.

'The article was ignored by the rest of the Press,' I said. 'Surely if there had been anything in that Company fraud business the other newspapers would have been after us like a pack of hounds.'

'Well, don't worry,' he said. 'I expect it will be all right when I put my report in.'

We sat and talked for about an hour and I explained, very carefully, how we had distributed a news-sheet in Bengali so the Bengalee migrants could see what the project was about. 'They were entitled to know,' I emphasised. Newman was extremely friendly and shook hands warmly when he left.

After he had gone we had a brief talk amongst ourselves and agreed that there could not possibly be anything to worry about. Newman understood all our points and seemed to be on our side. He knew we hadn't raised any money on the Bengali news-sheet, so how could a fraud have been committed? Newman was obviously just going through the necessary routine.

After a week or so Newman came back, as friendly as ever. He had made more enquiries, he said, and confirmed our story about the news-sheet. 'Have you seen this handwriting before?' he asked, handing me a manila envelope addressed to a particular room at the Department of Trade and Industry. I knew the hand that had written that envelope, immediately, for it was that of a man who had become an opponent of mine, and who had written long letters to me in the same handwriting. The moving finger having writ moved on, apparently to send an anonymous letter and bundle of documents to a Government Department. 'But how did he know your exact room number?' I asked.

'That was his undoing,' said Newman. Apparently the writer had previously been in touch with the department about the money-raising activities of someone else, so when the envelope came in they knew who it was from.

'Well,' I said, 'that proves our point. If this man can go to the lengths of sending you an anonymous complaint, that proves he is up to no good.'

'That's what we think,' said Newman. 'Don't worry, I'll deal with this in my report and I don't expect you will hear from us again.'

We relaxed and tried to get on with building up the Bank. But there was no denying it—the Bengalee community were not using the instrument set up for them. Few Bengalees opened current accounts and even fewer deposited their savings with BBT. A larger number came seeking loans and some were irritated when we had to explain, patiently, that the Bank, as a commercial organisation, had to judge each application carefully. We were not in the charity business and could not advance money to a cousin or nephew simply because he had an idea to set up a curry restaurant. It became clear that the slow development of the Bank in relation to the Bengalee community was not unrelated to the campaign of misrepresentation initiated by our enemies. Nothing travels faster than bad news, and it was all over the place. I valued the comments of the few Bengalee leaders who came to say how disgusted they were by these hostile activities. We were confident that the nonsense of petty intrigue and scandal-mongering would eventually die down, and gritted our teeth to brave it out. But we had not reckoned on Detective Inspector Grant. He came into our lives as a bombshell suddenly exploding weeks after a cease-fire.

The appointment was made on the telephone. 'This is Scotland Yard here, Inspector Grant speaking, can I come and see you for a chat?'

When he arrived I took him to the tiny room on the second mezzanine floor of the Bank offices at 27 Dover Street. It was a tastefully furnished room with a desk, swing chair, glass coffee-table and two deep armchairs. On the walls were some Eastern prints and some Indian mosaic work. I liked that room, which any Director or senior official could use for private interviews; it had calm as well as charm. Grant turned out to be a medium built man in his fifties with a slightly craggy face; he was accompanied by a fresh young Detective Constable who carried a notebook and later took everything down.

Grant, in accordance with normal practice, said, 'I have to warn you that anything you say will be taken down and may be used as evidence.' It was a well-practised phrase that he was required to use, and which no doubt he had used hundreds of times before, but which spelt dread and fear to the listener. Although I had no guilty feelings, a shudder went right through my body like a cold current of electricity deadening my nerve ends. 'What?' I said. 'Are you here on a criminal matter?' 'Yes,' he replied. 'I am from the Fraud Squad.' 'I must bring my solicitor,' I said, 'before I can say anything to you.'

When I contacted my solicitor, Andrew Kennedy, he was flabbergasted. 'That cannot be possible,' he expostulated. He came to the small mezzanine room and met Grant. The solicitor was still carrying a look of complete disbelief when he said, 'Tell us what all this is about.'

Grant explained that he was investigating alleged frauds under the Companies Acts. 'What are the frauds supposed to be?' asked Andrew Kennedy.

'It is the fraud in issuing the Bengali prospectus as revealed in the *Sunday Times*,' he said.

'Nonsense,' said Kennedy. 'That was no prospectus.'

Grant then started a cross-examination, working from a long list of prepared questions.

'When was the prospectus issued and circulated?' he asked.

'It wasn't a prospectus,' I answered. 'You should not come to this investigation with such presumptions.'

'Well, when did it go out?'

For a long, long time I dealt with his questions, which were very tedious to me. When, who, why and how? As the interrogation went on I imagined with horror that this man, probing into details the importance of which had long lost significance to me, was acting as if I was already guilty, and that all he had to do was to prove it. I tried to explain motivations. 'The Bengalees were entitled to see what had already appeared in the English Press and to read it in their own language. We did no damage to anyone,' I said in desperation. 'We collected no money from anyone.'

Grant arranged to come back and the young Detective Constable, who had said not a word, packed up the thickening sheaf of papers and they went away.

'They haven't a leg to stand on,' said the solicitor. 'It is a ridiculous business. Let me check up on the Companies Acts.'

He did, and in them found the obscure, but for us vital, clause saying that the issue of shares must be on the basis of the official prospectus, and on no other prospectus. The clause had been inserted to stop speculators raising large sums from the general public on spurious promises. Gullible people had fallen for such tricks in the past and the law was drafted to protect them. 'But this could not possibly be construed as applying to you,' said the solicitor. 'You were simply conveying advance information long before the prospectus, and you did not raise any money.' We nodded.

I was pleased by his confidence, but annoyed because I suspected that he did not gather what I was up against. I had been arrested in Northern Rhodesia and South Africa, I had been followed by the secret police in Uganda and Kenya, I had been near the firing-line in Bangladesh, but I had never been afraid. In those days my motives had been clearly understood. But this time I was consumed by a chilling fear. This time who would possibly want to make the effort of understanding if I were to be charged with fraud? Fraud, fraud, fraud—the word came back again and again into my consciousness, lurking like a ghost which refuses to be exorcised. Fraud! How could anyone grasp the truth? They would nudge one another and say, knowingly, 'There's more to this than meets the eye. Scotland Yard never take that up unless there was something more serious.' And in my case a man accused is a man ruined. 'A man is innocent before he is proven guilty,' is the most deceiving aphorism, because once a charge is made or once even a whisper of Scotland Yard investigations appears in the newspapers, a man in my position is paralysed. With a breath of suspicion getting out,I would be unable to conclude any important business deals, and certainly the Bank would suffer, and as far as politics were concerned my effective career would be finished for a long time, if not forever. No one in public life can operate with such a shadow looming over him.

When Inspector Grant returned to our offices he brought the Bengali news-sheet. 'How is this part translated?' he asked. I do not read Bengali but I gave him a general gist of the document—I had been over it before with Newman of the DTI.

'We must have it exact,' he said.

'Right,' I replied, 'we will get it translated for you.'

I contacted the Editor of *Janomot* and asked him to see me urgently. When he arrived I sat him down and said, 'Please translate that exactly as you remember the original English words you had in mind when you first wrote it in Bengali, and what you meant to convey.'

He sat down with pen at the ready, professional journalist that he was, and in the section dealing with the British Bangladesh Trust's development as a Bank he wrote that 'it could' be renamed as 'Bank' if the Bank of England approved.

'No doubt about the "could"?' I asked.

'Well,' he said, 'there is no doubt in my mind.'

Meanwhile, Grant, as Newman before him, obtained his translations: every one was different from the next. The problem of the Bengali language is that it was created for poetry, not commerce; it does not have the precision of English or German, nor their sharply defined tenses. The 'could' could be translated as 'would' or even 'will' so subtly altering the meaning of the sentence. It seemed that my whole future, and the Bank's, was hanging by this single thread of interpretation. It is said that in mediaeval times the philosophers argued vehemently about how many angels could dance on the point of a needle; in my desperation it seemed that this Scotland Yard investigation was becoming as irrelevant and arcane.

Grant went about his work thoroughly, spending weeks and weeks on the job. He obtained a list of all the Bengalee shareholders of the Bank, most of whom had only one or two ten pound shares, and worked through them systematically. He visited them in their homes and in the restaurants where they worked. It is not generally appreciated that most of the 'Indian' restaurants are, in fact, run by Bengalees from Bangladesh, and that almost all of them came from one area in Bangladesh called Sylhet. Grant probably had a lot of curry meals in his travels, but what he may not have realised was that we were getting regular feedback on his investigations. His questions, although perfectly proper, were intimidating to Bengalees, some of whom were illegal immigrants and scared of authority. He would ask them 'Have you seen this?' producing the news-sheet.

'Yes.'

'Did you subscribe to the British Bangladesh Trust?'

'Yes, I bought two ten pound shares.'

'Did you subscribe after you saw the news-sheet?'

'Yes.'

These good people had seen the news-sheet and had

subscribed—one action followed the other; it seemed as simple as that. But simplicity is damning. It is a trap for the unsuspecting: the commercial and company law jungle is full of such pits, covered with deceiving undergrowth, and to circumvent them the canny animal has to use all the guile and cunning available to him. The company law is so complex and so confusing it takes days and weeks for specialist lawyers to unravel it, and even then there can be no certainty that the act one is committing will not open up a trap underneath all those scattered twigs of detail. The innocent Bengalee *had* subscribed after he had seen the news-sheet, but *also* after he had seen the prospectus, which had not only been distributed in tens of thousands but copies had also been reprinted in *Janomot*, the Bengali newspaper.

My own lawyer for the setting up of the Bank was an expert in company law and had been recommended to me by Sir Charles Hardie, once Chairman of BOAC, Chairman of the White Fish Authority, Chairman of the British Printing Corporation and a large food chain and Director of up to a hundred other companies as well as being a Director of the Royal Bank of Canada and the big merchant bankers, Hill Samuel. Who better to guide me through the capitalist jungle than this man who had been sniffing out all the traps for three decades? And my own lawyer had never raised any doubt about the propriety of the news-sheet, nor indeed had the Bank of England, because the motivations behind its circulation were obviously moral.

During this period, which lasted for months, my morale dropped lower and lower. I was, for the first time in my life, facing an elusive enemy I could not engage, and police enquiries were harming the Bank. Suspicions had been aroused among Bengalees who thought, in their innocence, that an ex-Minister and a Privy Councillor could not be investigated by Scotland Yard unless something very serious had happened. They were therefore not willing to use a bank which was under this cloud, and certainly not prepared to deposit their money with it. We had been expecting thousands of Bengalees to use our services, but we never saw them. Caution is the better part of valour in such circumstances, and an immigrant in a new country does his best to remain inconspicuous and steer well clear of trouble.

I felt a real sense of persecution for I believed that the police investigation might never have taken place if I had been Joe Bloggs, unknown in the public eye, and I believed also that a Joe Bloggs was unlikely to have had a *Sunday Times* article devoted to him in quite such a way; and that without that article the investigation might never have got under way. There was a vicious circle whirling like a vortex, around and around, and pulling me down, down, down.

To be known to the public is an asset; eyes light up, knowing nods are exchanged and a certain reputation precedes one, generally making it easier to transact the affairs of the day. But fame can be a cruel burden as well, particularly when authority leans over sideways to ensure that preference is not given, or seen to be given. Civil servants sometimes protect themselves against that possibility by acting more harshly towards a well-known person than towards a mere private person.

Although I had no reason to believe that I had broken the law, intentionally or otherwise, a sense of guilt hung on my chest like a heavy weight. It constricted my body like a vice, holding me in an ever-increasing grip. Guilt dogged me everywhere I went. In the House of Commons I went about my job of asking Parliamentary questions, voting, writing letters to Ministers and talking to Parliamentary colleagues, and everywhere I went the guilt came with me. It would interrupt my thoughts as I tried to consider the political problems of the time; nothing would take it away. At nights I would wake up in the early hours, still exhausted, and the guilt would still be there. It obliterated everything like a dark thunder cloud obscures the sun. Try as I did, I could not shake off that awful malady; it infected my whole being. But the guilt was not the stirrings of conscience of a criminal or the feelings of remorse of a man who had done something wrong or shameful in any way. It was none of these. It was the knowledge that my position as a well-known politician had brought all this on my family, and my colleagues, and threatened the Bank itself. Through my person I was guilty of attracting this attention. My guilt was the public persona which I could not shake off my neck.

I suggested to my solicitor that we should consult counsel to see what possibly could be done to avert the horror of a charge. So far no news had leaked about the investigation, and that was a blessing, but Grant was burrowing on, and the possibility of a charge had to be considered. If I were charged,

I would be finished. How could I expect to become a senior Minister again, if Labour won the next election, with a fraud case in my past, even if I had been acquitted?

I went with K. B. Ahmed, who was as concerned about his own reputation, and the solicitors to the little chambers, in the Temple, of Victor Durand, the celebrated barrister. We sat around his desk, which was loaded with briefs, with the dusty volumes of law lining the walls. The place was impregnated with the lessons of litigation, as though each succeeding client had left behind an impression of the lesion he had suffered, until it penetrated the fabric, layer upon layer. Durand was very grave when we told him the story of the police investigations. The sense of foreboding within me deepened as he failed to give any sign of hope.

At his request I prepared a full brief on the whole affair, including all the documents, copies of the letters from Keogh of the Bank of England referring to our 'Bank', the schedule of the campaign to inform the Bengalee community, and pages and pages of notes. It took many hours and a lot of nervous energy. I was angry, not only that I was subject to what seemed to me unnecessary persecution, but at the distraction from the practical and useful things I could have been doing during those weeks. I was shocked that it was possible to waste so much time. I wondered how many other people who try to create, purposefully, are dragged down by the need to justify their actions; I wondered how many marvellous human achievements might never have been completed if justification rather than inspiration had been the order of the day.

Durand was impressed with my brief and suggested that it should go to the Director of Public Prosecutions for, by this time, he had discovered that Grant had submitted his report to the DPP. It was somewhat unusual for such a brief to go directly to the DPP but we wanted him to be able to consider our version of the facts as well as the police evidence.

We waited days and weeks for an acknowledgement, but none came. The legal system is a cruel torture for the person under suspicion as authority will never relax its dead wall of indifference or hostility. One can never know what is going on behind that wall. Durand tried to get close to Sir Norman Skelhorn, the DPP himself, whom he knew well, but beyond finding out that he was due to read the file on this or that day, he could make no contact. Durand became even more grave and I became quite desperate with worry.

I decided to consult Elwyn Jones, the former Attorney General, who had been my colleague in Government and was also a friend. There was a Division in the House at 7 pm that day, and in the 'No' Lobby I saw Elwyn and asked him to advise me on an urgent personal matter. He said he could see me after the 10 o'clock Division. Three hours later, after we had all trundled through the Lobbies to have our heads counted by the tellers for the second time. I waited for Elwyn in the crowded Members Lobby. It is there that most Members arrange their pairs and say their 'good-byes' on their way to cars, trains and taxis, leaving the Palace half an hour before the policemen, on their nightly ritual, strolling through the now near-deserted corridors shouting 'Who goes home?'

We slipped away from the others to find a small interview room below the Chamber—it was stuffy with the stale air of a day's meetings.

'I realise this is a difficult matter,' I said. 'I am about to be charged for fraud on what, at best, is no more than a fragile technical case. If this happens I shall be ruined—even if I am acquitted.'

Elwyn knew of my work for Bangladesh, and respected it. He listened with amazement as I unfolded the story of the repercussions of the *Sunday Times* article. I left with him a copy of the full brief, which I had previously sent to the Director of Public Prosecutions; he promised to read it overnight and discuss the case with me again the next day. At last, I thought, someone is prepared to look at the whole issue and not merely take a view on the minutiae of evidence completely out of context. I was not asking Elwyn to intervene with the DPP or any other law enforcement body: I simply wanted him, from his vast experience and as a friend, to advise me what a man in my unnerving predicament could possibly do.

On the next day I met him again, but my hopes were dashed. 'It's a very sad business,' he said, 'but there is nothing I can advise you to do. The due process of law must take its course.'

I was shaken. I was a mesmerised rabbit, waiting for its neck to be broken. 'The due process of law must take its course': the words rang out like a bell tolling for calamity. 'The due process of law must take its course.' For whom the bell tolls; it tolls for thee. 'The due process of law must take its course' piercing like an ugly lance into the depths of my being. And what is this 'due process' which is worshipped as a rite and intoned like a litany? It is an action, initiated by an ordinary human being within an institution which, however renowned, is proud and makes errors; then referred to a possibly overworked lawyer on the staff of the DPP, trying to make decisions on possibly inadequate files stuffed with material, according to law which even lawyers in their less pompous moments will admit is complex, confusing, esoteric, sometimes archaic and often quite unrelated to the moral and ethical needs of the situation.

One evening with my wife I attended a film showing at the Royal Geographical Society near the Albert Hall, at the invitation of a close friend, Aubrey Buxton, the Chairman of Anglia Television, who had produced the programme. It was a film about the Danakil, the remote tribe in northern Ethiopia, and it brought out vividly their resilience against the adversity of the harsh environment of the horn of Africa. It gave me some respite from my own environment. But mine was not a problem of dealing with the physical elements; it was a psychological enigma. The pressure of what I felt was unjust persecution was warping my mind and was making me incapable of normal rational relationships. I could now understand the degree of torture suffered by political prisoners in Nazi Germany or Stalin's Russia who were subjected to psychological bombardment; my suffering was not nearly so intense but I could feel it had the same paralysing quality of terror as that experienced by those hapless victims.

The film was followed by a reception in the Society's rooms, adorned with the maps and souvenirs of expeditions in past decades to the corners of the globe. Prince Philip was there, as charming and witty as ever. So were Lord Shackleton, the Antarctic explorer who became leader of the Lords and a friend in Government despite occasional clashes, and Rear Admiral Gordon Lennox, the Sergeant at Arms of the House of Commons. He is a most interesting man with many wise comments which must explode within him as he sits, struck dumb by office, in his Chair listening to the inane speeches of some Members.

Also at the party was Peter Walker, the Secretary of State for Trade and Industry. We both had to hurry back to the Commons for a Division at 10 o'clock, and, by chance, just before the hour I found myself running up the steps towards St Stephens Hall with Peter Walker by my side. 'Did you know,' I said, 'that I am about to be charged with fraud on investigations started by your Department?'

'That can't be true,' he said. 'I haven't heard anything about it, and I should be told if any MP is involved, let alone an ex-Minister.'

Along the corridor from the Central Lobby we walked towards the Lobbies where our paths would have to part on Party political lines. 'I promise you,' he said, 'I will look into this first thing tomorrow morning.' True to his word he did so, and I talked to his private secretary, a civil servant who had worked for me previously. 'The Minister is very concerned,' he said. 'No information on your case has ever reached this office and the Minister is going to find out why. There has been a breach of regulations. It should never have left our Department to go to the DPP without the Minister knowing.'

I could see that Peter Walker was in a cleft stick. If he intervened at this stage it could be condemned as political interference, but on the other hand few people would believe he had not known about the whole business from the beginning, and some might suspect a sinister politically inspired case, which it certainly was not.

During the next few days I saw Walker several times in the corridors at Westminster. He was always most sympathetic and understanding. He was, unlike so many other politicians, who are watchers from the sidelines, a do-er; as a do-er he knew the headaches of business and its pitfalls in a way the academics, the lawyers, the dons and the other fully professional and anaesthetised politicos can never do. 'It is a stupid case,' he said, 'and should never have been started.'

It became clear that junior officers in his Department had passed the papers to the DPP after the Newman report had recommended no action. Those nameless civil servants were 'keeping their noses clean' in the typical English way, passing the file and the buck to someone else so that they could never be accused of taking the wrong decision. When the DPP received the file he must have thought, 'My God, an ex-Minister, this must be a serious case for a Department of State to have felt compelled to send it to me.' He would, of course, have assumed that the Minister was fully informed. It was then that the doors of the arena were opened for the Fraud Squad of Scotland Yard.

Peter Walker said the best he could do was to make sure the file went immediately to the Attorney General, Sir Peter Rawlinson, for him to decide on whether to charge or not to charge. 'This is too important for the Director to make the decision,' he added.

I sent a copy of the full brief I had prepared for the DPP to the Attorney General. I received no acknowledgement. And again the fates were gathering: the Attorney, subject to all that groundswell of pressure, could hardly refuse the invitation to prosecute. It would need the courage of an exceptional man to turn back the tide.

As a last resort and in desperation, I turned to my other citizenship to aid me. This England, into which I was born and which had given its son a career and a chance to serve others, was turning against me; the lever was putting an intolerable, crucifying pressure on me: intolerable because it was unjust and crucifying because I was being sacrificed, not in the cause of justice, but in a collective homage by an inner circle to the rites of the 'due process of law' and by the English disease, of each individual in the process 'keeping his own nose clean', which had so deeply infected the body politic. And the lever turned on a tiny ball-bearing of an insignificant technical point.

I turned to Bangladesh, the new country which had adopted me as a citizen. I called Abdus Sultan, the High Commissioner, at his Putney residence, and he agreed to see me immediately. At the run-down former TOC H hostel in Notting Hill Gate which my wife and son, Mathew, had helped to furnish into a diplomatic headquarters years before, I told the High Commissioner about my plight and the danger the Bank faced if charges were laid. His reaction was immediate. 'I must ring the Foreign Office,' he said.

Within minutes he was through to the head of the Bangladesh desk and in my presence said, 'I know it is unusual for me to ring you direct, but this matter is urgent.' He said that he knew about some of the terrible troubles caused by political enemies of the Bangladesh regime, and expressed doubts about the veracity of the *Sunday Times* article. 'I saw the news-sheet,' he said, 'and it was issued only so the Bangalees could get full information about the Bank, but it has led to charges of fraud being considered against John Stonehouse. If that were done it would be most unjust and it would also harm relations between Britain and Bangladesh.' He rang off, turned to me and said, 'I wish I could do more, but I can't do more than that.'

Within days the 'case' was dropped. I felt a relief as though the beatings of months had suddenly stopped; but I was dazed and shocked by the psychological trauma of the terrifying experience. Perhaps I was saved by Bangladesh; my own England had seemed to want to destroy me.

After a week or so the telephone rang at the Dover Street offices. It was Detective Inspector Grant, smoothly confirming to me that it had been decided not to proceed in the matter.

12 *The threshold is shattered — breakdown*

BOLD ATTEMPTS WERE made to recover from the months of attrition. The Bank executives and staff who all knew about the Scotland Yard investigations were brave and discreet; they wanted to turn attention to the real job of building up the business. But, due to the wicked impression created by Grant's cross-examinations, the Bengalee community were unwilling to give support to the Bank which had been set up to meet their needs. Some English customers were obtained but, notwithstanding, we were not obtaining the volume of accounts we had been geared to service.

I found many other Bankers most helpful to us and, I was convinced that if we could survive the next few months and increase our paid-up Capital to £1 million, the Bank could get into the orbit of city acceptability. Edward du Cann, the MP for Taunton and Chairman of the 1922 Tory Backbenchers Committee, invited me to lunch with his Board at Keyser Ullman, the Merchant Bankers. They were impressed with the progress we had made in BBT, despite all the difficulties, and I found this encouraging. In Edward, I found a good friend. He is one of the most patient men in politics and has great reserves of ability which, for the sake of Britain should, sometime, be used in Government at the highest levels. He is also a man of compassion as I found during the Bangladesh campaign when he was one of the senior Tories to sign my Commons motions. I had found compassion and understanding in surprising places. Whereas some Labour Members doggedly refused to sign the Bangladesh motions, Conservative Members such as Sir Gerald Nabarro, whose death was a great loss, John Hunt and Hugh Fraser were enthusiastic. It was a revelation to me to discover how humane in their outlook Conservatives can be; many of them were more genuine than some of the Socialists who refused, in their ignorant way, on principle, to have anything to do with their opponents, mixing only with their own kind. But how can they understand Parliament when only Socialists they know?

I longed to get back, without any distractions into the political arena to work on trying to bridge gaps in Britain which were fast growing into yawning chasms. I resolved that when I had finally secured the Bank on firm foundations of success I would leave it to others, resign and return full-time to Parliament. My export business should also be able to stand on its own feet by that time.

But I underestimated the difficulties. Due to the strain he had borne during the Grant business, the General Manager of the Bank suffered two heart attacks and was away much of the time on sick leave. Early in 1974 he went into hospital and was on his back for three months. He had to resign. Meanwhile, his Deputy took over responsibilities temporarily, as I carefully sifted names for a successor as General Manager. It was a shock later to find that, although he had come with fine references from Lloyds Bank and the Bank of Cyprus, he was, in fact, an undischarged bankrupt. This situation of course worried me greatly as he was the one man left who had senior banking experience.

Problems also were building up in the secondary banking sector. London and County Securities, an old established Bank of which Jeremy Thorpe, the Liberal Leader, was a Director, went bankrupt and was followed by a whole succession of others. We just managed to get BBT's capital fully subscribed to £1 million before this debacle, but only after I had again thrown in every possible asset I had in my Companies and money borrowed elsewhere. The Bank set up a number of activities to try to make up for the lack of profitable business from customers but, due to the prevailing economic climate, they were failures.

We were getting deeper and deeper into the mire as we thrashed about trying to extricate ourselves. It was no consolation to learn that practically every other medium-sized or small Bank was experiencing similar problems, and even huge, solidly based institutions like the Crown Agents were losing millions of pounds.

I decided in my own mind on a strategy. The Bangladesh connection would be reduced and the main Company renamed London Capital Group so it could appeal to a wider public for business. The British Bangladesh Trust would be retained as a specialised subsidiary and new Directors would be recruited. Both Sir Charles Forte, the head of Trust Houses Forte hotel group, and James Charlton, the former Secretary of the British Aircraft Corporation joined the Board. They would eventually be great assets but I could not put all the burdens on them at once.

I still found that as no one else was available to take the strain, most of the burden for keeping the organisation intact rested on me.

John McGrath, who was one of the best Accountants in Britain, had been originally appointed a half-time Executive Director of the Bank, but shortly after our incorporation he suffered a severe heart attack and was in and out of hospitals for over a year. He could not help as his health was then too bad for me to ask him to take on any real responsibility. K. B. Ahmed, the other founder Director, had his own very complex financial problems which created embarrassments for the Bank and, eventually with sadness, I had to ask him to resign.

Some of the staff were excellent—Philip Bingham, the Bank's Secretary, for instance—but they could not take personal responsibility in the way I was forced to. My own Secretary, Sheila Buckley, who had worked for me on political as well as commercial tasks for six years, was a tower of strength dealing adroitly with the multitude of problems which blew up each day. She was an excellent sieve for the numerous demands made on me; the continual wear and tear on her must have been very great during this period. No one could have wished for a more loyal and painstaking assistant, and without her steadfast help I would have found those months completely unbearable.

As the weeks and months of 1974 wore on the burdens became heavier; I was being squeezed into a corner from which there was no escape. Together with the worries brought on by the Bank's incredible problems I had the suspicion that my senior colleagues in the House of Commons no longer respected me. Was this because the rumours had been spread that I had been the subject of fraud investigations by Scotland Yard, or because there had been tittle-tattle about my alleged spying for Czechoslovakia, or for some other reason? I shall never know; but I was wounded by it.

There was, however, another issue which obviously had also affected me deeply. In 1968, when I became Postmaster General, I enquired about the PMG's responsibility for supervising the bugging of telephones. I was told by Bill Ryland, the then Director of Telecommunications who later became Chairman of the Post Office, that no PMG had ever been given the names of persons being bugged. The order always came from the Home Secretary directly to him and was handled by a secret department.

What I do know now, on irrefutable testimony, is that from 1968 onwards, to the present time, my private telephones were continuously bugged by the special official agency established in Holborn for such surveillance. When I was Postmaster General, and later as Minister of Posts and Telecommunications, some of my senior staff must have known that their own head of Department was being watched. It was ironic that, on the recommendation of Bill Ryland, I put up the name of the Post Office man responsible for bugging for an honour in the Queen's Birthday List. Ryland knew I was being bugged and so did the man, who must have laughed all the way to Buckingham Palace.

The bugging went on after the change of Government in 1970 and, probably, several of my ex-Ministerial colleagues knew of it. No wonder I suffered from the atmosphere of suspicion. I seem to remember Harold Wilson, as Prime Minister, giving an assurance that no telephones of MPs were subject to official bugging. I, like others, accepted the assurance, but at that time his own Minister for the Post Office was, in fact, being bugged; this makes one wonder how many other telephones of Ministers, ex-Ministers or MPs are so important that similarly it has to be announced, wrongly, that they are not bugged when, in fact, they are. For defence and security reasons to lie about such matters is acceptable, but the lie is a cancer which spreads. Like the official lie denying an impending devaluation it leads to other lies, sending ripples of deceit through Society.

Now I look back, it is clear that my breakdown was contributed to by all these factors which had steadily affected my unconscious being. The miasma of suspicion was suffocating; no one in authority ever talked frankly to me to help to dispel it, and I could not grasp it myself because I had been guilty of no transgression.

I was also dismayed by the cant and hypocrisy and humbug in English Society and politics, and I became increasingly disgusted by my own part in the charade.

Half way through 1974 I found the only escape possible for me. I took on another personality in addition to my own. It was a relief which, strangely, helped me better to cope with the increasing problems of the original man. I found a renewed strength and threw more energy into trying to make the Bank a success. I also made bigger efforts to raise substantial business for the export companies. I went to Cyprus and North Yemen, Cairo and Beirut, Zurich and Brussels, New York and Los Angeles in search of business, and paid out more monies for agents commissions and retainers in the hope of securing some worthwhile contracts. One such contract alone could net my companies upwards of £500,000 in profits and that could help provide the sorely needed liquidity for the Bank to ensure, in turn, its survival. There was much at stake; I was coerced into even more feverish activity by the daily demands of other Banks for repayments of loans, overdue, and by the threats of business contacts who were themselves in great trouble. Some of them resorted to blackmail saying that, if I did not fulfil their demands for money or promissory notes, they would ruin my political career. One said firmly 'You know about Jeffrey Archer' (a Tory MP who had just been forced to resign through bankruptcy) 'We shall do the same to you if you do not agree to our demands.'

Another contact had been a friend at one time, but such is the pressure of business, it breaks friendships like dry twigs trampled underfoot. He also threatened me if I did not agree to buy the shares in the Bank which he could no longer afford to carry.

Life was becoming intolerable. I was a burden to my family, my friends, my colleagues and to myself. The effort to succeed in Banking, although I had sought no personal reward from it, had been thwarted by the succession of events started by the *Sunday Times* article. There was an inevitability about it which I had sensed at the time and expressed forcibly to the Editor, Harold Evans. Because of my public position I had created extra difficulties such as being subject to blackmail which other businessmen would laugh at. I was vulnerable and exposed and an ever-increasing liability to all around me. The strain became worse every day; I was distraught with worry and subject to frequent spasms of melancholia. I made every possible effort to break out of this condition realising, in my rational moments, that a solution must be available somewhere. But I was in a maze, as confusing as Hampton Court's; I rushed hither and thither always meeting an obstruction which kept me locked in the prison of my own unfathomable dilemmas. The sky was there and I could hear voices on the other side of the hedges; there must be a way out. Knowing this I made a superhuman effort to keep the original man exactly in the image as he was known. I went about my business, apparently rationally and sensibly; I went to Parliament and played my part there, so no one would notice my strain; I went to my constituency and performed the role expected of me; I even fought a General Election campaign without any one realising the turmoil within my psyche; I had to retain my normal shell so when I had cast out the contradictions, which had dragged me down, I could return to it and no one would be any the wiser.

The contortion of maintaining this pretence produced even more tension and I could not bring myself to release it by confiding to anyone about my psychosis. To a greater or less extent all people in public life maintain a public image, which is a distortion of the true man, because the public demands its leaders to be near-paragons. If the truth had been generally known about Napoleon, Theodore Roosevelt, Asquith, Lloyd-George or Nixon, who would have trusted them or followed them for more than a week. My pretence, however, was different in its character. For a long time I had been conscious of the philosophy of deceit and aware of its widespread application by politicians and others, and I found it repugnant. But now, because of my efforts to maintain the option of returning to normality, I was deceiving myself as well as others.

In ancient times men with problems made sacrifices to propitiate the Gods and the modern penance is a hangover from that. I reached the point of desperation when I was prepared to make any personal sacrifice, to pay any penance, so I could disperse the pressures on me. And I was prepared to be a lightning conductor to take away those pressures from others.

My health deteriorated. I could not sleep deeply, and when I awoke I was often swamped in perspiration. I developed a phobia about people and had to strain every nerve to maintain normal conversations; I had a phobia about telephones and could hardly bring myself to answer them; I had a phobia about newspapers and reporters, especially after a horrible and unfair attack which appeared in the satirical magazine *Private Eye*. All the time I disguised my phobias and I did not rant and rave, at least not openly.

Although I did not fully recognise it at the time, I was operating on three levels. One, the imaged man: cool, calm and apparently in command of all his senses carrying on the life normally expected of him. Two, the original man, who carried all the heavy layers of the imaged man as a burden and despised this role, suffering deep torment as the desperation of his position became more evident. Three, the Phoenix man: a make-believe person who was uncluttered with problems and tensions and, through natural relaxation, gave comfort to the other two. The first two men had to die for the strain of living for them was too great. I wanted them to want to die. I wanted them to die. I wanted to die. There was no other way.

13 *The politician's swan-song*

WHEN I WENT to the House of Commons that day, I did not know that it might be the last time I would speak in the Chamber. When Members are ending their careers they usually have some warning—such as an approaching General Election or the possibility of elevation to Another Place—but my category of retiring MP was probably unique. An inexorable process was under way towards the psychiatric suicide of the Right Honourable Member for Walsall North and the full emergence of another, less burdened, man in his place. For five months the parallel personality had been developing and gaining in strength day by day. But, ironically, the phoenix man also gave strength to the original man whose bodily shell he also occupied. On that dull Monday morning of 4 November 1974, the Rt Hon. Member went to Westminster confident; and he was consciously unaware that the approaching tragedy was so near. The new man within him provided the prop which a mentor or a Father Confessor might provide—someone outside himself who is always available as an ally or friend whatever the circumstances and wherever the situation.

Over the past few months I had been thinking more deeply about the political state of Britain and more sensitively about the condition of British Society. I felt possessed of an objectivity which had eluded me in the seventeen years since I had arrived in Parliament after the by-election in Wednesbury in 1957. What I saw and felt increasingly alarmed me and, most seriously, what we were doing in Parliament was, at best, irrelevant and, at worst, extremely damaging to Britain and her standing in the world. Parliament had become a raucous rabble concerned only to shout the ephemeral slogans of the day. The few intelligent leaders cynically pandered to the appetites of their supporters so they could ride along on their unthinking support. Principle, except on rare and isolated occasions, was thrown out of the window. What leaders wanted was power; their political aims as politicians were subverted to this end, rather than power being seen as the means to achieve those aims. Power and office became the cruel masters of men as ends in themselves.

On Monday mornings the corridors at Westminster are quieter than on other week days. The Northern and Scottish Members have not yet arrived off their trains or planes, and the Standing Committees usually do not meet until Tuesday morning. Members drift into the building after lunch — a handful to join the Speaker at Prayers at 2.30 pm and a few more to sit in at Question Time which follows. But the numbers attending the daily (except Friday) cross-examination of Ministers belies the impression given of Question Time being the outstanding Parliamentary Institution. Except for the Prime Minister's Questions at 3.15 pm on Tuesdays and Thursdays, the attendance only occasionally exceeds a minority of the Members. So on that Monday morning I had few colleagues around to distract me from my thoughts about my coming speech that afternoon. I had written to the Speaker to indicate my wish to speak and I knew the Speaker's Secretary would put my name on the long list which the Speaker kept on his lap during the big debates. As a Privy Councillor, the Speaker would give me some priority over other Members and I was almost certain of being called — unlike earlier back bench years when I would sit all day in frustration on the green benches. The debate was on the Queen's Speech — the Statement prepared by the Government on its general programme and read by the Queen at each opening of a new Session of her Parliament.

We had just been through the Second General Election in eight months and the result had been almost as indecisive as the earlier one. The Labour Party emerged with a majority over all others of only three. The significance of the election was the continued erosion of support for the two main parties and the increased votes for the splinter parties—particularly the Scottish Nationalists who made phenomenal advances and narrowly missed dislodging Labour from the few critical seats it needed for the overall majority. Notwithstanding the narrow victory, Labour was determined to carry through a programme of socialist legislation that had been inadequately thought out. The 1964–1970 Labour Governments had been conspicuous failures in the fields of National planning, but this did not deter Labour leaders from further adventures in state manipulation. In this they acted like alcoholics who had felt the effects of earlier drinking, but were not to be deterred by that experience, as the intoxication was already in their blood. Most leaders were not doctrinaire socialists but they were anxious—at all costs—to placate the vociferous Left-wing members of the Tribune Group and the Left-wing Trade Union leaders who had become the most powerful non-Parliamentary force in British Society. A lot of this Left-wing influence was indistinguishable from Communism and, indeed, some of the people concerned were Communists in all but name. Hugh Gaitskell, when he was Leader of the Labour Party, had drawn vigorous attention to the dangers of this trojan horse within the Party, but few had heeded his words, and the strain of his campaign had hastened his death. I had myself campaigned against the Communists within the Co-operative Movement and I knew from bitter personal experience how vicious they can be in the pursuit of their ends. Unlike most pragmatic social democrats they know what they want to achieve, and everything must be subordinated to that end. The religious intensity with which they pursue their objectives is, of course, their greatest strength, as is the discipline they can exercise over their supporters. So, the Party within the Party became the power house and the engine room, propelling the Movement further in the direction of Statism.

I had these heretical thoughts in my mind as I approached the subject of the debate, and I felt for the first time in my Parliamentary career that the truth was breaking through the veil of deceit which I had, in common with so many other Members, drawn over the problems of our time.

I went to my tiny room on the third floor in the new block above the Members Tea Room. It was like a cell with no window on the outside world, and the walls were so thin that every conversation held in adjoining rooms could be overheard clearly. The next room was occupied by a former Tory Minister of Health, and all his dictation to his Secretary could be taken down as clearly in my room as in his. However, on this quiet Monday I was not disturbed too greatly and made a few notes for my speech. As I wrote, the feeling of liberation came over me. It seemed that at last I could begin to express some true feelings on the floor of the House. I was sick to death with the way most Labour Members were afraid to say what they really thought about the Trade Unions because they feared the repercussions from the militant members of their constituency party organisation. I recalled with a shudder of disgust that Dick Taverne, the talented Member for Lincoln, had been forced out of his seat by such militants. It seemed to me that the State socialists in the Party were illogical. The Trades Unions were to be left out of the State structure. All other elements of the economic society were to be subject to State direction and control, but the key element of wages policy was to be left to voluntary agreement within a so-called social contract. It was rather similar to the feudal barons leaving the Church and the Monasteries out of their control because the Church was too powerful to be curbed and the priests had too strong a hold over their following.

In truth, State planning is impossible without co-ordination of wages, and a jungle of wage negotiations only gives preference to the strong groups of workers, while the weak go to the wall. This illogicality was born not from intellectual confusion but from fear. I decided on that Monday morning that in my speech I would try to speak out against this cancerous influence within the Labour Party which was sapping its moral strength. My own strength came not just from the Rt Hon. Member for Walsall North but from another man within me who was desperate to get out. He was saying imperatively, 'Give up this sham; escape these bonds of hypocrisy.' Feeling he was there gave me the courage to make my speech the most outspoken of my career.

I went down to the Tea Room to get a snack before the House started the afternoon proceedings. There were few Members around. The Labour regulars were sitting in the leather armchairs holding the usual desultory conversations over coffee; others were sitting at tables eating cheese salads or such simple dishes. There was nothing extravagant about the Members' Tea Room—the food was as ordinary as a

British railway station buffet and not so varied. At the far end of the second long room were a couple of Tory members talking together. Except on crowded days only one or two Conservatives stayed in the first room: that seemed always to be regarded as a Labour preserve. Tories hardly ever sit at the same table as Labour men. I always felt this convention of separation childish and unnecessary for ostensibly intelligent men. Most of my own colleagues regarded any social contact with Tory members as corrupting and frowned on anyone who engaged in it. Just after 2.30 pm prayers were over and Question Time was on. I finished my snack and strolled down the corridor linking the Tea Room with the Members' Lobby. I was walking down a corridor I had walked thousands of times before over the seventeen years of my membership of the Commons. This was the main thoroughfare and along this way lurked the Lobby correspondents of the accredited London newspapers who were allowed to approach Members either here or in the Members' Lobby widening out at the end beyond the swing doors. I nodded to fellow MPs as I passed them, occasionally saying, 'Hello George or Jim. How are you?' which is the standard House of Commons greeting, but to which no reply is expected. Members, by the way, will never shake hands with colleagues. On foreign trips I have seen Members quite embarrassed when expected to shake hands with another Member. Conventions die hard. Entry to the Common Market and MPs attendance at the European Parliament has, however, lead to a lot of handshaking, and some Members who spend part of their time on the Continent are becoming continental in their mannerisms. I passed through the swing doors into the Lobby and turned right to collect the Order Paper at the tiny office where a clerk stands all day dispensing Parliamentary Papers to MPs. The Order Paper shows the Questions put down for the day and the business, but a Member has to have a trained eye to unravel its complexities. I walked past the giant statue of Winston Churchill on the left and the diminutive statue of David Lloyd-George on the right, and past the eagle look of the attendant sitting at the entrance to the Commons. His job is to ensure that no 'stranger' enters the Chamber—a very difficult job just after a General Election when there might be up to 200 new MPs. I went through the swing doors to the Chamber itself—prosaic and practical compared to the ornate trappings of the House of Lords at the other end of the Palace of Westminster.

A Minister was at the dispatch box on the front bench to my left so I was able to advance towards the table on which the Mace stood resplendent and took the two steps to the third bench where I usually sat as a back bencher. I had not reserved a seat—under the rules of the House, Members can do so for Prayers by putting a card in the slot behind the place they want. Labour Members, however, are violently hostile to this rule and will not allow their colleagues to use it. On the 1969 Budget Day when we were in Opposition, I put a card in the place I had occupied for the eight years from 1957 to 1964, when I shared it with Manny Shinwell. I always gave way to him when he entered the Chamber as a courtesy to a Privy Councillor. But Eric Heffer, the violent Left-wing Member for Liverpool, wanted the seat and persuaded other Members to remove the card. The Sergeant-at-Arms was most upset by this breach of the House rules and so was the Speaker, but for the sake of peace I made no fuss about it. But it did illustrate to me how petty and narrow Labour Members can be. Question Time took its normal course. The Member calling out the number of his Question, the Minister reading his prepared reply (usually written by civil servants), and the Member asking a supplementary question (on which sometimes he had laboured long). Most Questions are put down so the Member can get a little mention in the newspapers back home in the constituency. As I sat and followed the proceedings I felt a foreboding. Would the man within me succeed in dragging the Member away from this place he had loved and where he had campaigned for so many causes. And yet, sometimes when I reflected on the inanity and dishonesty of the place, I wanted that release. I felt the ties of seventeen years holding me to those green benches, but the miasma which now pervaded it was almost suffocating me.

I remembered when the IRA supporter had thrown a canister of CS Gas into the Chamber and how Members staggered out choking with the noxious fumes in their mouths and nostrils. The noxious political fumes were affecting me in the same way. I had to get out somehow. If only politicians could say in Parliament what they really thought and felt, then the fumes of deceit would be cleaned out just as the CS Gas had been. But Members, particularly Ministers, were engaged so much in the game of posturing that it had become their real nature—the original men were suppressed. They were rather like character actors who were so typed that no producer could cast them in another role, and the poor creatures could never show themselves as they really are. In Parliament, however, we were locked in a game of pretence which had become so much a way of life that few could see it as it was— false and falsifying. At least the old actors, or most of them, would know themselves under all the years of grease paint. There was a Private Notice Question by Peter Walker, the Shadow Defence Spokesman, to Jim Callaghan, the Foreign Secretary, about defence arrangements with South Africa. I liked Peter Walker—a man of energy and enthusiasm, too much enthusiasm for many Tories who resented his pushing ability. But Peter was a man of integrity and human understanding. I had tested him when he was Secretary of Trade and Industry, and his sympathy to me was warm and genuine. Jim Callaghan is also a sympathetic man and one of the best Foreign Secretaries since the war, although disastrous, at some stages, as Chancellor.

I remembered when Barbara Castle was trying to get my scalp in the Cabinet Room over a Post Office strike and trying to make me, as the Minister responsible for the Department, take the responsibility for her own Department's mistakes, how Jim was the first voice in the Cabinet to be raised in my defence. Harold Wilson was upset that his favourite woman Minister was shown up in her petulant plan. But Tony Greenwood and even George Thomas, who was lovable as Secretary of State for Wales and was never outspoken against Harold, followed Jim and supported me. I was saved from Barbara's machinations and Harold never forgave me. Jim Callaghan is a skilful politico, always with his eye on the main chance; a man without the impediment of strong convictions, so he is able to kick the ball in the prevailing political direction at any time. One phrase he used in his final answer in the House that afternoon was to have greater significance to me than I ever realised then—'I do not always believe everything that I see in the newspapers.'

The debate was opened by Michael Heseltine, the Tory Spokesman on Industry, who is known as 'Goldilocks' because of his flowing blond hair. Bland, impeccable, capable, he is the prototype modern Tory, but lacking the depth of the older

more traditional Tories like Alec Douglas-Home. He launched
into the expected attack on nationalisation. Tony Benn, the
Secretary of State for Industry, replied. The man who
renounced the Lord Stansgate title to remain a commoner is
the most agile political performer in modern times. His flights
of fancy are, in my view, breathtaking. I had suffered from
them. As Postmaster General—his first Ministerial job—Tony
was determined to make his mark. No matter what the idea,
there had to be activity, hectic activity, with the result that the
Press always had plenty to report and the PMG appeared on
television frequently.

The staid officials of the Post Office used to the quiet waters
of a Reginald Bevins or even Ernest Marples or Charles Hill,
were thrown off balance by the onslaught from the pipe-smok-
ing and tea-drinking Tony. All the plans in the pigeon-holes
were taken down and dusted off as fodder for the Minister.
And he absorbed them like a hungry cat takes to milk. So a
succession of 'reforms' was launched—the setting-up of the
Post Office Corporation, the two-tier postal service and a Giro
banking system, among others. Giro, was well known on the
Continent as an effective money-transfer service, and where
joint-stock banking was not well developed, it had prospered.
Tony saw it as a possible jewel in his crown if he could introduce it in Britain. I believe it to have been one of the most
expensive single blunders of Government in postwar years
which will go on to rival the groundnuts scheme for its pro-
fligacy.

When I became Postmaster General in 1968, I was horrified
to find the Giro plans so well advanced. I had been pushed
on to an escalator which was already moving at a breakneck
speed. I tried to stop the purchase of expensive American
equipment, which would be a burden on our fragile balance
of payments, but the senior officials argued repeatedly that the
consumer poll showed that there would be a million customers
within a year or so. I didn't believe the results of that Market
survey, knowing, from my own experience as an interviewer
for a Gallup Poll organisation, that people's replies never cor-
respond with what they actually do—particularly in business
matters. Of course, if you stop someone and ask 'If a free banking service is set up to do so and so, will you use it?' the answer
is bound to be 'Yes'. But that is a long way from actually
filling up complicated forms and mastering the complexities

of a Giro system when a corner bank is so conveniently available.

I could not withstand the combined pressure of the officials and the momentum, and had to allow Giro to go ahead, as planned, soon after my appointment. I was left therefore, to 'carry the can' for Tony. It left a bitter taste in my mouth. And so did the fact that I became the scapegoat for what I believed were his errors in pushing for the Two-Tier postal system and the nonsense of Postcodes—a nonsense because the codes are useless until ALF sorting equipment is installed, and it was only available for several years in a very limited number of towns. The Postcode system, as initiated by Tony, is an example of the domination of technological thinking at the expense of everyday commonsense. The decision-makers become awe-inspired by the capacity of the machine and allow its needs to determine policy. In the case of Postcodes, by the time sufficient ALF equipment can be provided to justify the complications of a system which provides automatic sorting right down to the postman's walk, there are unlikely to be any postmen left to deliver the mail. When I was Postmaster General, I despaired that such schemes had been started on the basis of what seemed to me inadequate research. The 'Think-Tank' concept introduced later by the Prime Minister to evaluate major projects for the Cabinet was long overdue, not only for No. 10, but also for the departments like the Post Office. I was appalled by the lack of expertise in my department. There was no fully qualified accountant and the accounts were in a mess. The losses on the postal side—senior officials admitted—could never be properly assessed. There was never a cost-benefit analysis for new investments such as the Postal Headquarters in Birmingham, which could never pay its way by any stretch of the imagination. I felt increasingly that I was a fall-guy, a scapegoat in the Post Office taking over the schemes of Anthony Wedgwood Benn, which of course received Cabinet approval.

And so it was inevitable that on that Monday afternoon I listened very critically to what he had to say. I knew from bitter experience what he had done to one department by the pursuit of technological and philosophical perfection to the detriment of the good. I knew how, after all his grandiose 'restructuring', the ordinary men had to follow in the shambles of his wake to save what they could. What I heard in that speech confirmed my worst fears, that his thinking was now to be imposed not just on one Department or on one industry, but on the whole of British Industry.

By the time the Speaker called my name I felt compelled to expose the shibboleths of Bennery. 'We have had a failure by the Secretary of State for Industry,' I said, 'to analyse and explain some of the ideas which he has been ventilating in the past months. It is not sufficient on this important occasion to repeat in the House things we have heard many times before. We need detailed explanations from the Government as to how these great and imaginative ideas of social engineering are to be put into effect. We have not had them so far today.' I went on to point out that the opportunity for participation (which Benn had preached as the solution to all problems), had always been open through the Co-operative Movement, but there it had failed. In some big Co-operative Societies the democratic element has decayed so much that only one per cent of the members vote. I went on. 'We have had the mechanism for participation for 100 years but it does not work. The thinkers in the Labour Party who have now embraced the idea of participatory democracy must start to analyse the reason why it does not work in the Socialist area where it has already been available. We are in the throes of getting new systems of participation which may completely fail because in ten or fifteen years' time we may discover that the workers we are pushing into this participation in democracy do not want to participate. We have to apply ourselves to motivation as well as to creating new constitutions.'

As I warmed to my speech, strengthened by the ordinary man within me who could see through humbug, I felt the need to be frank. There was a quickening of interest in my speech. Both Front Benches were paying close attention. Tony Benn had left the Chamber—but Gregor Mackenzie his Assistant Minister was looking apprehensive. The Tories were rapt with attention partly because they approved, partly because they appreciated it was an honest speech and partly because it was bound to embarrass the Government and Benn in particular. The Left-wingers sitting near me were livid and I could sense their hostility. The trouble with such emotional people is that the holy writ of socialism—whatever it may be construed to be at any one time—can never be questioned. Objective thinking is anathema and thinking, such as it is, must be limited by the subjective confines of dogma and doctrine.

I went on. 'The period of this Parliament will be crucial to the future of the country. This is the time when the kidding has to stop. For too long we have fooled ourselves and have tried to fool others that Britain would somehow muddle through. For too long Britain has allowed itself indulgences which a successful and expanding country would hesitate to allow itself. Our problem is deep-seated, and can be best summed-up as "the end of Empire syndrome". It is a failure to adjust to our new situation in the world, which does not owe us a living and is making it extremely difficult for us to earn one.'

It had seemed to me that the constant electioneering in which political leaders had engaged for decades since the war had sapped them of the will to speak honestly about our problem, so I continued. 'The country demands honesty. It is not true that most other countries are more or less in the same state as we are and that we are all suffering from a worldwide disease. The truth about the state of our society is that in 1973 and 1974 political violence in this country has been worse than in any other country in Europe—including Greece and Portugal, which have both gone through some terribly traumatic changes in these years.'

Yes, I felt as I looked around the Chamber, the British problem is our innate sense of superiority. No matter how bad things are, we are better than anyone else. This attitude which had been our strength in the past was now the weakness preventing the truth from being understood. And, meanwhile, the country slid into economic decay as people followed the politicians' example of engaging in double-thinking and living in a multitude of fool's paradises. The truth had to come out. 'Our economic performance in the last ten years has been the second worst in Europe. A comparison with West Germany, a country of the same sort of population and resources as ourselves, shows the contrast. The West Germans have no balance of payments problem, even with the high oil prices. Their industry has high investment and there is a growth of productivity per man, year by year. Indeed, their productivity per man is, overall, twice and sometimes three times what we achieve. Factories in my constituency are still using machinery reparated from Germany at the end of the last war, but German factories today have the most modern machinery.

'According to some figures that I obtained from the Library, during the last ten years sterling has devalued against the German mark by forty-five per cent. The pound has not lost value simply because of the effect of worldwide inflation; it has almost halved in value against the German mark today in real terms. The pound would buy eleven deutschemarks in 1964. Today it will buy only six.'

As I said that, I felt a deep foreboding about Britain—we were declining at an ever accelerating rate. 'The implications of this trend are truly frightening. We emerged from the last war with our economy intact. Germany was devastated but it has won the peace which we are losing.'

I looked across the Chamber to Jo Grimond, the distinguished former leader of the Liberal Party and a man of exceptional integrity who would have made an excellent Prime Minister if only our Party system allowed the middle ground of politics to prosper. He had made a characteristically able speech before mine and I had to agree with him that North Sea oil would not be the solution to the country's economic problems. The price of oil could drop and the cost of extracting a barrel of oil from the North Sea is the highest in the world. It is fascinating to note, as I write only a few months after that speech, how the situation concerning oil has changed. The shortage has become a surplus and the North Sea could be a millstone, not a bonanza, for Britain.

My passion for frankness during that speech became stronger. My notes became only a guide to subjects, not the basis for content. This, I felt, was my opportunity to speak out. Tomorrow might be too late. I could feel the John Stonehouse succumbing to the increasing influence of the man within, and yet, at the same time, that inner man was liberating John Stonehouse from the inhibitions of a lifetime of politics. After Northern Ireland I turned to industrial relations, a subject plagued by as much emotionalism as the former. I remembered the meeting I had attended with Michael Foot, the orator who was now brought face to face, day by day, with the realities of human relations in industry. The myth of the noble worker dies hard in the breasts of saintly people like Michael Foot, but die it must as workers use every weapon in their struggle for a bigger advance in wages than another group had achieved. The appetites of the jungle do not mix with the sane tranquillity of socialism. Trade Unions pay lip service to socialism while destroying the concepts on which it could be based. It is a modern problem but it illustrates the dilemma of human history. How greed and power corrupts the soul of both the individual and the group as they search for the noble ideals of human relationships. I attacked the TUC weakness in failing to deliver their side of the social contract and said: 'The increases demanded by large sections of the population today cannot be afforded, and the Government must tell them so in forthright terms.'

'The nub of the problem is that the Government have failed to show how we should evaluate the various claims made on our economy. If the various sections of the community who are represented by trade unions do not behave in a responsible fashion the Government will have to step in. If the TUC and the trade union movement generally cannot keep their side of the bargain of the social contract, we shall undoubtedly have to have a wages freeze in 1975.'

As I spoke I could feel the hostility from some on my side of the House growing in intensity. It rose like a cloud of evil from the benches. But on the Opposition side there was obvious approval. The liberated politician, freed of the shackles, went on: 'I hope that we can break away from the depressing cycle of stoppages and strikes which handicap industry and sap the country's morale. I regard a strike as the last refuge of a bankrupt negotiator facing an inept employer, both operating within a flimsy structure which provides no real rules of conduct. The TUC and the Secretary of State for Employment must aim for the abolition of all strikes, unofficial and official. We should apply a little civilisation to this area of our affairs and stop inflicting terrible wounds on ourselves to prove our manliness.'

Now I was really into my subject. I was attacking the sacred cows of the Labour Movement of which 'the right to strike' is the fattest, but something more had to be said. The idea that groups of workers—because they were workers—had the moral right to do anything provided they came to their decision by a democratic process, had to be deflated. This, after all, was the central philosophy of the current Benn, and it was, in fact, anarchy not socialism, that it would serve.

'There are many misconceptions about democracy. I believe

that a democratic decision is valid for the community as a whole and is binding on the community as a whole, but that does not mean that democratic decisions taken by minority groups are thereby sanctified. Many minority groups make decisions to act against the community and representatives of those groups appear on television and say that it was a democratic decision, on the assumption that it will thereby be sanctified and everyone will accept it. I have never heard anything so ridiculous as the suggestion that if a group of people makes a decision in their own selfish interests which will hold the rest of the community to ransom it will be accepted because it is a decision democratically arrived at.'

The example which would prove this came to mind. And the place was Clydeside where, in the ship building yards faced with closure, Tony Benn had encouraged the workers into false hopes about their capacity to run their own industry. But the case I quoted was more graphic—the pollution of Britain by the antics of so-called Democrats.

'The decision taken by the men of Clydeside to pour hundreds of millions of gallons of sewage into the Clyde and pollute the river beyond recovery for two years I do not regard as a moral decision, although it was a democratic one. I think that the decision was wrong, and should be condemned. I hope that the Government, with four or five years in power, will be able to find an answer to the problem of creating a mechanism to prevent damaging strikes of that character, which destroy the environment and sap the country's morale.'

I finished my speech and sat down relieved to have, at last, got a lot off my chest. John Stonehouse was grateful to Joe Markham, the Phoenix/man, for giving him the strength to do it.

The reaction of the House to my speech was predictable, I suppose. The Labour speakers contrived to ignore it. They found it as embarrassing as the crowd did on being told by the small boy that the Emperor who was wearing the finest clothes in the land was, in fact, naked. The Tories were fulsome in their compliments: Sir John Eden said: 'I agree very much with the right Hon. Member for Walsall, North, to encourage a more constructive attitude on the part of unions and employees, especially towards schemes for improving productivity, whether of capital or of labour.'

And another relative of a former Tory Prime Minister

followed. Winston Churchill, who is a politician of tremendous latent ability and also an excellent writer, appears to prove the skip generation theory by taking after his namesake grandfather. During a thoughtful speech he said: 'Where is the social contract today in Scotland? There is paralysis over large sectors of Scottish industry. Where is it so far as it concerns the commuters who are seeking to get home tonight on Southern Region and up in Liverpool, and who face a total stoppage of all rail services?'

'I welcome the appeal by the right hon. Member for Walsall, North, to those people who take that action to think of the interests of the community as a whole.'

Julian Amery, the Tory ex-Minister, sent me a note of congratulations. Labour MPs were universally hostile except for Brian Walden who came up to me in the Division Lobby and said, 'I agreed with practically every word you said. It was a great speech.' He was the exception to prove the rule of Labour antagonism to frank speaking.

But my honesty had struck a cord in Tory hearts. Their front bench spokesman, Patrick Jenkin, called my speech 'robust', after pointing out that I had not received answers to my pointed questions. They did not know that the political opponent they praised was not the man who had sat on the benches for seventeen years, he was not the ex-Minister they remembered. The speech they had heard came more from the original man, who was unencumbered, than from a personality who was the product of years of political processing. The encumbered man, encrusted with the barnacles of all that time, was soon to sink, with the load of his accumulated burden, to the infinite depths of the seas of the Atlantic. But, perhaps, the death of the idealist had already happened.

14 *Miami—the final release*

WHEN I CAUGHT the National Airlines DC10 to Miami, I parked my Rover 3500 in the car park facing Number 3 terminal. There were just ten minutes to check-in time. There was no rush. Everything about the departure was normal. The friendly attendants accepted the ticket and checked in the baggage. One of them noticed me carrying John Le Carré's 'Tinker, Tailor, Soldier, Spy,' and said, 'He's not as good as Frederick Forsyth, is he?' I had to agree. Le Carré is obtuse. Forsyth is clear and yet dramatic; a brilliant writer with the tang of authenticity. I knew. His description in 'The Day of the Jackal' about obtaining a passport in the name of a dead man was true. I had done it myself. My second passport was safely in my briefcase.

That knowledge gave me a sense of elation. At last I had the prospect of finally escaping the terrible sham life of John Stonehouse and removing the awesome burdens of eighteen months, or was it eighteen years? The contradictions in the life of John Stonehouse had become intolerable and the relief of having Joseph Arthur Markham, the parallel personality, had become increasingly sweet. What a joy it had been for me to take up the simple tasks of Joe Markham. Organising the bank accounts, getting an accommodation address in London's St George's Drive, applying for visas and, above all, securing the migrant status for Australia.

Why Australia? It is a great country, created by migrants who—to a greater or less extent—had done exactly what I was

doing. They had escaped from the frightening conditions of
the old countries to be liberated in a continent where there
is enough room to move and where there is a genuineness in
human relations, born of a challenge in a new environment.
Furthermore, I would be 13,000 miles removed from the
hideous conditions of England; an England which I felt had
persecuted me; an England which was becoming twisted up
in the hypocrisies of its own decay, and where honesty and
frankness in business and politics had been suffocated by
layers of cant, deceit and humbug. To be Joe Markham, even
for a few snatched minutes between a business appointment
and Questions in the House of Commons, was a profound
relief from external tension and inner turmoil. To be Joe Markham for all day and every day and to destroy for ever the shell
of John Stonehouse would be a rebirth. For the first time in
two decades an uncluttered man could mix in human society
without the burdens of the ex-this or the future-that. For the
first time the problem of public image would cease. I wondered
how many men in public life before me had longed for such
relief. How the delights of being on holiday without being
recognised made one greedy for that anonymity for all time.
How the pressures of the media, always prying, always probing, made it so difficult for a real man to exist under all that
pretence. Oh what joy to escape:

My baggage was gone. 'Here is your boarding card, Sir.
Have a good flight.' She knew me as some VIP: my name had
a special mark against it on the passenger list. I hated the
special treatment. It reminded me of the oceans of unction and
pandering I had suffered before from people who put the
'public figure' in a category of untouchables for whom a
normal, unaffected relationship is not possible. And yet the
poor girl had done nothing. I must pull myself together. Soon,
after all, I would be free of all that humbug. Joe Markham
had already shown me the sweet simple pleasure of being
treated as an ordinary person.

I looked towards the car park. I would never drive that car
again. I would never drive my wife again to the Hampshire
countryside where we had enjoyed so much pleasure. I would
never again drive that hectic 120 miles up the Motorway to
the constituency. The old life was ebbing away. I turned towards the Departure lounge. What had to be, had to be. The
inevitability gripped me. I took the steps towards leaving

England for the last time; I took the steps towards my own destruction.

The Immigration Officer checked my passport and smiled knowingly when he saw who I was. If only he knew he held the identity of a man about to be extinguished. On the moving travelators I met Ernie Harrison, the brash and sharp Chairman of Racal, the fastest growing electronics company in Britain. His wife was with him. He was off to Florida to visit a subsidiary and to get sunshine. 'And how is Bangladesh?' he said. 'Bangladesh is in a terrible state. There is widespread famine and people are dying in the streets. The corruption is so rife the Government is breaking down.' The despair was evident in my voice, and the words choked in my throat. I felt a nausea that a country I had helped to create was in such a state. I felt pathetically helpless about it; then I realised that my escape was from this sense of helplessness too. Ernie Harrison did not respond to my remark but went on to say something inconsequential about Florida. I realised with a sharp shock that, of course, I had misunderstood his question. He was not asking about Bangladesh. He was asking a more pertinent question for him, 'What about the Racal business products in Bangladesh?' His company, through mine, had put in for some police communications business. He wanted the order. That was solely his concern: the circumstances of the country; the condition of the populace were matters of indifference. The priorities of business destroy the simple moralities even in a man as fresh and dynamic as Ernest Harrison. I was glad they had booked first class and I could slip away to the economy seats where I would have more space and solitude.

I settled down but the book was boring and the film about Dolphins seemed shallow. My own adventure had more to it than the fiction of print or celluloid. I was restless—the umbilical cord with my past life was being broken with every mile we flew.

At Miami we stood in line for the Immigration procedures. The officer looked me up in the big book of prohibited immigrants. I passed the test. 'How long will you be in the United States?' he asked. 'Just a week,' I said. He stamped the passport accordingly.

Admission to the States is a curiously democratising process. I suppose that Howard Hughes must get special facilities, but everyone, irrespective of rank, is subject to the same treatment on the conveyor belt before being privileged to enter. I remembered the ill-fated inaugural flight of British Caledonian Airways from Gatwick to New York, diverted to Boston because of bad weather and being held up on the tarmac by aircraft congestion for forty-five minutes. And how all the guests stood in line for another forty-five minutes. Admiral Lord Louis Mountbatten clutching his briefcase and standing like a real trooper in line like everyone else waiting for the officer to pronounce on his eligibility to be admitted. The former British Ambassador to Washington and a dozen chairmen of the largest British companies had no better treatment.

And here I was again submitting to the process, but with a difference. This time I had two personalities to submit: the old and the re-born. The old personality was in safely. After a brief moment in the customs hall I slipped past an unobservant officer, his head deep in his forms, and joined the line again, but this time clutching the virgin passport of Joseph Arthur Markham, my new personality. The line seemed to take longer to move. The others in the line were not from London. They had the more swarthy look of travellers from South America. I had plenty of time to study them until eventually my turn arrived. The check on the visa was fine; then the check in the big book of prohibited immigrants—no problems. 'How long will you be in the United States?' he asked. 'A few days,' I said. He gave me a permit for ten days. I had arrived as a new man. Officialdom had accepted me, ordinary Joe Bloggs or Joe Markham, it did not matter. I was beginning to be liberated.

But there were still many steps before my final freedom. A car to be hired from Hertz. The drive to the Hotel Fontainbleu on the north end of Miami Beach. The disappearance; the death of John Stonehouse had to be completed.

The baggage hall was crowded with passengers pushing and shoving their way through the customs examination. The customs check was exceptionally thorough. Miami, as an entry point from South America, was obviously a convenient centre for drug trafficking, and finding drugs seemed to be the customs' main concern. A negro porter trundled my bags through the swing doors along to the Hertz desk. Within minutes I had a big Chrysler car standing by for me. It was early evening and the drive across the causeway to Miami Beach was refreshing. The gentle breeze off the lagoon blew away the stale air of the long flight.

Miami Beach is less grotesque than Blackpool but that may be because the visitors do not promenade along the open front visiting a succession of Bingo Halls or Amusement Arcades. The delights of Miami are hidden in palaces which look as if they were built for the set of 'The Great Gatsby'. But the people are not Great Gatsby characters: the charm is missing. Indeed, most Miami Beach visitors seemed to me to be attending some convention or other, and within minutes of arriving they are on first name terms with all the other participants. In the corridors and lifts all is bonhomie of the hale and hearty variety, and almost everyone wears a plastic name tag with the 'pet' name prominent, to ensure that just no one could possibly miss greeting them as a life-long friend. A plastic relationship in a plastic world.

My suite was in the main building with a magnificent view of the sea; the rooms were ornately furnished but tastelessly. Little envelopes indicated there were two maids—day and night—and the tips could be left in the appropriate envelope, whenever the giver checked out.

I telephoned the Bank of Miami contacts and arranged to call on them the next morning; they invited me to lunch. It would probably be my last business lunch: my last lunch as John Stonehouse. The meeting was arranged to discuss the possibility of the US Bank acquiring a big bloc of shares in the London Capital Group. It was a sensible idea. Most US Banks wanted to expand in Europe, and the costs of setting up new enterprises were prohibitive. A shareholding in the London Capital Group would provide an inexpensive entry for them. For us it would provide backing which was sorely needed, and the absorption of shares which had been an embarrassment to us since the Bank was launched. It would also provide more banking expertise and systems.

As the non-executive unpaid chairman, I had been forced by the absence of qualified and able executives to take on more responsibility than I wanted. The exercise had turned into a nightmare. Whereas my intention had been to be a non-involved figurehead, circumstances had decreed otherwise. In order to keep the Bank from collapse, I had to throw in all my personal and Company resources. The amounts borrowed from other banks on my personal guarantee were immense.

I felt I was already drowning in the turbulent sea of debts. What had begun as an exercise in idealism and from the best of intentions now became a mad struggle for survival.

Sometimes I had felt like a patient in a padded cell unable to communicate my screams for help, because I was effectively gagged. At other times I was in an exposed canoe being swept down rapids, my paddle long since broken and the whirlpools and rocks all around. Survival meant putting on a brave face and engaging in the sham of success. In business, as in politics, no one can advertise his deficiencies. One's confidence must exude into every business discussion. How can 'they' have confidence if you do not show it? Falseness becomes the natural relationship in such circles. The strain on the inner soul is immense and I felt it, deeply and with a frightening intensity. My being was torn to shreds by the inner conflicts, but in the vain hope that something—oh something—would turn to advantage. I had kept up the pretence of outer strength. I knew that others had seen through such turmoils before and had lived to survive. In business one slight change in fortune can transform a situation. One major contract achieved could mean a commission of hundreds of thousands of pounds injecting liquidity into all the related activities of our group. And one major shareholder could bail out the problems of the Bank. The attempts to retrieve the position by other means had failed miserably. This might succeed. If so, I would gently withdraw from the scene and obtain respite and strength to deal with the political contradictions in my life. I felt stretched in so many areas of activity the strain was destroying me. The bundles of elastic in my brain were pulled out to breaking point, and yet, if only one of the pressures could cease, I would survive and recover an equilibrium, but a dozen stretching pressures were too much. The appointment with the Bank of Miami was a straw to clutch. Would it give me hope and pull me back from the brink of the extinction I was planning for myself?

I fell into a deep yet fitful sleep exhausted by the jet travel, time change and the enormity of my struggle for some sort of survival in a hostile world.

I woke early: A beautiful tranquil morning: The sea smooth and inviting. I checked my escape route. Surprisingly the hotel next to the Fontainebleau was shuttered and deserted. I remembered staying in that hotel years before as a government minister touring North America. It was strange to wander through the beachside facilities that once bustled and were now forlorn. My memories of the past were like dreams. Did this place once live or was I imagining it? Who was that man who stayed here? Can you recognise him? Is he even related?

Already I was looking at my past as a stranger. A man from a different existence, a man who had been separated from me by the twists and turns of fate. A man who had been separated from me by the distortions of a cruel environment. I felt, standing there by the deserted and now dirty swimming pool, as though I was looking back on myself through a long series of distorting mirrors. At the other end I could see the old me looking backwards through the same distorting mirrors with an expression of horror and incredulity. Is this what happened to the buoyant, confident and cheerful Minister of the 1964–1970 vintage. I looked over the passage of time—in both directions—and shuddered. The man I had been was broken. He was now a useless pathetic sham without confidence or hope. Useless to his colleagues who had expected too much of him, and to his friends, who misunderstood him, and to his family who loved him too much. He had to die. It was the final solution. He would perform a last valuable function for those who had relied on him. He would become the obvious scapegoat for everyone's problems. The business worries could be solved much easier in his demise; his death would be the lightning conductor absorbing all the electrical tensions that had built up all round the Dover Street financial enterprises.

I drove to Miami Airport and bought a suitcase and new clothing. My new identity was taking shape. I bought a ticket to Houston in Texas for cash in the name of G. Lewis. The name and the booking went on the computer within seconds. In Houston I would change to Joe Markham, take the plane to Mexico City and connect with the twice-weekly Qantas flight to Sydney via Tahiti. My passport already had the separate Mexican visa pinned inside. There would be no problems in leaving the US as the entry of Joe Markham had been so legitimate. It was stamped in the passport and the entry-exit form would be perfectly in order. In the computerised United States the system must be serviced, the forms must be correctly processed, for the aberrants will soon be discovered. If Joe Markham had left the US without the exit form marrying an entry form, then the computer's alarm bells would ring and the machine would search for the cause of the discrepancy.

I left the suitcase and a briefcase containing passport, papers and credit cards for American Express, Hertz and Avis, all in the name of Joe Markham, in a left luggage compartment, and drove back to the Fontainebleau Hotel. The stage was set for the disappearance. Only one thing remained to do to complete the preparation. I took a spare set of clothes—shirt, slacks and sandals—to the deserted hotel and left them in the telephone kiosk near the swimming pool.

At the due time I kept the appointment with the National Bank of Miami. The offices were surprisingly small and functional. John Odgers, Vice President, International, was affable and apparently personally keen on establishing a relationship between the two Banks. However, the decisions on such relations were made by the parent Company and not by the Bank itself. I would have to consult others. He rang through to another office and I was briefly introduced to another Vice President who was much preoccupied and obviously disinterested in my proposals. I felt the brush-off process was perfected when I was referred to yet another offshoot—a US/Canadian International Merchant Bank based in Luxembourg. In banking, as in business generally, there are two thousand and one ways of saying 'No'. Lunch followed. 'We can't have it in the executives' dining room, no alcohol,' said Mr Odgers, so we walked outside and along the pavement to a restaurant in the English style with Union Jack table-mats. My two hosts seemed to relish the opportunity of an expense account lunch with drinks, and they took their time over it. The delay irritated me. I was anxious to get away from this game in which effort is ninety-five per cent wasted and so much is pretence.

With relief I said goodbye to my hosts and drove back to the Fontainebleau, giving the car to the parking attendants. In my hotel room I changed into my swimming costume, slacks and sports shirt. I left all my Stonehouse possessions in the room—my passport, travellers' cheques, credit cards and money in a combination locked document case. My ticket with the flight booked to Los Angeles for the next day I left on the bedside table. My clothes were all in the wardrobe. I closed the door on my past life. On my way to the beach I gave the key for my room to the hall porters so it would stay—noticeably, I thought—in the room slot. At the entrance to the beach area I signed the check list for guests.

There were very few people about, a few hotel staff and one or two other guests, and nobody took any notice when I left my clothes on the verandah and set off to swim in the warm Florida seas. It was refreshing to feel the water washing away my tensions of the past; it was like a baptism of a new being. The coast shimmered in the afternoon sun and the buildings further down the southern coast came into view. They looked as if they came straight out of the 1920s. I had that in common, but now I was being recreated.

The sea was deserted and so was the beach when I swam back. How is it that pampered Americans come to Florida and spend most of their time indoors breathing the stale recycled air of the air-conditioning systems. I changed into the slacks, shirt and sandals retrieved from the empty Eden Roc Hotel, strolled through to the road and hailed a taxi. 'Airport, please,' I said. We seemed to sail over the tollway to Miami proper, and to me it was a dream, and within minutes the taxi dropped me at the airport arrival terminal.

The Markham belongings were in a big luggage cubicle— a case of clothing, and a briefcase with passport, travellers' cheques, credit cards and documents. My new personality was complete. In the name of George Lewis I bought the ticket for Houston and made the plane within minutes of its scheduled departure. As the aircraft circled over Miami Beach in its take-off pattern, I looked down to the place where I had cut the umbilical cord to my past life. It was a tremendous relief to be free of all that humbug, deceit and sham and all the pressures.

At Houston I changed planes in a magnificent airport. It was certainly the most beautiful complex I have ever seen. Each terminal was connected to others by underground and automatically operated railways—the trains running like robots between them. The buildings themselves were high domed like cathedrals and spotlessly clean, and the whole system operated so effortlessly that it seemed almost preordained. There was none of the hustle and bustle of a European airport. It was as if, here in Texas, the ultimate in the religious rites of jet air travel had been reached. The litany came over the soft amplification system 'Eastern Airlines announce the departure of their Whisper-jet to New York'. The aircraft were departing for every possible destination in the United States. But my destination was Mexico City and my terminal lounge was packed with dusky looking passengers, many of whom were speaking Spanish. It was late evening on a Thursday and I suppose many of them were returning home for a long weekend holiday. The Trans Texas plane was packed to capacity. For some reason the Americans fell down on their usual efficiency and the plane was forty-five minutes late in leaving. That delay turned out to be crucial to my plans. We arrived so late in Mexico City that I missed the midnight Qantas plane to Sydney, Australia. The Mexicans are a disorganised people, in sharp contrast to the Americans in the Texas we had just left. Perhaps it is the altitude or the Latin temperament that changes the atmosphere. Everyone was rushing about in a great chaos. My passport with its separate Mexican visa was passed from hand to hand in such confusion that I thought I might lose so soon this one link with my new life. A little Mexican air stewardess knew my reasons for haste and succeeded in getting me through the formalities of immigration and customs relatively quickly. I rushed to the Qantas desk to check in. 'Sorry,' the clerk said. 'The Sydney plane is already preparing for departure.' 'Can't you signal the Captain that a connecting passenger is trying to join the plane?' 'Too late,' he said, 'Ten minutes ago I could have got you on.' 'When is the next plane to Sydney?' 'Not until next week.' 'No other airline?' 'None.'

I had hoped to be in Australia, safely in my new country, before the death of Stonehouse was announced. That plan was defeated by ten lost minutes. There were no other aircraft out of Mexico City that night, but the following morning at eight or so aircraft began flying to Los Angeles. I would connect with a Sydney plane there.

That night I spent in a tourist hotel near the airport, booking in under my new name of Markham and using my passport and American Express credit card. The personality was complete.

But despite my fatigue the night was a turmoil. My dreams were so vivid that the interior of my brain felt it was coated with a Cinerama screen. The dreams were Technicolor and three-dimensional. The Stonehouse past kept coming back. The tape that had been erased was faulty. The memories that were killed in the baptismal waters of Florida were being replayed. Markham tried desperately to rerecord over these memories to erase them again, but they were still there, sounding more shrill.

The morning brought some respite. At least all was normality around me. I paid the account and caught the airport
transit bus to the terminal building. I discovered that within
an hour I could be winging my way to Los Angeles. I checked
in my baggage at the crowded counter. Before leaving I just
had time to buy some Mexican handicrafts as a souvenir of
my brief stay.

The plane to L.A. was absolutely packed and most of the
passengers were obviously well used to flying this route—they
were devout commuters. My contact with them was unreal.
I was part of them for we were all on the same plane, but they
were as distant as if they were players in one of my Technicolor
dreams. My state of mind was in suspense.

I re-entered the United States without trouble. The
immigration officer had no doubts about my passport or my
visa. Dealing with this formality seemed to remove my mental
suspense, for clearly I was Markham. This was all real—a passport, a visa and an entry stamp. 'Enjoy your stay,' said the
cheerful officer.

The plane to Sydney was not due to leave until late evening:
it was only early afternoon and it was Friday. I checked into
the Marriott Airport Hotel as Markham; another plastic
palace for plastic people. I had stayed there before as Stonehouse on my last visit a few weeks before; but it was a mistake
to come here; the memories came pouring back in a flood. Garrett Corporation, the aerospace company, was only a few yards
away—Stonehouse had an appointment with the President of
the Company, Mr Harry Wetzel, and even a date for lunch
to discuss the consultancy on the future of the British aircraft
industry. Impressions of the past, the present and the future
came swirling over me in huge waves. In a daze I picked up
the bedroom telephone and phoned Garrett. 'Is that Mr
Wetzel's secretary?' 'Sorry my plane was late and I couldn't
arrive in time for lunch.' 'Mr Wetzel was waiting in for you
but he's slipped out for a snack. Come in at 2.30. I know he
will be pleased to see you then.'

From the hotel I walked to Garrett which was situated
only just outside the airport area. With each step I left Markham behind and Stonehouse was filling my physical shell
like a vessel being filled with liquid. By the time I reached
9851 Sepulveda Boulevard, the shell was full and the
liquid was frothing over. 'Good to see you back,' said the

homely and friendly receptionist. 'Mr Wetzel is expecting you.'

Harry sat in his big office surrounded by the paraphernalia of the corporation President; the smart inter-office telephones, the electronic time clock, made, of course, by Garrett, and the souvenirs of successful business trips around the world. Incongruously, among the aerospace books on the shelf was the volume on Escher, the Dutch artist, whose prints Julia, my daughter, had distributed throughout Britain. Last time in this very office we had discussed the work of this amazing man whose drawings demonstrate the strange symmetry of life: how black merges into white, how up becomes down, how in becomes out and how in every situation there is a movement from positive to negative, and back again. Looking into one of Escher's drawings is like looking down the labyrinthine ways of one's own mind. For me at that time these thoughts were particularly poignant, for my mind and personality had been drained of John Stonehouse, but now—in the true Escher contrast of opposites—he had returned. In reality he was here talking coherently and sensibly to Harry and Jim, his Vice-President. The conversation took about an hour and a half exchanging points on the research project, and we all agreed on the next steps for its completion. Soon I would return to Los Angeles with the completed report.

I walked back to the hotel and, although Markham had booked the room, it was Stonehouse who was there to unlock the door. And on the other coast of the United States Stonehouse was missing from the Florida beach. I felt disembodied. Somehow the two halves of Stonehouse, one in California and one in Florida had to be joined. And other memories came back. The coming Sunday was Remembrance Sunday and I was due to attend the Cenotaph Service in my constituency at Walsall. I rang my wife Barbara to warn her that I would be late but I could not explain the unexplainable, that, in fact, I had to rush back to Florida to collect the other half of Stonehouse and, of course, his passport. There were no seats available on the direct trans-continent flight to Miami but, by changing planes in Atlanta, Georgia, during the middle of the night, I could still reach Miami on Saturday morning and then catch the Saturday night plane to London to arrive at Heathrow early on Sunday morning. It would then be feasible to drive to Walsall in time for the Remembrance Day Service—my God, I would have a death to remember.

As I flew across the United States over California, Arizona, New Mexico, Tennessee to Georgia, I slept fitfully in the aircraft. The pain and anguish of returning to Stonehouse was intense. Markham, for his part, resented the intrusion on his plans; he could see no point in returning to the empty charade in Britain, but Markham would not fight the blood ties which were dragging Stonehouse back like a powerful magnet.

Atlanta Airport at four o'clock on a Saturday morning is a hive of activity. Hundreds of people were strolling along the spacious corridors linking the terminal building to the departure lounges. There were smartly turned out servicemen with short haircuts and name tags proudly displayed on the left breast. There were family groups, businessmen, travelling salesmen, all alert and purposeful despite the hour. Nearly a third were negroes—equally smart if a little dandy, and certainly as self-assured as the whites.

I had sufficient time to make my connecting plane for Miami without rushing. No one took the slightest notice of me and I felt as though I really did not exist. Perhaps I was suspended between lives and my physical being was not evident to others. Within a few hours I was in Miami speeding in a taxi back to the Fontainebleau Hotel. The test was coming—would I find Stonehouse was missing, the police alerted and the Press already printing reports of a disappearance or death? At the Hotel Lobby my key was handed to me without question. I took the lift to my room which had been cleaned, and all my possessions exactly where I had left them two days before.

I went to the beach area to enquire about my clothes—the slacks, sandals, shirt and towel—left there. No one had any knowledge or recollection of them. The truth dawned on me. No one had noticed my disappearance at all. I returned to the room and fell into deep sleep born of utter exhaustion.

When I woke up about two hours later at one o'clock in the afternoon I realised that for once I had not dreamt. I was fresh and again fully capable. There was no doubt I was back into the Stonehouse personality. The horror of it hit me like a sledgehammer. Was it true that within hours I would be on the overnight plane to England back to that life of deceit and humbug and the stress of being all things to all men? It was intolerable. I had to escape. I quickly took a spare set of clothes for Markham to the deserted Eden Roc Hotel, and back in the room I surveyed for the last time—the possessions of Stonehouse which would remain as the evidence of his demise—the passport, tickets, cheques and money. At the entrance to the beach area I made sure I was noticed by signing the register of bathers against my room number. Surely this time they would realise Stonehouse was missing, surely this time I can succeed in destroying this man who was such a burden to me.

Within minutes I was in the baptismal waters of the Atlantic again, but with a difference. Markham was stronger and determined to succeed. The philosophical haze of the previous swim was replaced by a harsh strong light. I could see it all clearly now. Stonehouse must definitely die. My spare clothes were ready and I soon caught a taxi back to the airport. There were no seats on the direct flights to Los Angeles or San Francisco, where I could make connecting flights to Australia. The best plan was to fly to Chicago from where there would be many flights to San Francisco, the gateway to the Pacific—and the new life. The economy seats were full so I bought a first-class ticket and sat in the spacious front section of a Lockheed TriStar. For a moment Markham remembered wryly that Stonehouse had helped negotiate the Rolls Royce engine contract, which meant the aircraft would take off on power from Derby, England, but such thoughts were soon dismissed, for he was another person.

At Chicago the aircraft took a long turn over a darkening lake circling a pulsating Chicago where thousands of lights signalled the early Saturday evening of a great city. I reflected on the human dramas being played out down there. Should I spend the weekend here, I wondered, particularly as the girl in the next seat had spoken of her Chicago in such glowing terms? She was returning from a convention in Miami, perhaps she would provide some human companionship to relieve my isolation in my new identity. I dismissed the thought. I must put as much distance between Markham and Stonehouse as possible. This time the umbilical cord must really be severed.

O'Hare Airport is another palace of homage to the religion of communications and has the distinction of more passenger movements than any other airport in the world. But there was still the atmosphere of measured efficiency which pervades most of American society. I caught a plane for San Francisco

without difficulty, and settled down on the seventh plane in
seventy hours. It was my natural habitat this cocoon of an aircraft and the unchanging routine—seat belts, drinks, plastic
meals, the captain's announcement, and finally 'Deluxe Airways hope to have the pleasure of flying you again,' and the
nod and smile from the stewardess as the passengers spill out
to the tongue which links the plane to the terminal.

I felt suddenly oppressed, like a reluctant lemming. Why
should I throw my being over the precipice even if I was doing
it only metaphorically, and only in space and time, and with
the technology of jet travel to help me? From the depths
of my being an emotion of tremendous intensity rose within
me. I went to the rear of the plane into the tiny toilet compartment and screamed at the reflection in the mirror. 'Why do
you do this to me?' But who was screaming—was it Stonehouse or was it Markham? The struggle between the two
was tearing me to pieces. The inner turmoil was an agony.
I wept.

Stonehouse won the battle and when I returned to my seat
I resolved to turn round in San Francisco and recross the
United States. The umbilical cord was not severed after all.
I must return to Miami and recreate my own identity. For the
second night I flew from West to East Coast. The fates were
inexorable. The National Airlines DC10 engines broke down
en route and eventually at Tampa, Florida, on Sunday morning, I had to change planes to make the tedious onward
journey through Fort Lauderdale to Miami. My nervous
exhaustion was complete, and once in Miami late on Sunday
afternoon, I barely had sufficient energy to reach the Fontainebleau Hotel, check out my things and return the hired car to
the airport. Needless to say, no one had noticed me missing,
and my clothes had disappeared from the beach. Stonehouse
was fated—he could not escape.

On the overnight plane to London I felt like a condemned
man, with the noose already around my neck, being dragged
along to a hideous circus. Heathrow was bleak on Monday
morning as I staggered from my third consecutive overnight
flight. I steeled myself for what was to follow. I put on a brave,
confident face, went to the office and later to the House of
Commons. No one I met thought anything unusual had happened to me. Apart from missing the Walsall Remembrance
Service, nothing had gone amiss with my arrangements. At

least, so they thought. Oh, how different is the image from the reality!

The next days were painful as I went to all the appointments and dealt with all the business expected of me. The yoke was across my shoulders with a vengeance, heavier and more restrictive than before. The cloaks of deceit and pretence, which, like all people in public life, I had to wear, had hardened into a straitjacket. The man had become a robot, but with the difference that a spirit was still trying to break out. The House of Commons became even more oppressive and the childish banter even more irrelevant and irritating. In the Division Lobbies, as I shuffled through to have my name ticked and my nod counted, I realised that most Members around me were robots too, voting on issues which they did not bother to understand after debates to which they had not bothered to listen. The concentration of all that sham in one Division Lobby with the Members crushed against one another, after the ceremonial 'locking of doors', gave off a miasma of terrifying intensity. Parliamentary democracy had been reduced to a low level. I remembered when the reality of this charade had hit me. It was years before, when the Heath Government was pushing through the Industrial Relations Bill. The Labour Opposition, in an attempt to win favour with the Trade Unions, voted against every possible clause, and for every possible amendment, although debate was finished at midnight under a 'guillotine' procedure. Every night from midnight and sometimes to as late as 4 am Members were engaged in a perpetual voting charade. As the result of each Division was announced, another took place immediately, and Members streamed through the Lobbies yet again. Most Labour Members had the glazed look of callow, loyal slaves. My protest to this ridiculous humbug was not abstention, as it should have been, but playing chess in the Division Lobby with Douglas Jay—the former President of the Board of Trade, who felt as I did about the silly nonsense.

My 26th wedding anniversary came round and I took Barbara out for the evening to our favourite restaurant, La Bussola, in St Martins Lane. I felt as close to her as I always had—very close—but I could not bring myself to tell her what agony I had been through. As I saw it, my death would have been a release for her and for the family as well as for me. We were a marvellously happy family but I had feared what would happen to our relationship as I was gradually destroyed by the pressures and tensions and the miasma of disillusionment all round me. Better to die from one thrust than from a thousand cuts. Better the family to grieve me dead at an apparent peak than to be helpless witnesses of my slow decay. Barbara never knew that twice I had committed psychiatric suicide. Nor could she ever imagine I could resort to such action.

To follow up the contact I had established with the Miami Bank, it was considered wise for Jim Charlton, my fellow director, to accompany me to Florida on a return visit. The prospects of achieving an agreement on a share sale to the Americans seemed good, and it would be the solution to many problems. I was glad he was coming. As a barrister and as former Secretary to the giant British Aircraft Corporation, Jim was a man of experience, tact and charm. No one personified the English gentleman so well and he exuded confidence with effortless ease. I felt subconsciously that Jim's presence would help prevent me from relapsing into the Markham personality. With Jim it could be possible to achieve a success which would make my life—at least in one area—more tenable, and make Markham a less necessary adjunct to it. I felt also that a return visit to Miami Beach would help exorcise the effects of my psychiatric suicides.

And so I returned to the Fontainebleau Hotel with all its trappings of decadent affluence, and I returned to the Miami Bank and with its executives who had failed to give us the encouragement we expected. I returned to the restaurant with the Union Jack table-mats, and the shallow conversation, and with a deep disillusionment I returned to the same Miami Beach. This time I was determined. I could stand no more of the charade of that life. This time there would be no possible return. The disappearance from Miami Beach would be the final release of all my tensions.

15 *Escape to Australia*

I LEFT MIAMI without difficulty; catching a transcontinental plane in America is almost as easy as catching a bus in London. The non-stop flight to San Francisco gave me ample time to collect my thoughts about the future. The past, after all, was past. And this time the end was irrevocable; nothing of the life of John Stonehouse need be recalled. He had died just as surely as if the sharks in the South Atlantic had eaten him. Joe Markham had a lot to look forward to and the relief of emerging as this total person rather than sharing a life with another was a joy itself. The plane arrived too late to make connections with the Pan American or Qantas flights to Sydney, and so I took a taxi to the city. As usual, the taxi driver struck up a conversation—American taxi drivers must be the most garrulous in the world.

'Are you staying in Frisco?'

'Only for one night.'

'Are you a Canadian?' he pressed.

'No, I'm an Englishman but I'm on my way to Australia to settle.'

'Gee, that's the best idea,' he said. 'England sure is in a mess. What have you people been doing to it? It used to be a country we could all look up to; now it's fifth-rate, if that.'

'Well, you've had your problems here too,' I said defensively. 'Watergate is not exactly a tea-party.'

'Don't you worry, we can sort that out. What really has hurt this country has been the Kennedys and the foreign wars. We shouldn't get involved in other people's troubles. We've enough here for ourselves.'

I asked him to take me to a good hotel and he took me to what appeared to be the best. The Fairmont stands as a tall tower on the heights of the city with the steep streets falling away from it like Alpine slopes. It is not surprising that it is called Nob Hill; for those who live in the less salubrious areas hundreds of feet below, it is probably Snob Hill. I booked in for a single room. 'Sorry, Sir, there are no rooms available,' said the receptionist holding court behind a counter which looked over the spacious and luxurious lobby, reminiscent of old Vienna with its red plush settees and red carpets set in marble floors, 'But would you hold on for a moment.' She went away for a few moments and came back wreathed in smiles. 'You're in luck,' she said. 'We can give you our best suite and just for the price of a single room.' I said, 'Thanks a lot.' 'You're welcome, Mr Markham,' she replied.

I was shown to quite the largest suite I had ever occupied in any hotel. Even when I had been staying as the special guest of governments I had never had this luxury. The sitting-room was in itself the size of a small house and a reception could be held in it for fifty people without being crowded. At one end was a magnificently appointed bar complete, of course, with the inevitable refrigerator, and at the far end were deep armchairs and card tables. The colour television was huge and operated by remote control from one of the armchairs. The carpet was so thick I could cheerfully have slept on it, but the huge double bedroom made that unnecessary. The bedroom had its own colour television operated from the bed. It was surprising that the bathroom did not also have a television set. Double-sized book matches were scattered around the suite reading 'Fairmont Hotel and Tower symbol of the grace, charm, and dignity that is San Francisco.' I thought wryly that the new Joe Markham was falling on his feet.

The suite was so magnificent it seemed a pity to leave it to stroll down the hill. Stroll is hardly the word, to walk in San Francisco downhill is to slide. It is a mystery how the taxi cabs, let alone the cable cars, cope with that gradient. As I went down the hill the streets became seedier; there were as many massage parlours as bars and most of the bars had topless go-go dancers. Out of interest I went into one. The lights were low except for bright spotlights on a white girl dancing on the bar itself and a negress in a cage on the opposite side. For fifteen minutes I watched them gyrating to taped music as the sad men sat and stared. The atmosphere was almost completely without gaiety; the men sipped their drinks without any apparent enjoyment and the girls danced on and on like wound-up dolls. I found the synthetic titillation extremely depressing especially as San Francisco with its Fishermen's Wharf and Chinatown is a city of considerable interest and fascination, and the men in dozens of these bars were missing so much. The massage parlours were equally depressing and most appeared—even from the outside—exceedingly seedy. The life 'atop Nob Hill' at the Fairmont with its plush restaurants and the Starlight Room at the top of the Tower overlooking the whole of Frisco was far apart from the decay at the bottom of the hill. But perhaps the gulf was not as great as one assumed; the man from the top might creep down to the squalid level either in this or some other city because the pressures of life 'atop Nob Hill' demanded the experience of contrast.

But I had no more time or energy for these social researches and climbed my way back to my magnificent suite 'atop Nob Hill'.

On the next day I decided against flying direct to Sydney and caught the Pan Am flight to Honolulu. I paid the cheapest possible fare as economy tourist traveller and calculated that mile for mile this must be the least expensive jet air travel in the Western world by scheduled services. Onwards from Hawaii to Australia the fares are four times as expensive, contributing to the relative isolation of Australia.

The Hawaiian Islands are the most isolated archipelago in the world lying more than 2,000 miles from the American mainland and over 2,000 miles from the nearest major island group to the South. The Pacific Ocean itself is enormous— 10,000 miles in both breadth and width—covering a total area of 70 million square miles. It is therefore not surprising that these small islands covering only 6,500 square miles were not discovered by the Polynesians until the eighth century AD. What is remarkable is that the standards of navigation of these early pioneers were so good they were able to make frequent two-way voyages from Tahiti 2,000 miles to the South. Westerners did not discover Hawaii until a thousand years later when Captain James Cook with his two ships HMS Resolu-

tion and HMS Discovery landed early in 1778. It was to bring
an end to Cook's voyages, for a year later he was killed by
Hawaiians after a dispute about a stolen boat. It was a tragedy
as Cook had earlier established excellent relationships with the
Hawaiians who regarded him as a God. The English connection with Hawaii remains to this day, for the State is the
only one among the fifty in the United States of America to
retain the Union Jack in the State flag. The State flag flies
everywhere over hotels as well as public buildings, and the
Union Jack in it must be disconcerting to Limey-hating Americans.

I checked into the Sheraton-Waikiki Hotel which lies right
on the celebrated Waikiki Beach and was allocated a room
overlooking the magnificent Bay. Skyscraper hotels were
everywhere dwarfing the more attractive Royal Hawaiian
Hotel which still retains the charm of the earlier Waikiki. It
was difficult to believe that just 150 years ago Honolulu was
a hot, dirty, dusty village of only 300 grass huts. Today it is
a tourist jungle with every known delight available from the
amusement arcades to restaurants with full frontal nude
waiters. I suppose the latter delight—like Playgirl—is just
another American contribution to women's liberation.
November in Hawaii is slightly off-season, but the place was
packed almost entirely with Americans from the mainland, but
with a fair sprinkling of Japanese who are the new affluent international tourists. For the Americans a visit to Hawaii is as
necessary as a pilgrimage to Mecca for Moslems. It has everything for the great American dream. An air-conditioned con-
crete complex of plush bars, restaurants and shops superim-
posed on an island paradise where American culture ensures
that Polynesians, Orientals and Whites live together in a permanent Coca-Cola harmony. Yes, I have to hand it to the
Americans. There is a remarkable absence of tension—
the Hawaiians themselves seem to accept their role as
the providers of entertainment and services to the rich
or less than rich from the mainland with equanimity. And
the tourists for their part relax in a way I have not seen
Americans do anywhere in the world. According to the lists
in the Hotel Lobbies, the groups came from such far-away
places as Cincinnati, Chicago, Pittsburgh and Philadelphia
but, before long, they were all dressed in the almost compulsory attire of the matching his and hers Aloha shirt and

dress. The lei necklaces of fragrant flowers added even more colour.

I enjoyed the atmosphere and felt completely lost in this sea of happy humanity. My four or five days were spent swimming on Waikiki Beach—where the surf is nothing like it is cracked up to be—and touring Oahu Island, seeing the tropical parks and the incredible sea life park at Makapuu Point where the dolphins perform like human athletes. I never had time to visit the other islands of Molokai, Lanai, Maui and Hawaii, which I regretted as they were much less crowded and more attractive, according to all I heard.

Much as I enjoyed being free and accepted in this holiday paradise, I wanted to get on to Australia and to receive the final acceptance of my new personality with the migrant status. I felt it was also necessary to have confirmation that my old self was as dead. My previous attempts to escape on the mainland of the United States had failed; now with the whole Pacific to separate me from the past, it should succeed, but there were still lingering doubts. Despite this totally new environment in Hawaii and the stimulus of new experiences, there was still something pulling me back to the old self. That pulling had to be resisted; there could be no going back.

So I left glorious Hawaii, the sun-drenched islands of the Pacific, and caught the Pan American plane for Sydney. There were no emigration formalities and exit from the United States is simplicity itself. The foreigner hands to the airline staff the second half of the immigration card (which is then fed to that omnivorous computer) and the US citizen simply shows his passport to the airline. No Immigration Department officials are to be seen on leaving the country. Presumably the airlines are duty bound not to accept passengers who cannot produce passports. The system is an easy-going one and no doubt it has frequently been abused.

The flight was not non-stop, and in the very early hours of the following day, which was two days ahead as we lost a day crossing the International Date Line, the plane landed in Noumea, New Caledonia, part of France. The airport building with comfortable seats for six hundred passengers seemed unnecessarily large for such a small place. It was clear that the propitiation of the communication Gods was not confined to the Americans—the French also had to perform their religious rites.

During the stop over at Sydney I bought newspapers to see whether my death had been reported. The American newspapers had reported nothing and I felt still slightly in a state of limbo. It was extremely important for Joe Markham's peace of mind to know that the man whose body he occupied was accepted as deceased or at least missing, presumed dead. Unless he was so accepted there would always be the tugs and pulls on his consciousness, and I wanted none of that. The break had to be complete. But the newspapers had no news of Stonehouse.

The last leg of the journey to the Tullamarine International Airport at Melbourne took only an hour. Presenting my passport at the desk for returning Australians and migrants, I was accepted as a migrant without formality. The Immigration Officer only glanced at the large manila envelope containing the X-ray negative and certificate confirming that Markham did not suffer TB and then stamped my passport with the round stamp 'Permitted to Enter'. He waved me on to the customs area.

'Is that all?' I asked in amazement. 'Do I have any other procedures to be confirmed as a migrant?'

'None at all, friend,' he said. 'Mind you it will be more difficult after 31 December. Then you will need a visa. But, no worries, you are one of us now.'

I passed on, grateful to be in a form-free democracy where a single stamp in a passport entitles one to equal status to thirteen million other Australians. The customs examination was more thorough but not as prying as the American customs.

Through the swing doors to the arrival area there were crowds of welcoming families, mainly new Australians of Greek and Italian ancestry. They had lost none of their Latin customs and the embraces were exotic and tearful. As soon as I had checked into the Sheraton Hotel in Spring Street I walked through the city to the Bank of New South Wales to which my account had been transferred. The London office in Threadneedle Street had given me the address as Little Collins Street but the buildings were demolished and had been out of action as bank premises for six months. This lack of efficiency of the Wales did not impress me. However, at the Bank's Headquarters in Collins Street I discovered that all my documentation had been passed to them. The new business staff were very helpful and within twenty minutes it was confirmed that my money had been transferred from London and I had deposit and current accounts.

All seemed well for Joe Markham. He had arrived! Accepted as an Australian migrant complete with bank account, could there possibly be any further problems? Probably not, but a nagging fear was in my brain and it would not go away. Furthermore, the newspapers did not confirm the demise of Stonehouse. His presence—however slight—was oppressive to me. I had to put a further barrier between him and myself by escaping into another parallel personality: Donald Clive Mildoon. I felt a compulsion to go to Europe to confirm that John Stonehouse was dead. The compulsion gripped me and I could not shake it off.

Looking back on those days at the end of November 1974, I can now realise how irrational I had become. I had escaped from Stonehouse into the new, uncluttered and stable personality of Joe Markham, but the ghost of Stonehouse still haunted me. Joe Markham and John Stonehouse had been close associates for four months. Although they were separate and quite different personalities, they had intimate contact every day and were dependent upon one another like Siamese twins. The death of the one, with the traumas and the tensions, was a relief to the other who became free and whole. But the freedom could be real and permanent only if the twin were truly dead and no longer plagued by the problems of life. If only the ghost of the twin had been ignored, Joe Markham might still be alive today—and undiscovered—in the great haven of Australia.

I decided Clive Mildoon in Australia would be my protection against the ghost and that Joe Markham would travel immediately to Europe, if possible to England, to exorcise that ghost from my brain once and for all. To give flesh and bones to my second Australian personality I withdrew most of my cash from the Bank of New South Wales and transferred it to the Bank of New Zealand, a few doors along in Collins Street. The Accountant, Mr D. C. Rowland, at the Bank was all sweetness and helpfulness. 'We are very pleased to have your account Mr Muldoon,' he said.

'No, not Muldoon,' I said, 'Mildoon.'

'We have a leading politician in New Zealand with the name Muldoon, that's what confused me,' he apologised.

'Yes,' I said. 'I have heard of him, quite a character,' not daring to admit that years before I had met Muldoon on a Ministerial visit to New Zealand.

The transaction completed, I dumped my Markham suitcase at a cheap hotel—The Regal in Fitzroy Street, St Kilda—and rushed to Tullamarine to get the first available plane out of Australia. With minutes to spare I caught a BOAC plane to Singapore via Perth. My Markham American Express credit card was accepted without question and my passport was in order.

Reflecting on my actions, I can now see I had returned to the Lemming Syndrome, which I had, in fact, experienced weeks before in America. I was rushing and rushing and rushing, using jet travel to jump the precipices. I did not know where eventually I was going or why. Again I felt like a personality in limbo searching for an identity which remained ever elusive. But at least in this cocoon of the BOAC jumbo jet I was comforted. At least we were going somewhere. The stewardess brought English newspapers and I read of the Stonehouse mystery. The news did not add to my comfort. That ghost had to be buried. Perhaps in Europe—I could see it finally laid to rest and I could at last find the peace for which I had been so vainly searching. And then I could return to Australia before the 31 December visa deadline and take up my new life without ghostly memories to haunt me.

16 *To Copenhagen and back*

SINGAPORE IS ONE of the world's wonder cities. It is nothing but an island with a fine natural harbour, but its people—mainly Chinese—have made it a throbbing progressive industrial and commercial centre with the highest average standard of living in Asia, after Japan. Considering it has no natural resources, that is no mean achievement. And, like Hawaii, Singapore has been transformed in the last 150 years.

In 1819 when Sir Stamford Raffles, an agent of the British East India Company, first arrived, it was nothing but an island of fishing villages with few inhabitants. The British built up Singapore as a military base, and at one time it appeared to depend completely on military expenditure—a situation it shared with another island, Malta. I recall that in 1967 when Harold Wilson was proposing defence cuts East of Suez, the Singapore Prime Minister, Lee Kuan Yew, sent an impassioned appeal to London begging his fellow socialists to continue military spending. Lansbury must have turned in his grave at this demonstration of international socialist priorities. However, for domestic reasons, the Labour Government in Britain could not oblige Singapore and served notice that Britain would gradually pull out of the base. Rather than put the death mark on the island, it was the kiss of life. Lee, one of the world's most dynamic and intelligent leaders, galvanised the country into commercial and industrial activity. Through a series of tax concessions and other inducements, hundreds of foreign companies were persuaded to come and invest. The political stability helped also to establish Singapore as the financial Switzerland of the Far East.

But I was not to see much of the island; one night, in a second-rate hotel, was all the time I could afford. Europe was beckoning me with a fatal fascination. I had to discover what had happened to the ghost of Stonehouse.

On the next day I travelled by Thai International Airways to Bangkok and changed to the Scandinavian Airlines Systems Trans-Asian Express—one stop to Copenhagen and advertised, correctly, as the fastest route to and from the East. The plane needed the long runway to take off; it was loaded with a full payload of passengers and fuel. It flew over Burma, Bangladesh, skirted the Himalayas and onward over Afghanistan. The one stop was at Tashkent in the Soviet Republic of Usbekistan. At the bleak and desolate airport we had an hour's stop. The Soviet security guards in their heavy drab uniforms with the hammer and sickle red emblem on their caps came to the aircraft and solemnly collected our passports. They were mostly Scandinavian—Swedish and Danish, a few German and some Thai. My Joseph A. Markham passport was the only apparent British one in the pile. We were each given a numbered tag as a receipt and the corresponding number went in the passport rather like a cloakroom ticket. We all walked to the airport terminal through the wet slush of a mid-Soviet winter afternoon. The Soviet citizens walking nearby looked at us with idle curiosity—every week this DC8 from the West appeared among the Tupolevs and Ilyushins, confirming that another world existed outside the vast tight family that is the USSR. Inside the terminal the Swedes and Danes crowded round the souvenir stalls to buy Russian champagne or craftwork for foreign currency. The stalls with goods selling for roubles had definitely low quality merchandise. But the books were free. 'The Foreign Policy of the USSR.' 'The Place of Women in Soviet Society.' 'Milestones on the road to Socialism.' The books were in English, German and French. Around the building were blown-up photographs of joyous Soviet citizens happily going about their tasks. Their attitude to work was in sharp contrast to the desultory attitude of the women on the souvenir stalls or the hostesses who had to shepherd the passengers in and out of the building.

We returned to the DC8 and collected our passports. The security guards left and the cabin doors were shut. As the plane took off into the darkening grey skies of Soviet Central Asia, there seemed to be a gentle collective sigh of relief from the packed serried ranks of passengers. One thought united everyone: Copenhagen next stop. We flew over the Soviet steppes and skirted north of the Caspian Sea and then over Russia proper. Over the Baltic, the plane commenced its descent and the hostess said, 'Please fasten your seat belts; we are about to land at Copenhagen Kastrup Airport.' It was early evening in Denmark and the air was crisp with the hint of a hard winter on its way. I breathed deep and long; it was good to be in Europe again.

I booked in at the Grand Hotel on the Vesterbrogade near the Central Railway Station—a hotel I remembered from many years before in another life—and went straight to bed exhausted by the 7,000 mile journey from Singapore. After the first four or five hours I slept badly; the room was cold and the time change had left my metabolism unadjusted. I decided to move to a warmer hotel just around the corner. It turned out to be more congenial as well as cheaper.

My first task was to check up on the British Press and fortunately Copenhagen is well supplied with English papers. Sometimes—depending on the planes and the weather—they are on sale by 9 am. Wearing my corduroy trousers and jacket (and how grateful I was to have some warm clothes), I walked briskly past the Tivoli Gardens, padlocked and empty, to the Town Hall Square. One kiosk had only domestic papers, the other had English, Dutch and German papers on display. I greedily bought all I could lay my hands on including *The Times*, *Daily Mirror*, *Daily Mail* and *Daily Express*.

When I found a bench to sit down on and read them I was horrified. It was evident that John Stonehouse had caused a sensation. Instead of dying or disappearing, presumed dead, in a nice orderly fashion, so as to create the least possible pain and anguish; and instead of providing a short sharp lightning conductor for the release of tensions, the Stonehouse story had become a major scandal. Most disturbing of all was the fact that, even if assumed dead, many warped people were dancing on his grave. I read the accounts with incredulity. What John Stonehouse had always suspected deep in his subconscious was being proven true. Just below the surface of the body politic, there had always existed the pus of envy and spite. It had developed over the years like the muck in a human body.

The envy and the spite and the jealousy had grown up in certain fevered sores to such an extent that as soon as an object of this intense hate was presumed dead, it came rushing out like the bursting of a boil. From the newspaper accounts it was evident that some people—and certain sections of the Press themselves—were not only dancing on the grave of the missing man, they were trying to dig up the corpse to tear it limb from limb so it would get no peace. The allegations were fantastic. I searched Copenhagen for other papers and back copies to fill in on the story. Poor Joe Markham was distraught; his Siamese twin was under such attack! How could they be so unfair to an idealist who had worked thirty years in one good cause or another at great personal sacrifice. How could it be that the convoluted and confused events of recent years, which had unfairly caused so much distress to him, were now to dominate the newspapers to the exclusion of the decades of struggle for the disadvantaged and the oppressed. How is it that the merest hint of scandal, based on the flimsiest of evidence and propagated by obviously maladjusted or twisted men, can erase a lifetime of constructive endeavour motivated by the highest ideals. Some British newspapers were full of smears and innuendo and unsubstantiated allegations. And each report cut deep into the psyche of Joe Markham sitting lonely, isolated and without friends in a busy Copenhagen, preparing for Christmas.

It appeared that the first attack on John Stonehouse—from the Reverend Michael Scott, who, possibly on a basis of information given to him by a few Bengalee immigrants, some of whom may have had their own axes to grind, claimed that Stonehouse had been responsible for one million pounds missing from a Bangladesh Fund. The hyperbole was typical of certain Bengalees. The alleged missing sum could not be £50,000 or even £250,000, it had to be a million. But the facts were that John Stonehouse had been a Trustee of a Fund set up to help Bangladesh during the war of liberation from Pakistan, but that he had never handled any money himself which had been collected by local groups and paid directly into the Fund's Bank accounts. The other Trustees, Mr Justice Abu Sayeed Choudhury, who later became President of Bangladesh, and Alderman Donald Chesworth, likewise, had no direct contact with money collection or cash handling. The accounts had been audited to the complete satisfaction of both the Bangladesh High Commission in London and the Bangladesh Government itself. Most of the proceeds of the Fund had been handed by the trustees to the Leader of Bangladesh, Sheikh Mujibur Rahman, personally on the day he returned in triumph to Dacca from imprisonment in Pakistan.

The Reverend Michael Scott is one of a small breed of whites who are so genuinely concerned about colour relations that they are inclined to believe any allegation made by a coloured man against a white man. They are so psychologically enmeshed in the white/black problem that it becomes difficult for them to view certain problems objectively. I feel sure that he must have believed the truth of what he was told, but I believe also that he was misled.

The Press kept the story going for days, using the tricks of the trade to propel it along. One day an appeal for a Commission of Inquiry, the next for the Ombudsman to investigate, and on the next—good for a headline—the Prime Minister asked to intervene. And for good measure a non-story was thrown in—an alleged loss of the important file on the case in the Chambers of the Counsel, Mr Dingle Foot. The fact that the Bangladesh High Commission had issued a denial that there was any truth in the ridiculous story of a missing one million pounds was submerged in the orgy of press vilification of a supposedly dead man. And other stories appeared in profusion. John Stonehouse, according to the *Daily Mail*, was supposed to be Mr Fixit, MP in Bangladesh, where he had—so the story ran—been responsible for organising a major part of the imports, making for himself commissions on the deals of one million pounds. Again the Bangalee hyperbole—it had to be a million, not less! The facts were that, as an export promoting Company, Global Imex, in which John Stonehouse had the majority shareholding, had pushed British goods in the Bangladesh market against Japanese, German and French competition. What on earth was unpatriotic about that? It would have been possible for the Press, instead of smearing, to have praised the efforts to give jobs to British workers and promote British industry. It is an extraordinary quirk in Britain to regard the activities of Members of Parliament who are also Barristers as highly commendable, even when, for large fees, they defend men they know to be guilty.

It is also praiseworthy for Members to write memoirs, even including Cabinet secrets, and publish these for large sums of money. But for an MP—particularly a Labour one!—to engage in the 'sordid' business of promoting British goods abroad, is regarded with distaste, bordering on disgust, unless the MP is Mr Ian Mikardo promoting trade with Eastern Europe.

The facts were that John Stonehouse did not involve himself personally in the trade negotiations in Bangladesh; at the time of the Press attacks he had not even been to Bangladesh for nearly two years. The business was operated by full-time marketing executives including one experienced officer actually based in Dacca. But these facts did not make good copy for the newspapers concerned with muck-raking: the issues had to be personalised, the ogre-figure of John Stonehouse had to be firmly established in the public eye. The price of the free Press is to allow license to callow journalists, who have never had to take constructive responsibilities in their lives, to use their skill at words to destroy the men who try, in the interests of colourful journalism. Good copy, for this type of journalist, is scandal, affecting an easily identifiable public figure whom the general public can easily learn to hate.

The truth about the Bangladesh trade was not a one million pound commission for John Stonehouse but merely enough commission to cover the considerable Company expenses and to make a small profit for the Company. The idea that the person attacked in these ways can issue denials to put the record straight is a cruel myth. The newspapers won't publish denials except in small print, and even then they ensure they have the last word.

In the case of Joe Markham, walking the cold streets of Copenhagen to collect these daily attacks on John Stonehouse, the situation was even worse; he was powerless to defend the honour of his dead twin. He knew that John Stonehouse had died, in a next to ultimate suicidal sacrifice, to save his family from suffering his tensions, and to allow his friends and business associates the opportunity to recover the businesses in which his presence had been an embarrassment. Now Joe could see that the sacrifice had all been in vain. Instead of the peace and the tranquillity and the sympathy of death, the family had to suffer a steadily mounting campaign of horror. George Orwell's 1984 had arrived a full decade earlier as every day, without respite, the media taught the public to hate, to hate and to hate still more.

Joe Markham, eking out the days in a tiny hotel room off

the Vesterbrogade, could only watch like a paralysed animal because his very own identity gave the lie to the continued existence of John Stonehouse, and completely frustrated the ability of the dead man to defend himself. He tried to find distractions. Planning a ferry-trip from Esbjerg to Harwich took up some time. Would it not be better, it seemed, at one stage, to get even closer to the source of the evil pouring out in Britain. But how could that help? It was a foolish idea. One cannot snuff out a volcano as if it were a candle; and in any case how could Markham possibly do anything. I took to taking long walks around and around Copenhagen to try to throw off the terrible psychological pains which afflicted me. I walked past the Christianborg Palace and along the Harbour to the Little Mermaid statue to watch the tourists, even in December, taking their photographs. I walked to the museum showing the gallant resistance put up by Danes against the Germans during Hitler's occupation and reflected that their imprisonment was probably worse than my own. My own imprisonment was within a web of extraordinary circumstances which were partly of my own creation. At least I did not have to run the gauntlet of the guns of trigger-happy Germans as had those brave Danes over thirty years before. But the beautiful Copenhagen I remembered from another life from yesteryear was soiled by the excesses of the too-permissive society. The repression of the Hitler period had, after three decades, been exchanged for the doubtful freedom to see pornography blatantly displayed among the Christmas decorations. Is this what freedom-loving Danes fought for? I swallowed my disgust that along the beautiful pedestrian precinct of Strøget along the Frederiksberggade, just off the Town Hall Square, the children Christmas shopping with their mothers were passing sordid sideshows of obscene nudity. Standing on the pavement was a young long-haired sandwich board man carrying the advertisement. 'Turn here for the best porn in town. All sex acts including with animals displayed.' I spent two Sundays in Copenhagen. The porn shops were open; I hope the churches were too.

For the ten days I was in Copenhagen, from 29 November to 8 December 1972, the routine was compulsive. The morning search for the British newspapers (sometimes frustrated in dismay when fog or strikes stopped them arriving); and the fevered reading to gather what further horrors were being printed about the demised alter ego. In retrospect, I feel there are very few towns in the world where I could have borne that daily stress. Copenhagen was one. In the weeks before Christmas it is a happy city; the shop windows are full of beautiful things, the department stores like 'illum' are throbbing with people, and the cold weather, although not that bitter, is cold enough to make one walk and walk with vigour. I found a little modest first floor restaurant on the Nytorv Square, where I could sit by the big stove and sip *bouillon mit oeg* or drink a bottle of Tuborg and while away the hours. I was intrigued by the introduction to the official Guide by Urban Hansen, the Lord Mayor, '... Copenhagen is a town where the visitor is not solely judged whether he has a heavy purse, but by his intentions and goodwill to adapt himself to a different environment.' That was meant for me. Wonderful, wonderful Copenhagen!

The Press accounts became more bizarre, culminating in a story to the effect that John Stonehouse had died as a victim of a Mafia plot. I found myself looking at myself from beyond the grave; and yet it was not myself, as myself was surely dead. The Press reported myself as dead and yet—oh cruelty—they would not let the dead lie down. I searched into the inner recesses of my mind to make rhyme or reason from this frightening conundrum, but could find no solution. My attempts to travel to England were thwarted, and my attempts to exorcise the ghost had been a dismal failure. Joe Markham must return, I decided, to the welcoming embrace of Australia and escape into the relatively non-involved anonymity of Clive Mildoon.

I booked my return trip by the cheapest possible route—Aeroflot, the Russian airline through Moscow and New Delhi, back to that bustling Singapore and away from this daily horror of murder by the media. The aircraft to Moscow was packed. The Russians do succeed with their low fare policy in achieving high load factors. In another life, I had been to Russia leading an aircraft delegation; we had done our best to understand the economics of their air communications system. But it did not make sense. For every aircraft flying there seemed always two or three on the ground as stand-by planes, and the engine overhaul life was so short the planes were grossly uneconomic anyway. The Russians found, after a time, that they could not even give their civil aircraft away to foreign customers; only the captive markets in Eastern Europe bought them. The Czechs had told me they used Soviet aircraft very reluctantly.

On the Copenhagen to Moscow route I ruminated on the earlier visit by my other self. How we had been given the VIP treatment at the airport, how the Soviet Minister of Aviation had inadvertently confirmed that my hotel suite was bugged, how we had been the first Western visitors to see Concordski—the Tupolev 144—under construction in a Moscow factory that could have been a Heath Robinson warehouse, how I had been soundly beaten by Sir George Edwards, the designer of the Viscount, the VC10 and Concorde, at conkers on a Kharkov pavement, and how we had all sung songs with the merry Cossacks on a steamer cruising up and down the Dneiper at Zaporozhye. This time my mission to Moscow was different with a vengeance. What on earth would the Russians do if they recognised in me the ex-Minister of Aviation who was dead. But all I wanted now was to pass through Moscow as the simple Joe Markham wending his way like a lost soul trying to find the peace of anonymity. What a contrast!

At Moscow Airport we were disgorged on to the deep, snow-covered aircraft apron and made our way to the airport terminal and the waiting halls. The arrangements for checking off and on to flights were an untriumph of socialist planning. Passengers were wandering everywhere without direction and no check-out boarding cards were provided. The large hallway was pleasant enough with a black and white television in a corner, around which were huddled numerous airport staff and cleaners watching a skating competition. The souvenir shops were closed and the refreshment counter accepted only roubles. Most passengers spent their time either strolling around or thumbing through the ubiquitous literature: 'Soviet achievements in agriculture,' and the like. Eventually we were recalled across the snow-covered tarmac to the aircraft. The plane was still crowded but this time there were more Soviet citizens, presumably engineers and technicians heading for India and the East to fulfil the commitments of a State Aid Agreement. We trundled to the take-off point, the engines roared and the jet took off into the black Moscow skies. The stewardesses worked like beavers to tend to our needs, and the meals provided, although not the best I had experienced on my numerous journeys, were certainly not the worst. The tea was certainly the best ever served in the air. It was produced from a gigantic teapot that looked like a samovar. To pour that instrument a hundred times needed a strong arm; it could only be used on a Russian airline.

Sleep came with difficulty and the night was short as we were flying East against the sun. At Delhi it was already well past dawn when we arrived. The airport was a sea of pushing and shoving and gesticulating people with an atmosphere of friendly disorder that reminded me a little of Mexico City airport. When stopping at Delhi in the past life—as at other airports—I had invariably made a point of buying postcards and stamps so that the people back home would get a feel for my journeys. To escape the crowded transit lounge I walked through the customs area, past the passport control and into the wider hall of the airport buildings. My senses relished this relief from the cramped conditions of the aircraft, but I had a jolt when I looked at the postcard stand. This time I could not, need not, would not buy even a single postcard. This time I would not negotiate with the clerks at the tiny post office desk to acquire stamps. It would be so unnecessary and pointless. There was no one 'back home' to send a postcard to. The family of John Stonehouse, who had received and treasured these postcards from far-away places, could receive them no longer; they *knew* he was dead. And Joe Markham who had spent all his short life travelling could only stand in that airport building and reflect on the loneliness of his isolation. 'Fats' Waller's 'I'm going to sit right down and write myself a letter' came into my consciousness and it went on 'And make believe it came from you.' The loneliness in that poignant song is only matched by the loneliness of the long-distance traveller who has no one to whom to send a postcard. Strangely, I could feel more acutely now the need for human contact, although I was in this crowded airport with 400 million Indians just outside.

In India I had always felt the pressure of the human tidal wave, particularly in Calcutta with its tens of thousands of people living all their lives on the pavements, and in Bengal where one drives for hours through the countryside but always seeing people, people. And now here in this airport in the midst of all this humanity I could not stretch out—even with a postcard—to touch another human being who knew me as I really was in this new life. I returned to the Aeroflot plane, to the Russian teapot, to the fellow travellers, and sank into my chair. I had a curious realisation. To these people, and to others, I will always be the eternal stranger, a man with flesh and bones but none of the depth that a lifetime of human contact with family and friends produces. Man, I realised, cannot exist by himself alone; he needs to have the comfort of an intimate social environment, even if that environment is only carried with him as a memory of loved ones far away. If the memory is erased then something must fill its place because the vacuum of social isolation is painful. The sooner I could get to Australia the better, I thought. There I must fill the vacuum around me with the friends and contacts and, gradually, the new memories that would make my new life meaningful.

Soon we were in Bangkok where I shaved in the airport washroom, foolishly leaving too little time to buy the delightful knick-knacks which the Thais produce with such skill. And then on to Singapore, back again on the doorstep to Australia. I was feeling better, soon I would be home in Melbourne. A home where I had spent only a day of my new life, but a home for all that. At Singapore I had hours to wait which gave me the chance to see the airport shops with their profusion of gifts from all over the world: the transistors from Japan, the ivory carvings from China, the silks from India and the wood carvings from Africa. A duty-free delight for the overtaxed overcharged consumer of the Western world. I bought an American Sheaffer pen, which I am now using to write this chapter, a silk dressing gown and an ivory carved chess set; the comfort of possessions is second-best to the comfort of friends, but it is a comfort for all that. I was back to BOAC for the next leg of the return journey: Singapore to Perth. The plane was going on to Melbourne but I chose to stop at Perth to ensure that I would get that valued immigration stamp in my passport just as soon as possible. It was soon after midnight when the plane arrived Western Australian time. The Immigration Officer had no problems with my passport: it already had the magical round stamp of a migrant, and without more ado I acquired another magical stamp. It was early on 10 December 1974 a full twenty-one days before the visa deadline. I had made it. Here I was in Australia, firmly accepted and obviously acceptable, and here I intended to stay. This ceaseless jet travel must cease. I must now slightly disengage from the frenetic character of Joe Markham and put down my roots as Clive Mildoon.

I checked into a Perth motel on the airport road and slept soundly until the morning.

When it came to booking the air trip for Melbourne I came up against the special curiosity of airline timings. In my previous life I had, as the visiting Aviation Minister, been told of the competitive situation between Trans Australian Airlines (TAA) the State airline, and Ansett Airlines, the private creation of that remarkable Australian communications pioneer Sir Reg Ansett. The two airlines contrive to operate the same type of aircraft on the same routes and at the same times and, of course, at the same fares. At most airports there are two terminals for domestic flights TAA and Ansett, but the passengers are regarded as a convenience for the airlines not, as it should be, the other way around.

On my Ansett plane I sat next to a Canadian couple on a year's sabbatical from a university and touring the world. 'What poor airlines you have in Australia,' they said, assuming, I was glad to note, that I was Australian. 'We find the cabin service the worst in our experience.' They had a point. On the nearly four hour trip from Perth to Melbourne the refreshments served were minimal; it was a wonder that the regular travellers did not bring their own lunch boxes.

At Melbourne Tullamarine Airport I caught a taxi to drive to my modest hotel in St Kilda and bought a newspaper on the way. An advertisement caught my eye. 'Executive Apartments To Let': the address was 500 Flinders Street, near the centre of Melbourne City. I stopped the taxi there and discovered a new building with small but tastefully designed and furnished flats. Although it was near main roads, it was quiet in the recesses of the building as it was built around a quadrangle which, with its small pool and fountain playing, shut off the city outside. Compared to hotels—and even the squalid hotels in St Kilda—this place was inexpensive; it offered the opportunity to Clive Mildoon to find a haven with the other people in Melbourne who need to rent small furnished apartments. The proprietors, Bob and Joan Willcocks, were friendly people who emphasised—I thought sincerely—that it was their ambition to help not only in providing accommodation but also in providing a community atmosphere. I was impressed by the absence of pure commercialism and decided to stay. I paid a bond of 150 Australian dollars, paid the month's rent and moved in.

'We are glad to have you with us Mr Mildoon,' said Mrs Willcocks. 'You will be one of our big family.'

I said a quiet goodbye to my dear friend and twin, Joe Markham, who had taken me on such hectic journeys all over the world, and settled down to be a fairly ordinary chap, living among fairly ordinary people with a life neither excessively exciting nor excessively dull. To be normal, after all the abnormalities of my previous existences, was what I craved to be. As I settled down to enjoy that respite, I little realised that the vortex released by Joe Markham and before him, John Stonehouse, were already building up the violent whirlwind which soon would hit me like Cyclone Tracey of the Darwin disaster. As in Darwin there was a deceptive lull before the hurricane struck. Clive Mildoon had precisely fourteen days left to live in his make-believe nirvana. But he did not know it.

17 *One new migrant*

MELBOURNE, LIKE HONOLULU and Singapore, is a creation of the last century and a half, confirming the fecundity for cities of the first half of the nineteenth century. But, unlike the others, Melbourne continues to give the impression of solidity, ancestry and ageing respectability—at least in the central city area. The Melbourne Cathedrals, built to the designs of British Cathedrals, add to the impression of dignity and charm. The General Post Office, the State Parliament and the Town Hall are also all monuments to the faith, fortitude and confidence of the pioneers of a century ago.

Walking with the crowds on the pavements of Flinders Street or Swanston Street, it is almost impossible to conceive that the first pioneer, John Batman, arrived only in 1835, anchoring his schooner nearby in the Yarra River. He said then, 'This will be a place for a Village' which, if true, was one of the understatements of the century, for today Melbourne has a population of two-and-a-half million. According to the accounts at the time, he bartered twenty pairs of blankets, thirty knives, twenty tomahawks, ten looking glasses and some scissors, handkerchiefs and red shirts for an area of land totalling 600,000 acres. That purchase from the aboriginals of the Douta Galla tribe ranks with the purchase by Cecil Rhodes of most of Matabeleland as one of the least creditable transactions between colonists and colonised.

Today there are hardly any aboriginals to be seen in Melbourne. The population, originally largely British in origin, is now a melting pot of British, Greek, Italian, German, Croat and Turkish migrants. I met the daughter of an Irish father and a Norwegian mother who had herself married an Italian. Some of the communities are as big as the cities in the old countries. The Greek speaking population of Melbourne constitutes the third largest in the world after Athens and Salonika. The great difference between Australia and other migrant-receiving countries, such as the United States or Britain, is that the White Australia Policy has virtually excluded coloured people apart from a few Chinese, Filipinos, and more recently a handful of Mauritians.

Melbourne—so named, in 1837, after the then British Prime Minister—shares with Buenos Aires, in the Southern Hemisphere, the distinction of being a European city which, unlike their Northern counterparts, do not have any blacks on the streets. Years ago when I was in Buenos Aires, someone made a wager with a visitor that he would not see a negro during his short visit. The visitor won. He saw the American Consul; but there were certainly no other negroes around. The same is certainly true in Melbourne where almost the only negroes to be seen are the occasional diplomats or visiting pop singers and boxers.

I set about equipping and provisioning my new-found apartment on Friday the thirteenth. It was not an auspicious day. The Victorian State Police, as I learned later, had already been alerted to my presence in the city. They had no idea who I was, but assumed that as I had opened two bank accounts under two different names, I might be planning a bank fraud. There had been a spate of bank frauds in the city. The counter clerk in the Bank of New Zealand had seen me going into the Bank of New South Wales and discovered that the man he knew as Mildoon, was Markham at the other bank. It was this simple clue which led to the police being warned.

Unbeknown to me, the police put me under surveillance while I went about the daily job of establishing my new life. And with every day the death of my newest identity was drawing closer. Oblivious to this, I established new contacts and I found Melbourne a friendly city. There must be few places in the world where a stranger is made more welcome. On Saturday evening I went to the Victorian Jazz Club meeting at the Manor House on the corner of Swanson and Lonsdale Streets. It was like any English pub built 50 years ago; in the design of pubs the Australians have shown absolutely no imagination. They brought the pub culture from the old country, but instead of it evolving, the culture remained static as in aspic. Visiting such pubs—in almost any Australian town or village—is like seeing the re-run of an old movie. And from Perth to Sydney, over 2,500 miles, the pubs are the same dismal solid architecture. Those pioneer drinkers were determined that the pubs in Australia were going to stay! The jazz, fortunately, was of the old, uncommercialised, uninhibited style. It was vibrant and lively. I bought a pot of Fosters Lager and listened. There had not been anything like this since Humphrey Lyttleton played in the Jazz Club on Leicester Square in the late 1940s. Inspired that evening by the music of the Yarra Yarra Jazz Band, I enrolled in the Jazz Club.

Ian Collie, the committee member, said, 'Say, Clive, why don't you come to our house-party tomorrow?'

'Yes, I will,' I replied, glad, so soon that I could alleviate my isolation.

Ian said, 'We have parties most Sundays to raise money for the 29th Jazz Convention which opens in Melbourne on Boxing Day.'

The atmosphere in that upstairs pub bar was as informal as only Australians can make it. The sign outside read 'Guests must be properly dressed' which I had assumed to mean that the men should at least wear ties. There were, in fact, including me, only two men with ties. The rest were open-necked, short shirt sleeved and slack dressed. Most youngish men had the long hair which went out of fashion in Britain several years before. For a young country, Australia is remarkably old-fashioned in its styles; even its 'modern' ideas and young set are curiously out-of-date. One constantly has the feeling of *déja vu*; good for nostalgia and good for me as I was trying to re-create memories to fill the vacuum of my mind.

On Sunday, the next day, I bought the Sunday papers—more than double the price of English papers. They were all full of the most utter drivel. *The Observer* was the worst, and I remembered—from another existence—another *Observer* which, with its elegance and depth, was at the other end of the spectrum as far as newspaper styles were concerned. I reflected, 'I really am on the other side of the world. This *Observer* is an upside down mockery of its namesake over there.' The Australian Sunday papers do no justice to Australian society; they do not reflect it honestly; they make a mockery of its values. Australia is a country which does not get the Sunday papers it deserves. At least within ten minutes I had read them all; in England it would take a little longer!

I had bought myself a radio: A National Panasonic Three-in-one. Japanese, like so many Australian imports. It had capacity for cassette and record playing and turned out to be an excellent investment, for the quality of Australian radio stations is first class. The Australian Broadcasting Commission (ABC) put out superb radio programmes—particularly music; they are every bit as good as the BBC but avoid the British pedagogism (the BBC's hangover from Reith). I turned to the music as a joyful, deep contrast to the superficial and mucky Sunday newspapers. And I discovered that, unlike the image created for Australia in Britain and elsewhere, there is in this country a widespread and sensitive musical culture. Every State has its symphony orchestras and the quality of playing is excellent. I was especially pleased to hear a performance by the Queensland Symphony Orchestra and Queensland choirs of a rarely heard Mahler Symphony. 'Who,' I thought 'in Europe had even heard of the Queensland Symphony.' This country is badly promoted overseas. It has a lot of indigenous talent and should not give the impression to the old countries that it is a cultural desert which has wasted millions of dollars on a hideous Sydney Opera House simply to salve its cultural inferiority conscience. I took the train from Flinders Street, clutching a bottle of wine as my contribution to the house party. The train ran through a series of Melbourne stations with names which confirmed their English ancestry: Richmond, Burnley, Camberwell to Surrey Hills and on to Mitcham, Ringwood and Croydon beyond.

Those early English settlers were determined to keep as much of England with them in this new land—only occasionally do the aboriginal names intrude on the English scene. I alighted at the station of Surrey Hills and walked down the trim suburban streets with their bungaloid homes and neat gardens. The house party was in full swing with jazz records on the stereo player in the small sitting room and beer in the garden with desultory conversation.

'Come in Clive,' said Ian introducing me to the others. 'Clive has come to settle in Australia.'

I met Ron, the communications engineer who worked for

the PMG and who spoke with enthusiasm about the Australian Post Office and its mission in uniting the country. 'What were you doing in England?' he asked.

'Insurance,' I said, vaguely, not daring to reveal that another me had been the British PMG.

'Have you been to England?' I asked.

'Yes,' he said. 'I took six months leave to go round the world.'

'Six months leave,' I said incredulously.

'Yes, after twenty-years service everyone in the PMG can have six months paid leave.'

'Good gracious,' I thought, this is a welfare state with cream on top.

'Where else did you go?'

'America; I did some good recordings there. The big stars never complained when I set up my equipment at their concerts. The jazz community is very free and easy,' he explained.

Australians do nothing by halves. The party which began at 2 pm was going on throughout the evening. I took my leave around 6. The following Saturday I met up again with my friends of the jazz scene at the Manor House. This time another band, The New Harlem. Where, I thought, does Melbourne find all these excellent performers, most of them amateurs? Certainly the economics of playing jazz in Melbourne were not such to justify the dozen or so really good bands which exist. The evening had the elements of a real jazz session, with members of the audience getting up on stage to participate. One of these, Nick Polites, played the clarinet simply beautifully. I congratulated him and discovered that, as is the case with many others in Melbourne, jazz is simply a hobby for him; Nick is an economics graduate involved full time in commerce.

This was my second evening in a week, just sitting in a pub, listening to music and being totally accepted by other people as an ordinary person who was one of them. It was a revelation to me. My new personality lapped it all up, hungry for this simple acceptance. It was such a contrast to that other existence, where pubs were associated with the pressures from constituents and others, who treat the politician not as a man but as a receptacle for all manner of complaints, or ideas to put the world right, and pleas for help of one sort or another. In my other life, like so many other politicians, I had been swamped by this constant deluge which flowed in any social circle until I came to loathe the idea of visiting pubs or clubs. I had done so week after week out of a sense of duty, but every time feeling the strain of it because the real me was drowning in this surfeit of false relationships. Oh! Thank heaven for my new self! What a joy! It took me back two decades of my life. To have had two whole evenings in that atmosphere of unforced human relationships was a luxury which my other self could never have enjoyed, except perhaps on holiday. And even then, one never escaped properly, because one still carried around a heavy cloak of humbug. It was necessary to have a holiday of six months to disengage; to enable the heavy layers of sophistry to peel away.

'How are the arrangements going for the Jazz Convention?' I asked Ian, who came to sit at my table.

'We are expecting a super turn-out,' he said. 'You can bring a tent and put it in the grounds of the Dorset Gardens Hotel at Croydon. Lots of people are bringing their tents.'

'Where are the bands coming from?' I asked.

'All over Australia. Some of the States give grants to enable their groups to come. They simply play and play,' he said. 'Its a beaut!'

These simple conversations helped to clothe the new me with a genuine and uncomplicated identity. I was no longer distorted by the need to perform, or the need to deliver the expected responses, or the need to be ever sympathetic and receptive to the inanities of others, or the need to impress for ulterior purposes.

Yet another house party the next day, appropriately at the home of Dick House, at Railway Crescent, in the suburb of Moorabbin. There was a bigger crowd in the garden and a barbecue. It was an 'American' style function, with everybody bringing their food and sharing it out. Someone cooked me a marvellous steak. I talked to a young surveyor who spent most of the year in remote areas of Australia, mapping the countryside. He was healthy and weatherbeaten. The others at the party were doctors, accountants, tool makers and factory workers. Dick House and his wife had arranged for everyone to win a prize for Christmas from an improvised Christmas tree. Father Christmas arrived on a bicycle. The whole scene was sweet and innocent. I bought a Jazz Convention tee-shirt, meaning to wear it when I went to the sessions on Boxing Day.

On week evenings I went to the Melbourne Chess Club,

which meets on the second storey of a miserable warehouse at
the top of Elizabeth Street, half a mile from the city centre.
In a long drab and ill-lit room there are serried tables with
well-worn chess boards, the pieces standing ready for the game.
Every day the place is open for the chess enthusiasts, and there
are many of them. Chess both unites and divides the world.
The Fischer/Spassky contest demonstrated a passionate con-
flict between Capitalism and Communism. But for me, on
those evenings, politics could not have been further from my
mind; the game gave me yet another feeling of identification.
Chess is also a remarkable technique of distraction from any
other thoughts one might have. One can play for six hours
and not think another thought. It is a wonderful way to clear
one's brain, like sluicing it with clean spring water, carrying
away all the impurities left behind in the crevices by the gar-
bage of the thinking man.

I recalled that in that other life I had achieved that same
cleansing of the mind in the Chess Room of the House of Commons, where Members can indulge in the only game allowed
in the Palace of Westminster. Under an age-old rule, enforced
strictly by the Sergeant-at-Arms, games of chance are forbidden. Chess is considered a game of pure intellect, so it is
sanctified with a room of its own. I would play there for hours,
particularly during all-night sittings, reaching an ecstasy of
play at 4 o'clock in the morning, when the physical senses were
deadened by fatigue but the mental processes still operated,
at least for chess. How beautiful it was to escape from the squalid conversations of the Tea Room or the ludicrous intrigues
of the corridors or (worse horror still!) the Members in the
bars drinking their way through the night, carefully remaining
sober so that when the Division bells came they could go past
the counting clerks.

I could not help but look at that other person and feel grateful that I had escaped that prison, where the falseness of the
constituency relationship is only exceeded by the sham of that
enforced and enclosed community of Parliament. The impression given to the outside world is that the House of Commons
is the best club in the world, where interesting personalities
engage in scintillating conversation about the political and
moral problems of the age. Parliament, according to this thesis,
is a crucible of the wisdom of 600 Members drawn from various backgrounds who bring to Westminster, the mother of all

Parliamentary democracy, the experience drawn from all levels of British society. Members of Parliament and most press lobby correspondents like to give currency to this myth. It is indeed a myth. Although one cannot dispute that there are interesting personalities and there are occasionally scintillating discussions, most of the discourse in the corridors of power is either abysmally trivial or concerns some squalid intrigue.

I had only a limited amount of money and I did not want to fritter away my scarce resources. As soon as the essential preliminaries of establishing my third identity of Clive Mildoon had been completed, I wanted to start some paid job. I went to obtain a driving licence in the offices of the State Police in Fitzroy, a northern suburb of Melbourne. To my surprise I was shown into a large room, sat at a desk and given an examination paper to answer. The Police in Victoria will not grant anyone even a Learner's Licence until they have passed the preliminary written test. The Australian driving rules were strange to me and I failed the test badly, but at least they gave me a book to study, and on the following day I passed with flying colours. I made an appointment to take my actual driving test, after which I would have to have a 'Probationer's' Licence for some months. I was on the way to a little more official acceptance for the new me.

I walked everywhere, not only to save money but to get exercise. The taxis, in any case, were very expensive, and the trams, though quaint, never seemed to be going in the direction I wanted. Through careful budgeting I managed to keep my daily expenditure down to two Australian dollars, apart from newspapers which I still had a compulsion to buy every day. I lost weight day by day, which I thought was all to the good.

I read newspapers because I was not yet convinced and indeed had grown not a little concerned, that that other man, John Stonehouse, had not been truly accepted as dead. Day by day I went to McGills Book Shop, opposite the GPO to buy *The Times* newspaper (for the surprisingly high price of 65 cents), and every day I felt a terror as I read the continuing saga of the dead man who had been one of my parallel personalities. I did not realise then that *The Times* was a pale reflection of the horrific stories which were still appearing in the British 'popular' newspapers which could not be bought in Melbourne. I felt welling back within my breast the pain of anguish that I had felt sitting in that tiny hotel bedroom in

Copenhagen, plumbing the depths of despair. That alien world in England would not accept that Stonehouse was really dead. I knew that he was dead. 'Why, oh God, wouldn't they accept it?'

One day, horror of horrors, the Australian newspapers, *The Sun* and *The Age of Melbourne*, both, for the first time as far as I knew, featured the story of the missing MP. The trigger for this treatment was the allegation that he had been a spy for the Czech Intelligence Service. One of the newspapers even had a large photograph, and that day, for the first time, I wondered would Clive Mildoon be confused, mistakenly of course, with that other man? A certain Czech Secret Service-man, Major Frolik, who had, at the time of the Russian crackdown in Czechoslovakia, defected to America, had made the allegation. Some of the English newspapers were, it seemed, making a meal of the story. My anguish became even more intense. That poor man had no way in which to defend himself against these ludicrous and sensationalised allegations.

On the Radio I listened intently to the news programmes. Incredibly, yet another allegation was being flung at the demised John Stonehouse. What is there in the English character which makes it so easy to kick a man when he's down or, worst of all, dance on a dead man's grave? A Labour MP who had never met John Stonehouse publicly asked whether he was an agent of the CIA. This confirmed to me that Clive Mildoon, living innocently in that little flat in Flinders Street, was better off away from the atmosphere of Parliament. The questioner was the new Member for Selly Oak in Birmingham, Tom Litterick, who was actually a member of the ASTMS trade union group of MPs, of which John Stonehouse himself had been the most recent Chairman.

The news announcer reported that the British Prime Minister, Harold Wilson, was to make a statement on the issue in the House of Commons. The next morning at 7.30 am on the ABC programme 3AR, I heard the BBC report of the Prime Minister's denial that John Stonehouse had ever been a spy and he said something which John Stonehouse had never been told officially, or unofficially, that there had been a complete security investigation which had cleared him of all suspicion. Clive Mildoon then realised that John Stonehouse had been suffering the miasma of this suspicion without being fully conscious of the reasons for it. The Prime Minister and senior colleagues, who must have known, had never told him, even later when they were in opposition. There had been no attempt to 'clear the air'. But they had shown by their strange attitude a subtle change in their relationship with their once very close colleague. Clive then could see that this had been one of John Stonehouse's big traumas; the unspoken and the undispelled cloud had been weighing on the Privy Councillor for six whole years and nobody had felt the compassion or considered the matter important enough to mention it. Nobody had done the decent thing and said, 'That is all past, now the slate is wiped clean, your conscience can be clear.' Instead his subconscious had been warped over the years by this evil influence. That revelation helped Clive to understand something John could never fully appreciate.

The Press publicity dismayed Clive who was unable to do anything to help John Stonehouse as he was so far removed from him. But the shock forced the memories to come back involuntarily. I made no attempt to recall. It was like a dream which constantly brings back images to the screen of the mind without the sleeper having any control over the projector. In a previous life I had jetted across the vast Australian continent, the size of which never ceases to amaze: across Australia is further than from London to Baghdad and my journey from Perth to Melbourne was as far as London to Istanbul. But on my previous journeys I was a cossetted Minister from a Labour Government in Britain visiting a Liberal Government in the Antipodes; the circumstances were very different from those of Joe Markham or Clive Mildoon squeezed on a crowded plane and thinking that in Australia he knew virtually no one. The jet travel before was mostly by the Government VIP aircraft — a BAC111 which, with two others, had been suddenly purchased from a surprised British Aircraft Corporation who had had no idea that there was even a requirement for such planes. It was said afterwards — particularly by US aircraft companies who were dismayed by the deal — that the purchase was simply a sop by the Australians to the British to compensate for the pro-US line being taken by Australia in foreign affairs.

The visit to Woomera came into my mind: that research station which failed to become the successful centre for rocket launchings in the Southern Hemisphere. What a barren, inhospitable place it was with no concession to creature comforts for the officers transferred there from the lively towns of Adelaide, Melbourne or Sydney or the graceful, beautiful Canberra—one of the most beautiful capitals in the world. I had thought at the time 'although the Australians have so much in common with the Americans in their pioneer mentality and in their brash energy the US make better efforts at the outpost.' I remembered that it was very difficult even to get a soft drink at the Woomera Rest Centre—the Americans would have had dispensers and ice everywhere. I had met Reg Ansett, the airline leader and he had impressed me as the type of entrepreneur Australia really needed—blunt, hardworking and pushing. Ansett did not suffer fools gladly; although friendly to the old country he showed little inclination to allow sentiment to influence his aircraft purchasing decisions.

'Whatever the Government wanted to do about RAAF VIP fleets was their business,' he said. 'I am in a commercial business and I can only survive by buying the most efficient planes and they happen to come from the States.' So Ansett bought Boeing and TAA, the Government airline were forced to follow. So today there is hardly a single British aircraft flying in airline service in Australia, except for the little Britten-Norman 'Islander'.

I remembered my frank discussions with another blunt Australian, the head of Civil Aviation, Don Anderson, big, bluff and breezy. It was a joy to talk to him after years with stuffier English civil servants. I thought then: if only Britain would introduce some of this freshness and honesty of approach into the higher ranks of its Establishment what a better place Britain would become. It was obvious to me and I was extremely irritated by it, that the British civil servants looked down on their Australian counterparts with great superiority for which they had precisely no justification. In fact they still seemed to regard them as 'colonials'. The informality of the Australian Government hosts was very impressive. When, in Canberra, I expressed greater interest in a weekend skiing than in the official programmed tour of the Snowy Mountain project, they responded with alacrity and one official volunteered to take me to the skiing resort of Perisher on Mount Kosciusko for the first snow of the season. We were in fact so deluged by snow that we had to dig ourselves out on the Monday morning.

I met Gough Whitlam, the Leader of the Labour Opposition, in his offices at Parliament in Canberra. He was also breezy and friendly. I kept in touch with him and later introduced his son to Harold Wilson when he came on a trip to the British Parliament. The new migrant—the unknown Clive Mildoon—wondered how the Prime Minister would react to the arrival of this reborn ghost from his past.

When the press made so many announcements about my visit, as they tend to do about any 'celebrity' visiting Australia, it seemed to me then and the impression has been more than confirmed since, that this tendency of the Australian media to play up the visits by overseas film stars and overseas personalities, however *passé* they might be and however minor they may have become in their own countries, Australia gives them a ball. It seems yet another confirmation of Australia's unnecessary inferiority complex.

When I was in Australia as a Minister I was taken to see the Commonwealth Government aircraft factory. It was a disappointing complex and it seemed a pity that this great country with so many resources could not develop a more successful aircraft industry. If one considers what Sweden has achieved, with a smaller country, one can appreciate how far behind Australia is in this respect. In Melbourne, of course, my visit caused the usual publicity associated with a Minister from overseas, not only did it appear in the press but I was given a radio interview with an excellent interviewer who turned out to be the brother of Michael Charlton, who had a similar and successful job in London. As a result of this publicity I had an approach from an old school friend whom I had not seen for over twenty years. He was 'Griff' Bartlett, a delightful and genuine man who had become successful as an architect in Melbourne, but despite many years in the new country had not lost his essential Englishness or his Hampshire burr. Griff and I had been founder members of The Citizens of Tomorrow, a youth organisation in Southampton and we talked a lot about that period in our late teens when the future ahead looked so malleable to the intense idealism we young people felt. I remembered and felt a deep dismay that that other man had been so disappointed that the great ideals of their earlier years had not been realised. The new man looked on these memories as belonging to another life and never considered contacting these friends of the original man.

During these days the Police were watching me with an eagle

eye. At the City Centre Flats an opening celebration cocktail party was held and I attended along with other tenants. It was a very chummy affair and I made a lot of new friends. Bob and Joan Willcocks were excellent hosts, introducing people to one another. Both of them knew, but did not tell me, that I was being watched. One of the other tenants in the block was, by chance, a policeman. When Joan said she was going to collect him to come to the party, I little realised the significance of the amused glint in her eye. Soon after this two or three policemen quietly moved into the flat facing mine and kept a round the clock surveillance; with the aid of walkie-talkies they had me followed wherever I went. One day—it was actually Christmas Eve, although Christmas did not have much significance for me (I had bought one solitary Christmas card to give to the Willcocks), I took the train to St Kilda to call at the Regal Hotel, where Joe Markham had been living, to collect any mail which might have been sent to him by the Bank of New South Wales. For the exercise and also to kill time, I took a sight-seeing tour around St Kilda. The part I chose, I now understand, is well known as the 'Red Light' district of Melbourne. I walked down towards the coast where the promenade skirts the harbour, where the St Kilda pier juts into Port Phillip Bay. I turned along the side streets, doubling back to the St Kilda station, and passed down a street which has a series of delicatessen shops which would do justice to Soho. The community here is mixed Russian and Viennese with a sprinkling of German. The merchandise in the shops reflected this continental influence. I strode on, feeling that I had got into my walking stride after the weeks of walking in Copenhagen and Melbourne. Behind me, apparently, one of the most athletic of the Victoria State Police was panting to keep up with me. At St Kilda station I bought a ticket and ran to the waiting train. Almost immediately three men pounced on me. 'Are you Mr Markham?' they said. 'Will you come this way?' They led me into the deserted booking hall and sat me down on a bench. The three men stood over me, holding my arms back. I was dumbstruck and dumbfounded. One of them looked straight at me and said, with a gleam of a friendly smile, 'Don't worry now; its all over.'

18 *My arrest and liberation*

THE THREE MEN HUSTLED me into a waiting car. They were tough and determined and two of them sat on either side of me on the back seat and insisted I keep my hands on my lap. The car drove fast into the city along the Kings Way Road and over the Yarra River. Apart from directions to the driver, hardly a word was said. Just over the Yarra I stole a glance at the apartment block at 500 Flinders Street, where I had been living, and thought Joe Markham had let Clive Mildoon down. Joe was in a mess. Clive could do nothing to help him. I was a disoriented being. I was now firmly gripped by authority who was dragging me backwards from the paths of escapism. Whereas I had trod those paths in three separate personalities in a leisured, if sometimes erratic way, the return journey was anything but leisured. And it was not erratic. It was a consistent rush of horror as they dragged me by the scruff of my neck from the far end of unreason. It was as if a person had suddenly been exposed to the bright light of the mid-day sun after weeks in the half light of a darkened room or, as if someone who had been wandering free as if in a dream, carefree and light-hearted and floating without effort, was suddenly dropped like a stone into a dungeon and manacled to a post which spelt 'reality'.

During the journey one of the police officers asked me to pull up my right trouser leg. He looked at the inside of my right knee.

'Oh yes, I thought so,' he said.

We arrived at the Russell Street Police Headquarters and drove into the car park. I was escorted to one of the upper floors and taken into a small interviewing room. Here I was frisked and everything in my pockets was laid out on the table. There wasn't much as I was only dressed in slacks and shirt, but they wrote it all down on a sheet.

'Now, who are you?' they said.

I said nothing.

'Do you know who you are?'

I said nothing.

'Are you Mr Joseph Arthur Markham?'

I said nothing.

The three detectives looked at each other with a slight shrug of despair and thought they had been through all this before, they had infinite patience, and in time they would get what they wanted because time was on their side—time and authority.

Two of them were dressed in suits whilst the third had wide bottomed denim jeans and a denim shirt. It later transpired that this was the detective who had followed me for much of the past fortnight and his 'gear' was his disguise.

They returned to the questioning.

'Where do you live?'

They picked up the keys to suite 411, City Centre Flats.

'We saw you look at those flats on the way here. Now will you admit that you live there?'

I said nothing. I felt utterly drained, as though the spirit of the man had been taken away as in a blood transfusion. This intense questioning could get me nowhere because the reality was not only too difficult to grasp, it was totally beyond my comprehension at that point. My mind could only register the small sparsely furnished room, four chairs around a desk and the three men facing me, one lounging back with his feet up, and one with his elbows on the desk, and the third staring intensely into my eyes. Within me were three men struggling to get out, wanting to escape from this torture.

'Perhaps we can help you,' said one of the detectives, and he drew a sheaf of documents out of his pocket. I could see they included a copy of Clive Mildoon's application to be a tenant at 500 Flinders Street, and details of Joe Markham's bank account at the Bank of New South Wales.

'Are these yours?' they said.

I said nothing, trying in a fevered moment to disentangle Joe from Clive and to establish a true identity.

'Why did you go to St Kilda?'

I said nothing.

The questions became more insistent and nearer to the truth and finally,

'We believe you are John Stonehouse; is that true?'

'Yes,' I said weakly, hardly believing my own voice which seemed disembodied, admitting to something which did not relate to the body to which the voice belonged.

I had been in a cataleptic state, with my being paralysed by the tension. John Stonehouse did not want to return to the world of reality. He could not return to the world of reality. He could not return to the world at all. He was dead. Weeks before his being had ended. What these three men were trying to do was to exhume a corpse and force it to live again. And both Joe and Clive, who each, in their way, contested owner-ship of my mortal being, could not and would not accept that John Stonehouse had any right to it. His rights had been bequeathed a long time ago, but the catalepsy was broken and the consciousness was flowing into my mind like a torrent. The swirling whirlpool of my thoughts took me back to another day, another month, another year, another life. Joe and Clive were swept aside by this stream of consciousness called realism.

'Yes,' I said, stronger, 'I am John Stonehouse.'

One of the detectives half stood up, stretched his hand over the table and shook mine. I took it involuntarily. The second detective did likewise, and then the third, and by this time it was a conscious John Stonehouse who shook the hand. I was a man transformed. I could then realise that the catalepsy had not lasted half an hour, or was it an hour, since these men had seized me; it had lasted weeks. My real John Stonehouse had been buried in the recesses of my mind, just as surely as if he had been buried in the warm waters of the South Atlantic. With their patient but blunt treatment of their suspect the three poli-cemen had, perhaps unwittingly, succeeded in opening a path-way to those inner recesses and releasing the consciousness of the man trapped inside. Who, after all, is a man? He is not a body, merely. He is not the image or the impression that he gives to others. That is not the reality. That is what they see. The reality is in the mind; usually open and communicative, but in my case the mind had been locked and the stream of consciousness dammed—so for that period, however long it had been—the man did not exist.

I was now willing to talk to these three men, and in a halting way told them as much as I could. Fortunately they did not press me, perhaps realising that the strain would be too great for me. The tension was now relaxed. Through the experience we had been through together, an understanding had been established between us. They introduced themselves. The two men in suits were John Coffey and Hugh Morris, and the third man in jeans was Tom Clarkson. All were Detective Sergeants in the Company Fraud Squad of the Victoria State Police. They were obviously quite pleased with themselves. They had got their man. And they told me how they did it.

'Look,' they said, 'Here's a signal from Interpol which gives a description of you.'

'That was why,' said Hugh Morris, 'I asked to see the inside of your right knee. You have a scar there, haven't you? Actually, the Interpol signal said it was a six-inch scar, but I couldn't believe that and was relieved that I was right. I thought it must have been a misprint for one inch,' he said.

John Coffey said, 'Do you know when we first started following you we thought you were the Earl of Lucan. You were such an English gentleman and we knew Lucan was missing in England and wanted as a murder suspect.' Surprisingly, they were talking more to me than me to them.

Hugh Morris said, 'We only got on to you because you opened two bank accounts. We had no other reason to be suspicious of you at all, and for a time we almost gave up, thinking we were on to a false track, but the Lucan suspicion kept us going. And then the possibility that you were Stonehouse came through, and we sent to Interpol for a full description, and you seemed to fit. Especially when we received these,' they said, showing me copies of my passport photograph blown up to four inches square.

'Let's have some lunch,' they said.

'Difficult today, its Christmas Eve. Everybody is having parties. We can get some food from the Chinese take-away,' said another. 'Hold on, I'll set it up.'

They dispersed to make these domestic arrangements and I found myself left alone in the room with the sheaf of documents still on the table. I had no inclination to tamper with them because the over-riding feeling I had was one of relief, relief that the true me had been, at last, released. I regarded my three captors not as enemies but as friends, not as gaolers but as liberators. They had, and I don't think they realised it, captured a Joe or a Clive, but in the process had freed another who had been locked away. Physically, I was shaken and broken, but mentally my senses were beginning to recuperate.

They soon brought back the Chinese food in plastic cups. We ate it with plastic spoons. It tasted quite delicious, although it was nothing special.

After lunch the policemen questioned me closely and I co-operated fully. I told them how I had to establish a new parallel personality to escape from the inordinate pressures on the original man. How J. A. Markham had eventually won the battle and Stonehouse had to die. I told them a few of the reasons for the pressures—the disillusionment with the sham and hypocrisy of public life in Britain; the deep dis-appointment with the intrigues of business and the falseness of human relationships in the business world; the steady build up of contradictions of a combined political and business life; the unjustified suspicions of my colleagues in Parliament about my activities which I could never dispel, because they would never be frank with me; the press campaign which had undermined the ideal of the British Bangladesh Trust; and the blackmail by business associates who knew the public figure would be vulnerable, and who, like Shylock, were prepared to stoop to any level to get their pound of flesh. I could only show the top tip of the iceberg which had dragged me down, but what I did was self-therapy. These three sympathetic policemen did more for me than they will ever know. They be-came my psychiatrists, gently releasing the pent-up passions that were locked up inside my soul.

'I can't go back to England,' I said.

'Why not?' they asked.

'England is the cause of my psychological problem. England and English attitudes made my breakdown possible. I could not return; my breakdown would happen all over again. I could not exist in all that sham and cant. The English would let me have no peace.' I was speaking to two men with English back-grounds and one with Welsh ancestry; none of them more than two generations removed from the old countries. But they could understand what I meant by the prissiness of the English poms, the snobbishness of the English Establishment and the vindictiveness of the English media towards anyone who transgresses the conventional norms of behaviour. At last I had found people I could talk to about my deep-set problem.

'You will have to stay in Australia,' said Tom Clarkson, one of the policemen. 'You can still apply to be a migrant here.'

The others looked a shade surprised that their colleague had been so forthcoming.

'Do you really think so?' I asked.

'Yes, of course. There are people coming here all the time who enter illegally and are then allowed to stay. Seamen for instance.'

The others agreed it would be a good idea. They then admitted that having followed me for a fortnight they had established something of a rapport with me. They were impressed that I had done nothing illegal, entertained no women and had not visited any massage parlours nor any other murky establishments, even in St Kilda.

They said the 'Super' had arranged a press conference at 3 o'clock to announce their find. Superintendent Patterson came in.

'Is it all OK boys?' he asked.

'Yes, he's been as good as gold,' they said.

I was left in the room alone with Tom Clarkson, the policeman in the denim jeans.

'You should be all right if you apply to stay,' he repeated. 'Wait a minute, let me make sure the tape is turned off.'

Our earlier conversations had all been recorded. Not that I worried; I felt I was among friends. I wasn't even under arrest—just detained as a suspected illegal immgrant.

The British Consulate General sent an Information Officer to see me. He was about the last person I wanted to see, but it was an invitation I could hardly refuse. He turned out to be called Manville, a typically worried English civil servant: not worried about the realities but worried in case someone should think that in all the circumstances he was not sufficiently worried. To be seen to be doing the 'right thing' for the English civil servant is more important than to do the right thing. That is perhaps why so much time is wasted by the English bureaucrat in preparing the ground for an event and then covering up the effects of the event afterwards, rather than on the event itself. 'Oh dear,' I thought, 'What problems my re-emergence would cause for the English bureaucracy!' They would find it so difficult to cope with and explain such an unusual occurrence. I felt, instinctively, they would not want to go for the kernel of truth but would rather thrash about producing endless investigations. It is a pity that many sensible and intelligent politicians get polluted by the English bureaucratic Establishment, and instead of using their instincts get drawn into the 'English' way of dealing with problems. But there was one man I felt would appreciate my situation: Harold Wilson. Ten years before he had met me just after I had exhausted myself physically and mentally in a struggle with the Communists in the London Co-operative Society, of which I was then the President. Harold was having lunch with his political Secretary, Marcia Williams, in the St Stephens Restaurant, just across Bridge Street from Parliament, and came to my table.

'You're not looking well,' he said. 'What you need is to get away to my bungalow in the Scillies. You can rest and relax there. Don't you think that is a good idea, Marcia?'

And so I took my wife and four year old son to the Scillies to stay in the little place which is the Wilson's retreat. It did me a lot of good. Harold could show such human sympathy and understanding because basically he is a genuine sympathetic person. His generosity of spirit and his idealism are his great unsung virtues. Because he is so much a professional among professionals (whether it be politicians, economists or journalists), very few people have known the real Harold Wilson. Over the years—particularly as Prime Minister—he has had to wear the cloak of office with the fine flourish of the actor on the stage, but, because of the incredible pressures of modern Government, the show never stops, and so the leading actor can never switch off.

But Harold will understand, I thought, so I asked Manville to send a message to the Prime Minister apologising for the trouble I had caused, explaining that I had suffered a breakdown, and thanking him for his statement clearing me of the Czech spy allegations.

Now I was transferred from the custody of the Victoria State Police to the Commonwealth Police and I learnt something about the problems of administering the Australian Federal system. Two police forces operate in parallel in all States (except Australian Capital Territory: Canberra), and in most places view each other with suspicion. The Victoria Police had kept my case a secret from the Commonwealth Police, who were strictly speaking responsible as they handled all Immigration matters. The Victoria Police were very sensitive that the investigation of my case should be handled properly after the way they had, allegedly, let the Great Train Robber, Biggs, slip out of their clutches. They were good enough to acknowledge that there were few parallels between the two cases, but for all that they did not want another international bungle on their record. And there was the bizarre position that sections of the Press, who intercept most police cables sent to Interpol, knew about me days before when the Commonwealth Police had no knowledge. I was handed over to Acting Superintendent 'Call me Bob' Gillespie of the 'Commonwealth', an avuncular and cheerful character who did much to cheer my spirits on that and subsequent days.

At no time did I feel that either Police force was harrassing me. My feelings were quite the reverse. I was grateful to these men, not for arresting me, but for liberating me from the lunacy of attempting to live in a fantasy world. They had brought me back to myself in the kindest way possible.

But to assist me in the inevitable negotiations to unravel the dilemmas of my status I needed a lawyer. The Police recommended several, among them James Patterson, who had represented Mrs Charmian Biggs with distinction years before. They could not have done me a better turn. He was called from his home on Christmas Eve, and we sat and talked in the police offices. He was—and is—the most patient and understanding lawyer I have ever met; a great contrast to the brash 'too clever by half' lawyers of the big English cities, or the lawyers who spend nine-tenths of their time worrying about the interests of the practice rather than the client. The caricature of the super professional in the play 'The Latent Heterosexual' by Paddy Chayefsky is the ultimate in the worst type of lawyer who, in devising ways ostensibly to help his client, pushes him through a whole series of metamorphoses and ultimately to his death, because from the lawyer's and the accountant's point of view, those changes were 'in his own best interests'. There was nothing in James Patterson's make-up to remind me of that type of lawyer.

I was smuggled out of the Police headquarters, avoiding the Press hounds, and driven to the Maribyrnong Detention

Centre for illegal immigrants. It was a fine warm Christmas Eve and the rest of Melbourne were beginning celebrations in earnest as I was taken behind the barbed wire and security fences and locked in a sparsely furnished hut which was to be my Christmas Holiday home. The policemen on duty were all very friendly, especially a Mauritian who had emigrated to Australia four years before. He remembered, as a Sergeant in the Mauritius Police Force, guarding me when I visited Mauritius as Under-Secretary of State, and stayed at Le Reduit, the Government House. Our separate circumstances had somewhat changed! All my possessions were taken away, including my toilet bag—in case I should attempt to cut my wrists, although to attempt to do so with a Gillette double-two blade would have been very frustrating. Officialdom has its ways and they must be adhered to, however illogical. However, they did allow me to keep my three-in-one National Panasonic radio: I was grateful for that: it gave me music and contact with the world outside. During the night I slept fitfully, disturbed every hour or so by the guards who inspected inmates regularly under regulations. Two detainees had recently escaped so the guards were especially vigilant.

At two in the morning I awoke to see a figure at the barred uncurtained window shining a torch on to my bed. When he saw I was awake he waved and grimaced. I wondered, on such a Christmas morning what manner of Santa Claus is that? I heard him unlocking the door. He came into my room, sat on the bed and asked: 'Would you like a cup of tea?' Dreamily I said 'Yes' and before many minutes he returned with two mugs of hot tea. This was a curious way to greet the Christmas Day, but despite the hour I was glad to have his company. This guard was the friendliest of them all, cheering me up with bright inconsequential conversation and bringing me extra cassettes to play on the National Panasonic.

At 7.30 am I turned on Radio 3AR and heard the BBC news beamed for overseas. The news about me was the main item and I heard Ted Short, the Leader of the Commons, interviewed and commenting that it all seemed like a detective story. He appeared to show no compassion for me. Strangely enough I knew that I could expect little compassion from most of my colleagues in Parliament. It seemed to me that they were too steeped in the English hypocrisies to be able to appreciate the torrent of anguish I had suffered, or to understand the violence to my idealism which had caused my trauma. How could I expect them to understand what it meant to be under investigation by Scotland Yard for three months? How could I expect them to understand my dismay and anguish as, without respite, this Scotland Yard pressure built up? How could I explain that the basis for investigation had been the issue by us of an information handbill, in the Bengali language, so that the Bengalee immigrants would have equality of information with the English readers of the *Financial Times*, which had already reported the proposed setting up of the new British Bangladesh Trust? How could I explain that the Bank of England and the professional advisers had been told about the handbill at the time, and had raised no objections? Indeed, the idea of involving the Bengalee migrants had been applauded. How could I expect them to understand the action of the junior officials in the Department of Trade and Industry, who had passed the papers to the Director of Public Prosecutions, without advising Peter Walker, the Minister responsible at the time? How could I tell them that the DPP, having received the papers from a Department of State, must have considered that the case was serious? How could I convince them that the whole business was a nonsense, that the handbill was not a prospectus and that no money had been raised on it? How could anyone understand how I had felt during those months as I saw the noble ideal eroded by the death-watch beetle introduced into our timbers by the *Sunday Times* article?

How could I explain that I had been caught in the vicious trap of English Society, which is best described as 'the ability to keep one's nose clean'? How could I convince people that, in pursuing a minor technical offence under the Companies Act, the authorities were in effect crucifying people, including myself, who were motivated by the best intentions? How could anyone understand the awful trauma that a completely innocent man suffers when his life-long sense of idealism is totally denied and misinterpreted, and he has to contend with the English system of grinding the kernel on and on to dust until there is no truth left? How could I explain that I had to appeal to my second citizenship of Bangladesh to save me from the relentless persecution of the very English Society into which I had been born and which had given me my career?

Now here I was, in consequence, locked in a Detention

Centre waiting for Boxing Day when I would appear in Court, as an alleged illegal immigrant, and begin the long task of appealing to the Australians, or some people somewhere, to accept me as an ordinary person. I could see 1975, the new year, coming soon. For me it would be the year of the recon-struction of my being and my soul, when I would seek to break away the images about me which had hardened like some per-spex screen, distorting the view in and the view out. It would be a chance to cut away the canker collected during my life and find the real being underneath it. At least, I felt, Australia is a good place to start.

*   *   *

In the Melbourne Magistrates Court on Boxing Day I was handed a bundle of cables. One of them read: 'GLAD TO SEE YOU ARE ALIVE AND KICKING. WILL YOU WRITE AN ARTICLE FOR THE *SUNDAY TIMES*? HAROLD EVANS.' The request had come two years and two months too late!

Epilogue

'UNLOCK.' The loud cry could be heard through the heavy iron door of the cell. It was seven o'clock and time for the gaolers to arouse the remand prisoners in Her Majesty's Prison, Brixton. This was the routine every morning; at the end of my fourth week in number 6 cell on Floor one in 'C' Wing, I had learnt the routine well. The first recognition of an approaching day is the rustle of the latch on the Judas spyhole in the door as the gaoler peeps in to check that the inmate is still present. Time for a last stretch on the iron bedstead and a quick recollection of the dreams of the night before. But how elusive are the dreams like mists that disappear in the hot morning sun; like the ideals in life, ultimately as insubstantial, burnt up as they are by the harsh realities of a relentless, insensible world?

I turned on the old Roberts portable radio held together by elastic bands but still serviceable, and tuned into BBC Radio 4. The news hit me like a bombshell. A coup in Bangladesh! President Mujib is deposed by the Army and is either killed or under arrest. Some fighting is reported around Dacca. Martial law has been declared and the situation is now said to be quiet. And then a recording of the Sheikh's strong accented voice with the words of the dreams from three and a half years ago, full of poetry and emotion even after the passage of so much cruel time. 'Bengal is rich, there will be no exploitation as we will be a democratic and a socialist state and a secular one too.'

The gaoler jangled his keys and opened the cell. This was the time for me to hurry to slop out my chamberpot before collecting my breakfast of porridge and sausage. There was no opportunity to ruminate on the fate of a nation, even if one happened to have been made a citizen of it, for the immediate prison pressures had to be obeyed. As I returned to the cell the news was concluding: 'The Labour Party in Walsall has disowned Mr John Stonehouse as their MP; they say they have severed all relations with him.'

This news was more predictable than the first item, but still a shock: I collected breakfast in a daze, and ate it, as usual, alone in the cell. It is twenty-eight days since I ate a meal in the company of another person; I had never realised before how isolated one can feel to eat, day after day, and week after week, on one's own. The breaking of bread with others—particularly with one's friends—is an essential element in a normal person's existence and to be deprived of that simple opportunity is a cruelty itself. The gaoler, pursuing his daily routine rather like an automaton, could never understand how brutal his innocent actions were. He was after all—like the millions of other Government servants—'only doing his job', and who was he to question the machine as he 'banged' the doors of the cells? For another hundred minutes at least, according to the routine, I would be left alone with my breakfast, my books and my thoughts. That morning, August 15, my thoughts were on Bangladesh and Walsall. I wondered how many other listeners to the BBC would have realised the hidden link between the two seemingly separate news items. Without the emergence of Bangladesh and my traumatic involvement with the creation of new links between Britain and that new nation, the progression of events which led to my breach with the Walsall Labour Party, after eighteen years, might never have taken place.

The double news items were a final confirmation of the demise of my ideals—the collapse of any pretension of popular democratic rule in the country I had helped to create and the breaking of a constituency party's links with the Mother of Parliaments through the repudiation of its Member. It would not be true to say I was shattered, for how can a man who is shell-shocked anyway be so moved when other bombs go off in his head? It is too late. He is numb.

I reflected on the long and tense and bitter months of 1975, the year of my gradual retreat from the breakdown of the preceding years. It had been like crawling out of the dark tunnels of the mind, slowly and painfully reaching the bright light of a world outside. It was not the same world that I had known. The light was stronger, shining into corners and recesses which I had not even seen before, and the colours were more pronounced. The myths and the mirages of a previous life had been dried up in the harsh reality of that light. And I could see the elusive truth not only about myself but about others.

It had been the humbug and hypocrisy of the political and business life of Britain which had caused my breakdown; above all I had become, in those terrible days of three and two years ago, increasingly disgusted with that person who masqueraded as me. Disgusted that he had participated in the grotesque charades which warp genuine human relationships. During my recovery process it was essential to speak the truth as I felt it and compromise no longer with the duplicity which affected human relationships at the decision-making level. It was extraordinary what effect my frankness had on the Press and on my erstwhile colleagues in Government and Parliament. They did not want to believe it and they could not bring themselves even to grasp the basic rudiments of what I was trying to say. It was as though any acceptance of my narrative would undermine their own belief in themselves and in the integrity of the society in which they operated, a society which provided them a relatively comfortable environment in which to exist. The philosophers through the ages have speculated on the question 'What is truth?' and the answer has invariably been distilled as 'What we want to believe or what we must believe in order to survive.' For someone in my position to imply that deceit is the currency of contact in high places is, of course, anathema to those who inhabit the high places. It questions not only their moral authority but their way of life. So the heretic must be disowned. But not through a full frontal attack, for that would be too indecent and would raise too many awkward questions. Not the attack by exposure and argument but the more subtle and devious and, shall we say, deceitful, technique of pillory. To ridicule an unorthodoxy is easy when most of the media is caught up in the prevailing mood and is busy filling the news stories about the heretic with rumour and innuendo and never allowing his own account to get through clearly to the manipulated public.

The antics of the British Press deserve a fuller exposure than is possible here and I hope to do so in a book to be called *Murder by Media*. However it must be noted now that the constant reiteration of adverse, and sometimes completely untrue, stories have had the effect of warping almost all views about me, including those of formerly close colleagues and friends. The barrage of attack was such as to cause even the most steadfast supporter to wilt. I was falsely accused of being a Czech spy, a CIA agent, a thief of £1 million from the Bangladesh Fund, being implicated in the murder of a Nigerian businessman, associating with the Mafia, and of stealing a wife. Needless to say, none of these particular accusations has resulted in charges being made against me.

My tiny voice reiterating the fact that I had suffered a breakdown brought about by the collapse of my ideals and my disgust with the humbug and hypocrisy in English society could not be heard in the cacophony of abuse generated by some of the Gentleman of the Press. The truth perhaps was not palatable to them, or more likely it was not newsworthy. The destruction of a public figure made better headlines and copy than an examination of the deep problems of modern society to which his breakdown drew attention.

The British Government were advised through the first message I sent to Mr Harold Wilson on Christmas Eve, 1974, that I had suffered a breakdown. In retrospect it may be asked why the Government did not ask a qualified man to see me in Australia within a short time after my reappearance to check and report on my story.

The British Government was probably anxious to get rid of an embarrassment. It showed no inclination that it wanted to solve a mystery; and it in no way revealed compassion for a colleague. Its only wish was to get me to resign as a Member of Parliament and then let me stew in the problems which I had apparently created for myself. Not a single colleague in the House of Commons attempted to contact me—not one letter—and some erstwhile friends were the most vitriolic in their attacks on me, although they had at that time only heard one, highly sensationalised, side of the story. Mail addressed simply 'John Stonehouse, Australia' actually reached me in quantities.

The Press, particularly sections of the British Press, did not let up their campaign of vilification which became hysterical in its intensity. Looking back through the press cuttings of the early months of 1975, it is difficult to find a crime for which I was not condemned. The 'popular' papers all had their reporters specially sent to Australia to report on me. It cannot be imagined how persistent a reporter can be to find some exclusive point, however irrelevant, in order to justify his expense account and gain some credit in a branch of the profession which thrives on sensationalism. This period deserves deeper and more extensive treatment. I mention it now because when I look back, I can see that my recovery from breakdown in the first three months of this year was much hindered by the pressures of reporters, ferreting out my 'secret' addresses and harassing my family, my friends and even the distant families of my friends. It was a nightmare for all of us, and I felt driven out of my mind because I had so much to say about my experience but I could not speak to reporters because their inane attitude was so totally unfeeling of the situation I had been in. They wanted good sensational copy, not an analysis of a most complex experience which I was not myself, at that stage, in a position to explain adequately.

During that period the Australian authorities were wrestling with the dilemma I had put them in: to admit me as an immigrant or to expel me. I had been released from the Maribyrnong Detention Centre after Mr Clyde Cameron, the gentle ex-sheep shearer who was the Minister of Labor and Immigration, had spoken to me on the telephone from his home in Adelaide and confirmed that I was, in fact, a Member of Parliament. Under the Parliamentary conventions Australia admits any member of a Commonwealth Parliament without restriction. Although I had arrived in the country on another passport, Mr Cameron accepted me as an MP with a right to stay. It was a neat way out of the dilemma and shows that South Australia breeds wisdom as well as sheep. Furthermore Mr Cameron was good enough to say that I had not committed any offence against Australian laws. So far so good. But problems developed for the Australian Federal Government when some Australian newspapers began to agitate for me to be thrown out on the basis that I was getting privileged treatment. Those papers were out of step with the ordinary Australians I met who were wholly on my side, accepting that I had had a tough time, although they could not be expected to understand the background, and that I deserved a break.

I think in retrospect that if, at the end of January, things had been allowed to cool down I would have been given permission to stay in Australia, I could have resigned my seat in the House of Commons, which I wanted at that stage to do, and then had a period of rest and rehabilitation which I sorely needed. But that was not to be.

My Australian solicitor, Jim Patterson, advised me not to send my formal resignation from the House of Commons and his advice turned out to be very wise. I was under incredible pressure to resign, and during the terrible weekend in New South Wales when my wife and I were pursued for hundreds of miles by teams of British Pressmen, I got up in the middle of the night to compose a letter to Ted Short, indicating my willingness to resign. The leader of the House represents Newcastle upon Tyne, Central, in the House of Commons so it was an unhappy coincidence that I wrote the letter in the Noahs Hotel, Newcastle, New South Wales. It lent colour to the association of names that, as with Tyneside, the NSW Newcastle had Stockton, Wallsend, Gateshead and Hebburn just down the road. Driving back to Melbourne in a second-hand car a day or two later, I delivered the letter to a Counsellor of the British High Commission in Canberra. We met in a hotel car park after I had arranged the rendezvous by telephone. He brought his official briefcase as evidence of identity, and received the letter, which might have severed a Privy Councillor's association with Parliament after two decades, with the perfect equanimity of a typical British Civil servant. At the end of the episode he wished us a safe journey back.

When I rang my solicitor during the night from a call box at the little town of Yass on route to Melbourne from Canberra, I told him the letter had been delivered. He nearly dropped the telephone in shock. It was clear he did not approve, and indeed within weeks he was proven right. Mr Cameron, the Minister, was forced to make a statement by the Liberal Opposition and revealed that he had already made a firm decision that I would not be granted residence status and that as soon as I resigned as an MP I would have to leave the country within hours.

Probably the British Government knew all along that the Australians had made this decision and that was why they put so much pressure on me to sign the formal application for an office of profit under the Crown: I think the designated office

was Bailiff of the Manor of Northstead. The hapless Consul
General in Melbourne, Mr Ivor Vincent, was told to persuade
me to resign. On his own initiative he invited me to stay for
the weekend in his large mansion at Toorak. It was pleasant
although the Filipino servants had all left in an unfair blaze
of publicity about low wages. (I had a lot of sympathy from
the Vincents about the Press because of that.) One minor disaster of the weekend was my attempt to make pancakes for
Sunday lunch which ended in failure because I smothered them
with lemon and salt instead of castor sugar. The next disaster
came an hour later when the British High Commissioner, Sir
Morris James, who had just heard I was staying with his Consul General, telephoned to give instructions that I was to leave
immediately. The Vincents were very upset but I went quickly
to avoid giving them any more headaches. My fourteen-year-
old son Mathew was supposed to be joining us that night after
flying out from England to be with me, and I had to arrange
for us to stay together elsewhere.

In view of the Minister's eventual decision it was just as well
that I had not sent in my formal resignation. My psychiatrist
had advised me that I had not yet sufficiently recovered to go
back to England which had been the scene of my worst
traumas. A premature return, he thought, could do more
damage. My original intention had been to resign and stay in
Australia, but when this no longer appeared possible I had to
find another country as a haven of rest to enable me to complete the recovery. So at the beginning of March I wrote to
eight countries whose Heads of State or Prime Ministers I
knew personally, and explained that I needed travel
documents—the British having completely refused to return
my own passport or provide another. I also explained that if
I had somewhere to go I would resign from the House of Commons, and on obtaining another passport renounce my British
citizenship. To an uninformed person that might sound a very
dramatic or hysterical action but those who have read my story
will understand how desperate I was at that stage to achieve
some tranquillity. Nobody had allowed me peace for over two
months; I badly wanted to get well again and that needed rest.

Furthermore there was no apparent reason why I should
not travel to another country. I had not gathered either from
the Department of Trade Inspectors, who had been sent out
to Australia to conduct enquiries concerning my business

affairs, or from Scotland Yard that they wanted me to stay in Australia. Indeed, the final confirmation that I was free to travel was the statement made by the British High Commissioner to the Australian Minister for Immigration, and quoted by him, that no criminal charges were contemplated against me by the UK authorities.

The House of Commons pulled back from the brink of expelling me just after my article in *The Daily Telegraph* which, unusually for the paper, was given the lead on the front page. In that piece, which I think heralded my return to coherent thinking, I argued that such an expulsion without hearing evidence would be Star Chamber treatment. Instead of expulsion the House decided on the inevitable compromise—it set up a Select Committee. In the debate Enoch Powell, among a few others, again showed his sturdy intellectual independence from the motley crowd of bitter attackers.

The Chairman of the Select Committee, George Strauss, who happened also to be my own Member of Parliament for Vauxhall, Lambeth, wrote to me to ask for my comments. It was the one and only time I had been asked to give evidence, and the significance of this will be seen later. I replied that I wished to return to the House as soon as I was well enough. That was quite true. Although not yet fully recovered, I felt determined that, when I was, I would brave my fellow Members in their own den before resigning with some dignity. Dozens of other Members had suffered illnesses before me and had been allowed long periods—sometimes years—away from the House without question so that they could recover. My case was only different because my disappearance had made me a target of a vitriolic press campaign. The Select Committee took my point and in their first report published on March 19 recommended no action on expulsion as non-attendance, in itself, was an insufficient ground.

I breathed a sigh of relief. Now perhaps I would be allowed the respite I needed to complete my recovery. But the peace was shattered within two days by a visit from Inspector Bob Gillespie. 'Sorry, John,' he said, 'I've got some bad news for you. I have here a warrant for your arrest.' He then read out fifteen charges.

Later that day, after I had spent my first hour in the squalid cells of the Watchhouse, the ancient police cells in Melbourne, I appeared in Court to hear the prosecuting counsel proposing that I should be refused bail because the Chief Metropolitan Magistrate, 12,000 miles away, had advised against it. My solicitor caused a ripple in the Court by pointing out that Australia was no longer a colony and its Courts were independent of direction from Bow Street or anywhere else. I got bail for the relatively low surety of 1,000 dollars.

Meanwhile the replies to the letters I had sent to the eight countries began to filter back. Sweden was the first to react. The letter had gone to an old friend, Olaf Palme, the Prime Minister, but in Sweden unbelievably—and unbeknown to me—all official mail to the Chief Minister can be examined by newspaper reporters, and my letter appeared in the world's Press before he even saw it. I had a charming reply from a secretary in his office explaining that I could not have a Swedish passport unless I resided in that country but that I could apply for residence status. Mauritius responded warmly—the Prime Minister, Sir Seewoosagur Ramgoolam, demonstrating the compassion of the gentle old-fashioned socialist and medical practitioner that he is. As Jane, my daughter, had the opportunity of going to Mauritius with her boyfriend, I asked her to take a message for me to my friends there explaining that I would have to deal with the criminal charges against me before taking up their offer of a passport. Botswana sent a very formal and negative reply from a secretary in the office of the President. I had not expected Seretse Khama to be so brusque. Presidents, Kaunda of Zambia, Nyerere of Tanzania, Kenyatta of Kenya and Mujibur Rahman of Bangladesh did not reply. Prime Minister Pierre Trudeau of Canada eventually wrote a friendly personal letter in which he revealed that he had discussed my problems with Prime Ministers Wilson and Whitlam 'at the Commonwealth Heads of State Conference in Jamaica'.

The extradition trial dragged. The daily reporting to the police headquarters was a bore particularly as there were restrictions on my movements, because I had to report daily to the same police station.

It has been a matter of concern to me that Sheila Buckley, the secretary who has worked for me for eight years, should have been charged with six offences relating to my case. Obviously I am not allowed to comment on matters which are sub judice at the time of writing. However she had been almost as badly pestered by the Press as I have. Indeed, one of the reasons she went out to Australia was in the hope of escaping from their attentions. I met her when she arrived, and she went to stay with friends in Sydney.

Subsequently, I was arrested at my home in Melbourne, and ten days later, when I heard that she might be arrested, she drove on the advice of my solicitor with a boyfriend towards Melbourne so that the solicitor could handle her case also.

While we both had to report daily to the same police station, we were naturally frequently in each other's company, much to the delight of the newspapers.

I found the *Daily Mail* particularly objectionable. One strange article early in May purported to be an account of my day. A snatch photograph had been taken earlier of me coming out of the solicitor's offices accompanied by Sheila Buckley, and Jane, my daughter. For the paper's purposes Jane was 'painted' out of the photo, and the fact that my daughter was living with me at the time was not mentioned in the article, leaving the impression that I was almost exclusively in Sheila's company.

Possibly in view of the continuing adverse stories in the British Press, the Select Committee brought out another report, which I thought a massive injustice. It acknowledged that it would not recommend expulsion from the House of Commons on grounds of non-attendance but went on to report that expulsion would be justified as the Right Honourable Member for Walsall North had 'not submitted himself to the processes of justice as established by Parliament'. This allegation was curious. I had perforce submitted myself to the Queen's Courts established by Parliament in Australia. There was in any case no other action I could have taken as the Prosecution were determined to pursue the extradition proceedings and had even laid six extra charges. All the adjournments of the case had been proposed by them and a delay caused by a legal dispute on the relations between State and Federal Law in regard to extradition was certainly not my responsibility. But to add insult to injury, the Select Committee had not bothered to tell me on what issue they were judging my future membership of the House and in no way did they consult me on this part. Their report was, in my view, hurried and against the traditions of British justice. A further anomaly was the delay of one month in the implementation of their report 'to enable the Rt. Hon. Member to return to the House'. But the report appeared a day after another appearance at the Melbourne Magistrates Court when the Prosecution proposed an adjournment which, together with the mandatory delays in extradition, would have ensured that I could not possibly arrive in Westminster until after the month was up.

In view of this impossible 'Catch 22' situation, I decided to stop all legal arguments on my case, dismiss my lawyers and fly back to London under my own steam. What I was doing was tantamount to extradition as I was willing for the Scotland Yard escort to travel with me. In addition there would be a large press corps on the plane and the prospects of my being able to stop or change en route were nil with those fellow travellers. I wrote a 4,500-word petition to the Queen to describe exactly what I proposed to do and in it I explained that the extradition proceedings were quite unnecessary as if Scotland Yard had warned me that they wanted to prefer charges, I would have travelled back to England voluntarily. I also gave the details of the plane I was booked to fly on.

My daughter Jane and son Mathew both boarded the British Airways plane at Melbourne's Tullamarine Airport after we had fought our way past over a hundred Pressmen and TV camera crews; but I was arrested by Inspector Gillespie. This time I tasted prison at the notorious Pentridge Prison in Melbourne—for four days until the Magistrate granted me bail again. The Leader of the House, Ted Short, despite the open demonstration of my anxiety to return, arranged for the expulsion debate to go ahead, and only after I had gone on hunger strike in Pentridge did he withdraw his motion on the eve of the debate. It was a last-minute conversion to reason. I was saved by the bell, and the extradition proceedings went on to the bitter end.

I returned to England, under escort, on 18 July 1975. Seven times I was denied bail, although it had never been refused in Australia. I was incarcerated in a century-old prison—overcrowded, insanitary and claustrophobic. As I looked through the eighteen bars of my cell window, my only vision was of the Brixton skyline—four television aerials on sixteen chimneypots on four houses. Sometimes I saw pigeons or an occasional seagull. Apart from solicitors or social visits and the brief moments for 'slopping out', I was in my cell for twenty-three hours every day.

I was not allowed near the House of Commons to make the

statement which the House itself asked me to return to make months before. Even my Parliamentary mail was censored. The one consolation, as far as my function as an MP was concerned, was that I was fast becoming an expert on prison, prisoners and the iniquities of the bail system—all of which information may be put to good use one day. Ironically, my interest in these matters had first developed when, in the Probation Service, I was on the other side of the fence.

Eventually, on August 27, I was suddenly granted bail, and I found myself a free man again in England for the first time since my disappearance. Although I still await my trial, I am a freer man than I was nine months ago. I feel myself liberated from much of the clutter of earlier inhibitions, pressures, tensions and pretensions, and I can face the future, whatever it may be, with the confidence of a reborn man. But the idealist is still dead.

John Stonehouse
London, September 1975

Index